John Comer's first brush with the Military (1928) was with the 112th Cavalry (National Guard) while attending Trinity University in Waxahachie, Texas. The writer has never had a high regard for horses since then. In 1943 Comer flew the missions from England on which this book is based. He was a fl.ght engineer – top turret gunner in Flying Fortresses. In 1944 fifty missions were flown from Italy. After the war, Comer became Sales Manager in the Northeastern States for a large manufacturing company, then served as Zone Manager for the Southern States. After retirement he did market research in Europe, Asia and South America. John Comer now lives in Dallas, Texas where he teaches business subjects at a nearby college.

COMBAT CREW

by
John Comer

SPHERE BOOKS LIMITED

SPHERE BOOKS LTD

Published by the Penguin Group
27 Wrights Lane, London W8 5TZ, England
Viking Penguin Inc., 40 West 23rd Street, New York, New York 10010, USA
Penguin Books Australia Ltd, Ringwood, Victoria, Australia
Penguin Books Canada Ltd, 2801 John Street, Markham, Ontario, Canada L3R 1B4
Penguin Books (NZ) Ltd, 182–190 Wairau Road, Auckland 10, New Zealand

Penguin Books Ltd, Registered Offices: Harmondsworth, Middlesex, England

First published in Great Britain by Leo Cooper 1988
Published by Sphere Books Limited 1989

Printed and bound in Great Britain by
Richard Clay Ltd, Bungay, Suffolk

"Combat Crew" Is Dedicated
To The Memory Of

James Counce, Corinth, Miss.	*K.I.A. Jan. 11, 1944*
George Balmore, Bronx, N. Y.	*K.I.A. Jan. 11, 1944*
Herbert Carqueville, Chicago, Ill.	*M.I.A. Oct. 9, 1943*
Raymond Legg	*K.I.A. by German civilians*

And To The Memory
Of All
The Men Who Gave
Their Lives
In The Air War Over Europe
That The Rest Of
Us
Might Continue To Live
In Freedom

CONTENTS

FOREWORD

The ultimate objective of "Combat Crew" is to make the combat missions come alive for readers of this book. In particular I want the wives, the sons, the daughters, and the grandchildren of the participants, to feel that they are experiencing the extreme cold, the constant dangers, and the traumatic events that were common to all the men who manned the Flying Fortresses in the high thin air over the European Continent. To the extent possible my purpose is to take the reader along with us on the combat missions.

This account tells how one combat crew handled the boredom and monotony of barracks life, all the while sweating out the missions as the air battles unfolded. Every crew was different, reflecting the discipline desired by the pilot. However, I flew with thirteen air crews during the war, and I found that all crews were far more alike then they were different. The well researched documentary books about this period may leave the impression that all of the missions were life and death struggles. It was not like that: each crew had some very rough missions and some easy ones. Often the accounts of the air battles over Europe are concerned with the commanders and the generals and their agonizing decisions. Again, it was not like that for us: we knew nothing about where we were going or why until two or three hours before takeoff. Once in the air we merely followed the formation, not being concerned about tactics.

What happened to "Gleichauf's Crew" was much like the experiences of men in other crews who succeeded in completing their quota of missions. Each crew could see only that part of the action within its range of vision. When our crew had a rough go, sometimes crews in another part of the same battle had it easy. And even on the missions we called "milk runs", almost always some unlucky crews were shot down. Death was never more than a few feet or inches from the men in the Flying Fortresses.

PROLOGUE

As we approached the site where Ridgewell Airdrome once stood I was overcome with memories. It was June, 1972. All at once I was transported back three decades in time. I could hear the raucous roar of Flying Fortress engines revving up for takeoff in the damp pre-dawn cold of an English morning. I could smell that mixture of oil and gasoline that filled the air when engines coughed and started. I could feel again the vibrations of those over-loaded aircraft struggling to escape the runway and lift up over the mists. I recalled that uncomfortable feel of an oxygen mask fitted tightly against my face. I remembered the hours I spent recalculating the odds of surviving and the daily realization that they were not good.

Suddenly I shivered despite the warmth of the summer day. I could not shake off the chill of the past. Was this return to Ridgewell going to be a mistake?

One by one I recalled the faces of my crew — a group of young men from diverse locales and backgrounds, thrown together by chance and placed under intense pressure. We were such ordinary men from whom the extraordinary was demanded. We were half trained and woefully inexperienced. Most of our men had been in military service barely a year. We were expected to face the fury of Germany's superbly trained and experienced Luftwaffe and survive. Some of us did. During those months together we formed bonds of friendship I have never experienced before or since.

We were getting closer and I strained to catch a glimpse of something familiar — anything — that would confirm that I had once been a part of this place. Ridgewell had been home, prison, and refuge — the center of my world for so many months. I squinted ahead secretly hoping for rain, but there was none. That seemed so strange! Ridgewell — without that eternal drizzle and everlasting mud? But that week England played a trick on my memory. The sun made daily appearances and the sky remained uncharacteristically free of moisture. Then it happened! About a hundred yards from the site of the base a gentle drizzle began to fall from skies that up to that moment had shown no hint of rain. It was eerie, as if it had been staged just for me. I was tempted to look upward and say, ''Thank you.'' And I knew I was right in returning to Ridgewell.

Then I was jolted back to reality. The site had long since returned to grain fields. Two old hangars were still standing, but now they were filled with farm machinery. They had traded airplanes for tractors! Part of me knew this was as it should be. Another part reached back through the years remembering how those hangars were once alive with men — and Flying Fortresses needing major repairs. I wanted to regain for a few moments the experiences that could be relived only by those men who flew from this field in that long ago time of war. I stood there silently in the soft rain for a long time, remembering.

My wife and two close friends were with me but they could not participate in my nostalgia. Nor did they try. To me, it represented the most intensely lived year of my life. To me this was ground as hallowed as Lincoln's Gettysburg. Although I flew out of other combat airfields far distant from England, none was burned as deeply into my memory as Ridgewell. It was from here that I had the first traumatic shock of combat. It was from here that so many of my friends, some of the finest men I have ever known, began their last flight.

PREFACE

November 24, 1942

A thousand men were assembled on the parade ground at Sheppard Field, Texas, on that November day, just eleven months after Pearl Harbor. A dapper Major strode to an elevated speaker's stand. I will remember him as long as I live. The man was a spellbinder, a military pitchman with superb talents. I listened in hypnotic fascination as he described the adventurous life of an aerial gunner. Carried away by his fiery enthusiasm, I could picture myself holding off a swarm of Japanese Zeroes! With exciting fervor the speaker challenged those of us who had an extra share of guts. Some might, he hinted, be accepted for aerial gunnery. The Major concluded his remarks: "Those of you who want to escape menial assignments for the next three or four years, and live a life of excitement, fall out to my right for physical examinations."

About fifty of us, whose judgement at the moment was questionable, lined up as directed. An hour later I was still sitting in the silence of the reception room at the base hospital awaiting my turn.

The hypnotic spell was beginning to wear off. Men were leaving quietly until there were only a few of us left. What the hell was I doing there? Did I really want to trade a safe aircraft mechanic's job for active combat? Since when had I developed an extra share of guts? Slowly rational thinking returned, and I wondered if a thirty-two-year-old man belonged there. I got up and began easing out and was ten feet from the exit when a door opened.

"Comer!"

"Here," I responded automatically.

"That room on the left. Strip down, they'll be with you in a few minutes."

How often the timing of a trivial incident shapes our lives. If that orderly had been five seconds later I would have been gone, and the war for me would have been a vastly different story.

I suddenly remembered the crushing blow ten years earlier when an unexpected visual depth perception change abruptly ended my hoped-for aerial career at the Air Corps Flying Detachment at Brooks Field. I had to conclude that the defect would still be there and I was sure the medical exam would be the same as for pilots.

But now a strange feeling came over me: I wanted very much to pass those tests. And I did great until it came to the depth perception. Once more it floored me. When I showed such obvious dismay at the results of the depth perception gauges, the examining officer asked, "Are you in the Aircraft Machanics School?"

"Yes, Sir, I am."

"You might qualify for aerial engineer."

"Aerial engineer?" I had never heard the term before.

"Yes, a flying aircraft mechanic who is also an aerial gunner."

It was certainly an interesting new possibility.

"We are not as strict on engineers as on the other gunners. The Colonel might O.K. you."

When I got to the Colonel he used a new instrument I had not seen in the past — an electric depth gauge. He studied the results, then looked at me.

"Comer, you're close enough that I can waive the defect if you are sure you want to be a flight engineer. It will probably mean combat. Is that what you want?"

I had no time to ponder my decision.

"Sounds great to me!"

"O.K. I'll mark your records as medically qualified for Flight Engineer-Gunner. Good luck!"

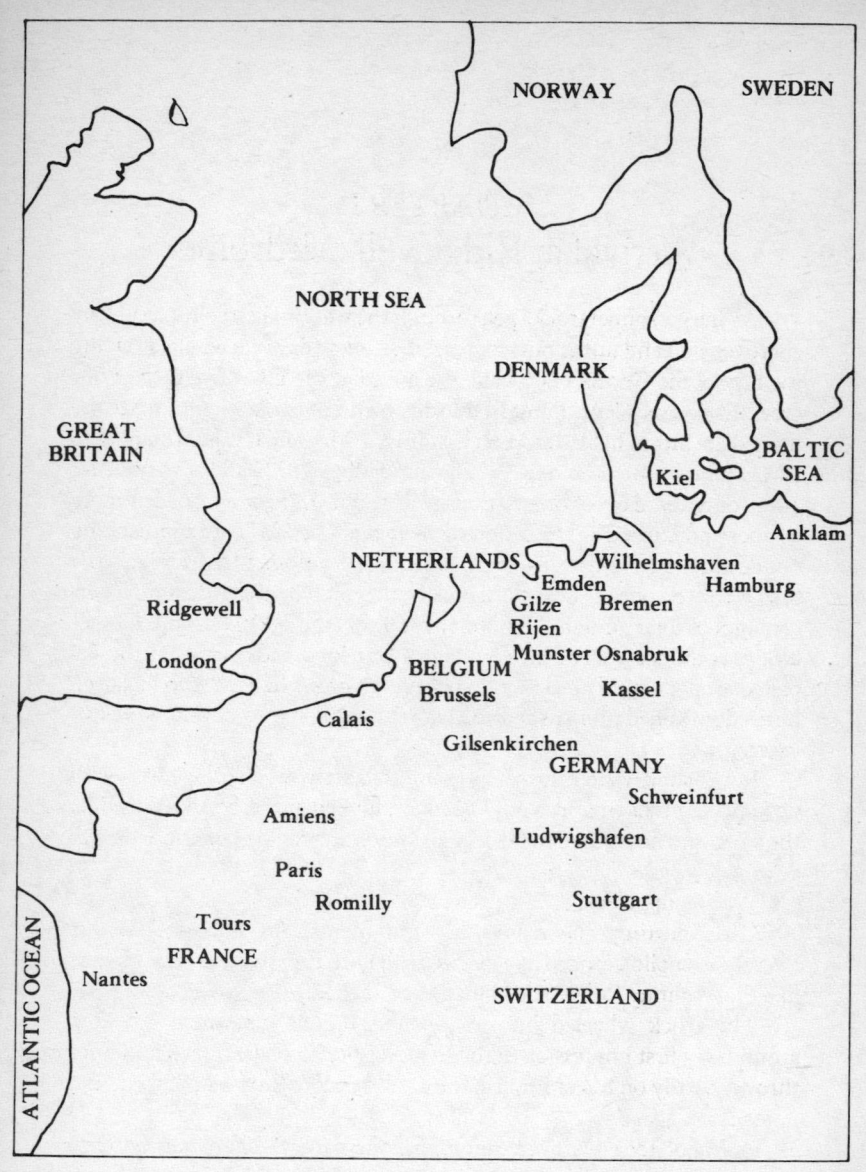

The principal targets for the period covered by this account.

CHAPTER I
Arrival at Ridgewell Airdrome

As the personnel truck sped through the wet English countryside my apprehension and uneasiness increased. In a few days we would be facing the fury of the German Luftwaffe. I glanced at the other five men of our crew. Each was silent, immersed in his own contemplation of what the immediate future held in store. It was July, 1943, and it was all coming to a head for us quite soon now. What would it be like? Could we handle it? After only ten days of orientation in England, I knew we needed more gunnery practice. The truck slowed down and I saw we were approaching our destination. All day I had been dreading that moment. Most likely the base would be one of those hard luck outfits who regularly lost high percentages of their aircraft. The worst of all was the 100th Group. Please! Not that unlucky snake-bit command! But logic indicated that the depleted groups would need more replacement crews like us, who had been hurriedly trained and rushed to the 8th Air Force to cover the heavy losses.

It was shortly after dusk, a poor time to arrive at a strange base with no conception of what it would be like. I looked at Herbert Carqueville, the pilot, and he pointed to George Balmore, the radio operator, who was dozing.

"Wake up, George. We're coming into the base."

Carl Shutting, the navigator, straightened his uniform. George Reese, the copilot, looked like he did not have a care in the world. He was like that. Johnny Purus, the bombardier, looked worried — as I was.

The truck wheeled into an obviously quite new base. Looking around, my first impression of the base was prefabricated metal buildings thrown hastily on top of English mud. At headquarters we piled out and unloaded baggage.

A Major took his time examining our papers. There was another crew with us, from the same training command in the States. "I know you are wondering where you are. You are now assigned to the 381st Bombardment Group at Ridgewell Air Base."

What a relief that was! The 381st was not one of the high loss groups we had been hearing about.

"I am sending you to the 533rd Squadron, under the command of Major Hendricks. They are low on crews. A driver will take you to the squadron headquarters. Good luck on your new assignment." From what I had seen since reaching England, we were going to need some luck!

"Major," said Carqueville, "we've heard so many stories, how tough is it? What kind of losses are you having?"

The Major hesitated before answering and studied a large chart on the wall crowded with names. "See that chart? That's the combat roster. We've been here sixty days, and so far we've lost a hundred and one percent of our combat personnel."

That seemed impossible! Did he mean a lot of replacement crews had arrived and were already lost in addition to originals? Surely the Major would burst out laughing in a few seconds. I watched his face for some sign that it was a joke pulled on new arrivals. The smile did not come. The message was clear. I did not know then if that frightful loss figure was factual, or inflated to get across his point that the playing was over. (Those were his exact words! But months later I found out that the early losses, while serious, were not that bad.)

The Major continued, "You'd know it anyway in two or three days. I guess it's just as well to let you have it straight right now. Our strength is down and we are happy to have you with us."

I glanced at the other men and noted that the color had drained from their faces. No one said anything as we loaded the baggage into a transportation truck. Each of us was trying to digest the startling high loss situation and struggling, with scant success, to translate those figures into what they meant to us individually.

At the Squadron Headquarters we were greeted warmly by the Operations Officer. "I'm Lt. Franek. Welcome to the 533rd Squadron. We're glad you're here because we have only four combat crews in the squadron, and our minimum strength is suppossed to be seven."

Carqueville asked, "Have you any information on our four gunners? They were supposed to arrive about the same time we got here."

"Yes, we do have information," Franek answered. "They're due tomorrow."

That was the only good news I was to hear that day. It was a great relief to know Jim Counce and the other gunners would definitely rejoin us. It would give our sagging spirits a lift just to see them again.

A truck transported us to the combat site, and the driver pointed out the small, metal Quonset huts that would be our quarters. The officers would be in one hut and the enlisted men in another, not far away. The driver said, "Note that here we are widely dispersed to prevent serious damage from German bombing raids. Personnel trucks make regular rounds of the field perimeter during the day time, and early in the mornings when there is a mission. Combat personnel are quartered separately from the permanent personnel." I picked up the nuance in his voice: what it meant was that combat people were not expected to be around very long.

The driver continued. "You men have a separate combat mess because your hours will be so different from the other men. As soon as you can manage it, I suggest you get into Cambridge and buy a used bicycle. It will make getting around the base a lot easier."

"How far is Cambridge from Ridgewell?" I asked.

"About eighteen miles. A supply truck makes a run every day, and there's also train service from a nearby village."

I doubt if I ever had a more miserable evening in my life. The dingy hut, designed for twelve men, was a dirty, dimly-lighted, depressing place. It was bare except for twelve crude cots. A single low watt bulb hung in the center of the small metal building. I decided on a bunk and opened my bags, but before I could get my gear unpacked, some veteran gunners started drifting in to look us over.

"Where you guys from?" one asked.

Balmore answered, "I'm from New York, and Comer is from Texas."

"That's a helluva combination! You got some more men comin' in?"

"Yes," I said. "Our other four gunners will be here tomorrow."

"Your pilot got a lot of high altitude formation time?"

"Nope," said Balmore. "Not much."

A second man entered just in time to hear what George had said. "I feel Goddamned sorry for you guys if your pilot can't fly tight formation."

"Oh, I think he can do OK on formation," I offered.

"It takes seventy to a hundred hours of high altitude formation experience to be a fair pilot in this league. Your pilot got that many hours?"

"Far as I know he's never been in a high altitude formation, and has only a few hours of low altitude formation," I said.

"If they don't find you a new pilot who knows what he's doin' at high altitude formation you're in trouble. Those Jerry sonnuvabitches can spot a new crew on their first circle aroun' the formation and they—"

"— They'll tear into your ass on their first attack," interrupted another Vet, " 'cause they always pick the easiest Forts to knock down."

A third man came in. "Don't worry about it, you might make it — sometimes a new crew does get back from its first raid. This week it wasn't too rough: we only lost twenty Forts — mostly new crews!"

Another voice added, "As soon as the Jerries approach us they look for you fresh jokers."

"How can they tell which crews are new?" asked Balmore.

"Damned easy, friend. Green pilots can't stay in tight formation. They throttle-jock back and forth — might as well flash a neon sign!"

A new voice spoke up. "Relax! Don't get lathered up. Mebbe your crew will be one of the lucky ones. We were once new and we're still here!"

"When you hit a German fighter with some good bursts, what happens? Does it break off the attack?" I asked.

The six Vets laughed uproariously. "Hell, no! You can see your tracers hit those 190's[1] and 109's[2] an' they bounce off like it's a God-damned flyin' tank! Those square-headed Krauts keep comin' at you no matter what you throw at 'em!"

The most vocal of the group continued. "The worst bastards they got are Goering's Abbeville Kids — those yellow nose and red nose ME 109's[2] are the roughest you'll ever see." He turned to Balmore. "Hey kid, you're about my height. What size blouse your wear?"

George replied testily, "None of your damn business!"

"Don't get your guts in an uproar, friend. I need a new blouse, so I spot all you new gunners my size — one of you jokers don't get back, I grab me a blouse before those orderly room pimps get over here to pick up your gear."

One of the Vets explained it: "At the 381st they don't issue any replacement clothes. If you tear your pants, or ruin a blouse, you sweat it out until a gunner your size don't make it back."

"That's how we do it over here," said another. "That way ain't no red tape — say, any of you men wear size 38?"

"I do," I replied. "But don't get any ideas — 'cause I'm gonna make it!"

"Maybe! But the first rough raid will thin out these huts — a lot of you new bastards won't get back — maybe one of you will be my size."

"Say — there was a nice lookin' kid had that bunk over there for five

[1]Focke Wolfe 190 (F.W. 190)
[2]Messerschmitts 109 (M.E. 109)

or six days," one of the Vets remarked. "Saw his plane blow up — no chutes!"

He pointed to an empty cot. "The fellow who slept there — they brought him back with no balls."

"Well," a voice added, "that poor bastard don't have to worry no more about findin' a pro station open at four a.m.!"

Ribald laughter reverberated from the thin metal walls, but I couldn't share in their hilarity. My insides were tightening into knots, and I wondered if all those tales were true. I knew they were trying to scare the Hell out of us — and succeeding! I kept thinking about those high losses the Major told us about, and realized the Vets didn't need to embellish their stories. The plain, unvarnished facts were frightening enough for me.

"Hey, you guys gotta watch those 'lectric fly suits. If a shoe or glove goes out at fifty below zero you can lose a hand or foot."

"But the big thing is an engine fire," from another voice. "When you rookies see that fire you got mebbe thirty or forty seconds before the explosion!"

The Vets finally tired of their oft repeated initiation game and drifted off. George looked at me for a long time without saying a word. He didn't need to for I knew what his thoughts were. Sleep for that night was completely out of the question. The reality of what we faced was almost too much to absorb. Always ringing in my ears were the Major's words: "We've lost a hundred and one percent of our combat personnel." The Vets told us we would get in about three missions a month, and the odds stacked up four to one that we wouldn't make it! (Which later proved to be quite accurate).

Balancing the bad news of the last six hours was my memory of how grand those Flying Fortresses looked in proud formation heading out toward Hitler-held Europe. The second morning we were at Bovingdon, the orientation base near London where replacement crews reported for induction into the 8th Air Force, we were awakened by the roar of many engines. In a matter of minutes the barracks was empty. The Fortresses were passing overhead on their way to strike the Mad Dictator and none of us wanted to miss the sight. I have had many thrills in my life, but I believe that picture-perfect formation of American bombers headed for a clash with Goering's best was one of the most emotional experiences I have ever had. I wanted to be up there with them. All that day I worried about what those men were going through over the Continent. In the early afternoon I was in an aircraft recognition class when someone whispered, "The Forts are coming back." In one minute the classroom was empty. Where were the proud eagles of the dawn? They returned, but not in the style I had seen that morning. A few were in formation, but most were scattered across the sky. There were feathered engines and many trailed smoke. But where were the other planes? I counted only half of the number that went out that morning. I did not know then that ships in trouble, or low on fuel, broke away from the formations as they approached England looking for a landing field. For the next half hour, I watched wounded Forts straggle in, a few on two engines.

July 20

There was an agreeable surprise at Ridgewell. The food was good. The Combat mess hall was a hundred yards from our barracks. We were in a country where part of the food had to be imported, and all of ours had to come by boat from the States. So those mess officers did a great job with the materials at their disposal.

On the way back from noon mess I said to George, "We're gonna have to get into Cambridge real soon and buy bicycles. I notice all the men here at the base have bikes."

"John, when the other men get here, don't say anything about what the Vets did to us last night."

"You mean let 'em get the news on their own?"

"Right! It oughta be interesting to see how they handle it. One thing for sure, they're in for a shock!"

An hour or so later a truck pulled up near the hut and out jumped our four gunners.

"Damn! I thought we were gonna get four good gunners and now you jokers show up again.," fumed Balmore. "Come see our Country Club Quarters."

Now that the gunners were back, our crew was all together. James Counce and Carroll Wilson were our two waist gunners. Jim was 23, single, and came from Corinth, Mississippi. He was an engineering student from the University of Tennessee. Jim served as second engineer and was fully as capable as I was, and a very solid man. Carroll Wilson, twenty, from Tulsa, Oklahoma, was assistant to Balmore in the radio room. Carroll was a likeable youngster but had not grown up yet. He had married just before leaving for England. The tail gunner, Buck Rogers, thirty-nine, was a rugged individual from a small Ohio town. I am not sure of his marital status. He had many rough experiences, but he was a loner and had little to say about some phases of his life. Nickalos Abramo, nineteen, from Massachusetts, operated the ball turret guns. He was an impetuous young man of Italian ancestry.

We were sitting around talking about going to Cambridge to buy bicycles, and the possibility of buying a radio for the hut. Suddenly the door opened and five or six Vets entered. ''What do you know? We got us some new gunners,'' one of them said. ''Where you guys from?''

I knew what was coming and glanced at George. We sat back in morbid fascination to watch how our four friends responded to 'the treatment.' A few months later initiating new arrivals was one of my favorite amusements.

If there was a crew favorite, I suppose it was Jim Counce. Carqueville had a special trick we played on Jim. I would go back to the radio room and make sure he was looking out of the waist window. Herb would put an engine into an extra rich carburetor position to create some smoke on Jim's side of the aircraft. As soon as Counce saw it he started toward the cockpit, and Herb quickly switched back to automatic lean. By the time Counce reached the cockpit the smoke would be gone.

''Smoke? I didn't see any. John, did you see any smoke?''

''No. You're seein' things, Jim. Are your sure you're OK?''

''I did see smoke from number three engine,'' he would protest vigorously.

Herb would look at me and shake his head as if to say, ''I'm afraid Counce is cracking up.''

July 21

From the first night at Ridgewell, it became slowly apparent that Carqueville did not have the experience at high altitude formation flying to be a first pilot in the big leagues of combat over Europe. It was difficult to understand how the training command in the States could have neglected the one indispensable requirement for a B-17 combat pilot. For the time I knew Herb in training, he was given no high altitude formation practice. Only two hours of low altitude formation flying! A copilot should have had fifteen or twenty hours of holding a B-17 in formation over twenty thousand feet.

Late in the afternoon Carqueville opened the door to our hut and stepped inside. I knew instantly he was upset. ''I've been cut back to copilot. I'm takin' Reese's place.'' (Reese had come down with an infection and was grounded for the time being.)

''What!'' Even though I was expecting it to happen, the news came as a shock. ''It's not fair.''

''Wrong! They had to do it. A pilot has to have a lot of formation time, and I don't have it. Believe me, I don't like it one damn bit, but that's how it's got to be.''

Jim spoke up, ''We hate like hell to lose you. Now we'll start all over with some pilot we never saw before. We could have made it with you I'm sure.''

"Thanks, Jim, but Hendricks couldn't permit that risk. He made the right decision. Reese is goin' to be the Assistant Operations Officer.''

Regardless of what he said I knew Carqueville was hurt. Who would be the new pilot? There was much conjecture and concern about what kind of man would take over the crew. The next afternoon Carqueville introduced us to the man who would hold our destiny in his hands. The officers had already met him.

"Men, this is Lt. Paul Gleichauf, our pilot. He's got the formation experience we must have if we are going to make it in this league.''

"Lieutenant, I'm John Comer, Engineer.''

"Glad to know you, John.''

The rest of the men introduced themselves and shook hands. It was an awkward moment, with Herb standing there watching his men accept a new leader.

"I'm glad to be your pilot,'' said Gleichauf. "Looks like we've got good men, so I think we'll do OK.''

There was more small talk but it was mainly verbal sparring while we sized him up, and the pilot got a good look at what he had to work with. Since Herb was to be copilot, it was much like a new football coach keeping the ex-coach as his assistant. Lt. Gleichauf was younger than I expected, but he did fit the image of an Air Force Pilot more than Herb.

One the way back to our hut there was silence for a while, then George turned to Counce. "Well, what do you think of our new pilot?''

"Looks OK. He doesn't talk much but we need the experience he has.''

"John, what do you think?''

"About the same as Jim — only thing, I wish he were a little older.'' (Actually, he was twenty-four, and two years older than I thought at the time.)

Buck said, "That ain't important — we gotta have somebody who can fly tight formation. That's what all the Vets say — to hell with the rest of it!''

Paul Gleichauf was originally from Lakewood, Ohio — a suburb of Cleveland. He was a handsome young officer — dashing, slim, and very attractive to women. He came overseas as a first pilot several weeks ahead of us. Just before flying a new Fortress across the Atlantic, a heavy fire extinguisher fell on his foot. He arrived in England with a bad case of hemorrhoids, wearing a moccasin on one foot, and certainly in no condition to handle a B-17 on formation flights. By the time we badly needed a pilot he had recovered enough to resume flying status.

Lt. Gleichauf would have been dumbfounded had he fully realized the low level of combat "know-how" of his new crew. He was aware that Carqueville was short on formation flying, but he had no idea how little gunnery practice the crew had logged before coming to England. He would have been further dismayed had he known that our total experience with oxygen equipment added up to only thirteen hours.

Who was to blame for this woeful lack of training? How could the Second Air Force Training Command have been so ignorant of our needs? I suspect that the Command was overloaded with ex-educators who let their passion for classrooms supercede the substance of what was actually needed where we were headed. In a new situation people usually fall back on what they know best. What happened to the communications between the 8th Air Force and the stateside training command? So much time was wasted on classroom trivia and not enough on the essentials necessary for a crew to survive in combat with the enemy.

The 8th Air Force was made up of two units: Bomber Command and Fighter Command. Bomber Command was composed of three divisions, each of which had two wings. Three groups made up a wing. The bomber group was the basic fighting unit of the Command. A combat group had four squadrons who handled the personnel. At that date a group was expected to put up a minimum of eighteen Fortresses on a mission. Sometimes it would be a few more. In most cases a group occupied one air base, and had about two thousand men in combat and support personnel. We found out in the first week that we were in the 8th Air Force, First Division, First Wing, 381st Group, and the 533rd Squadron. The First Wing was made up of the 381st, the 351st, and the 91st Groups.

It took me a while to get used to Gleichauf's cockpit procedure. He was as different from Herb as day is from night! He had none of the easygoing, relaxed characteristics of most four-engine pilots. He was all business from the moment engines started, and prone to issue short, concise orders, which at first sounded irritable on the intercom. But I knew we were lucky to get Gleichauf's kind of experience and ability.

Herb Carqueville was from Chicago, where his family operated a lithographing business. Prior to the war he was quite active in the business, and expected to return to it when the war was over. A good relationship developed between Carqueville and me, partly because both of us had been in the business world for a number of years. Herb's background gave him a different perspective from young men fresh out of college. At twenty-seven, he acted more like a mature man of forty.

Our Navigator, Lt. Carl R. Shutting, was from Chattanooga, Tennessee. I had a mental picture of a navigator: he would be a neat, orderly, well-organized person with cold, mathematical efficiency, and precise methodical habits. Carl Shutting was at the opposite end of the spectrum from such an image. He had been married before entering the service, but had recently been the recipient of a ''Dear John'' letter. Carl was twenty-four, and prior to the war had worked in the post office in Chattanooga, Tennessee.

Johnny Purus, the Bombardier, was from the Boston area. He was in his early twenties, and as dependable as a person could be. He was a bit shy, soft-spoken, and not easy to evaluate immediately. For a short period he had worked as an aircraft mechanic, but not on B-17's. It was good to have another man with mechanical aptitude on the crew. There might come a time in the future when his help would be crucial.

When the war broke out I was thirty-one, married for not quite two years, and living in Corpus Christi, Texas. My education had been at Trinity University and the University of Texas. I was a competent outside salesman for machine tools, equipment and auto parts. I had a solid background in the field of mechanics and supply, and also some electrical experience (fortunate because a B-17 was operated and controlled mainly by electric circuits). My position was flight engineer and I fired the top turret guns. The turret was mounted in the cockpit directly behind the pilot and copilot.

It did not occur to us that we were already on combat status. No one had told the gunners a single thing about the 381st procedure for gunners. In fact we had not seen a gun since we reached Ridgewell. We were still waiting for the briefing that the Operations Officer promised shortly after we arrived. I understood that we would get at least one gunnery practice flight that would outline the 381st gun and armament procedures. We should have asked questions. Where did the crews keep the guns? Where did we get parts or supplies needed on a mission in a hurry? What about the briefing procedures on mission mornings? Did we report to the Briefing Room or go on to the aircraft? But military life discourages initiative, so we waited and waited for the instructions, so vital, that never came.

July 29

At 0230 (two-thirty A.M.) the lights snapped on and six startled men roused enough to hear the Operations Officer:

''Now listen to this, Comer, Counce, Balmore, Abramo, Wilson, and Rogers. You're flyin' 765 with Gleichauf. Briefing at 0400 hours. Chow's ready now. Come on! Out of that sack!''

"This is a combat raid!" said Counce. "Why didn't they tell us we were on combat status? No one has told us one thing! Do we go to the briefing with the Officers?"

"Don't know," I answered. "We gotta catch Gleichauf before he gets to the Briefing Room and get orders."

There were fresh eggs for breakfast but I was too nervous to be hungry. I watched the men come and go in anxious fascination. Our crew seemed to be the only newcomers there. I had a tight feeling in my chest and was beginning to feel nauseated. I envied the confident air of the Vets who appeared totally unperturbed. I wondered if I would survive long enough to develop such a carefree attitude. Probably not! I was under no illusions as to what generally happened to new crews. Not many made it back!

Trucks were lined up to ferry us to Operations, and in the dark they assumed ghostly shapes. Men talked, if at all, in subdued whispers. Most were silent except for an occasional curse as some new arrival stepped on a foot. It was a black, gloomy pre-dawn, and our spirits were in complete harmony with the cheerless atmosphere.

Just before the truck pulled out I recalled, with a feeling of panic, that my electric flying suit was back at the hut. I had taken it there to make some needed adjustments. I had no idea if I could survive the intense cold without it, so there was no choice except to jump out of the truck and run through the dark and mud to the hut. When I got back to where the trucks were parked, all had left. I had to run all the way to the Operations Office, following the indistinct shapes of other men in the darkness, and quickly drew my equipment. I found the rest of our men huddled together in a corner of the room, with their flying equipment piled around them.

"What did you find out from Gleichauf?" I asked Jim, who had been the first to get to Operations.

"He was in the Briefing Room before we got here. Everybody who knows anything is in the Briefing Room."

"Don't you see the other gunners are headin' out to the planes?" Jim said.

"Yeah, I see that, but they got orders to do so. We don't. Suppose Gleichauf expects us to be waitin' here," George answered.

About that time the Briefing Room doors opened, and I made a dash for Gleichauf. "Are we free to go to the aircraft?"

"You gunners oughta be there now. Hurry it up or we won't be ready in time!"

We made a run for the trucks and got a new driver who took far too much of our time wandering around the perimeter trying to locate the aircraft. A quick check of the plane showed no sign of any guns. The only man at the plane was a sleepy PFC mechanic.

"Where th' hell do they keep the guns?" I asked.

"Guns? I don't know nothin' about guns," he answered. It was obvious he didn't give a damn, either. "Ain't they in the ship?"

We had only one flashlight and searched everywhere. I was getting very nervous as the time ticked away.

"Don't you know any place the guns might be? We're running out of time."

"Sometimes Armament pulls out the guns while a ship is laid up a spell with heavy damages," he replied.

I hailed an empty truck and the driver agreed to take Abramo and me to Armament, wherever that was. When we got there no one knew anything about our guns. I turned to an officer who had just arrived.

"Sir, we've got to have twelve guns for 765 — and real quick."

He turned to a Sergeant. "Get these men some guns and I mean right now!"

"Wait! See those guns in the corner over there, all stripped down? Maybe they're from 765," someone said.

Our ship number was painted on the barrels. Every gun was disassembled and Nick and I tore into them at top speed and got them more or less together. There was no time to make a careful inspection of each gun to be sure there were no missing parts. When we got back Jim checked the guns and asked, "Where are the bolt studs? Didn't you or Nick bring them?" (A bolt stud was a one-inch-long metal device required to insert a round of ammunition into the firing chamber to permit the firing to begin. Unless that round was in place to start the action, the gun would not fire.)

"You mean there are no bolt studs in the ship? Check again. They're supposed to be tied to the receivers," I responded. But there were none in the airplane that we could discover. An obstinate habit of each gunner having his own bolt studs had developed in defiance of regulations to leave them in the airplane. We did not know this at that time. (Before long I was carrying them in my pocket wherever I went).

An Operations Jeep drove up just then and Carqueville hailed the driver. "Take off for Armament and get us twelve bolt studs. Hurry! You got to get back before we taxi out." The Jeep tore off at high speed. All of the hurry-hurry and confusion was enough to create a panic situation. This was no game we were preparing for! Planes would take off with or without guns in working order! Would he make it? Two minutes before taxi time the Jeep slid to a halt and the driver fought his way through the propeller blast to hand Jim the twelve bolts studs at the waist entry hatch. What a relief that was! Without them, not a gun would have fired.

There was no time for a briefing on the target before takeoff. As soon as we were settled down in the formation Gleichauf came on intercom: "Pilot to crew, Pilot to crew — we're heading for Kiel in Northern Germany. There are several hundred fighters in the area and you can expect a hot reception. Be ready for attacks half way across the North Sea. This is your first mission — now don't get excited an' let 'em come in on us!''

The formation was far better than I expected. Hour after hour we droned on. It would not be long now: if only we could be lucky enough to get by this one! The way Gleichauf was holding tight formation, I hoped the fighters would not pick us out to be a new crew. Of course I was keyed up to a high pitch and I wondered if I would forget what little I knew about aerial gunnery in the excitement of the first fighter attacks.

Number four engine began to vibrate too much and I watched in alarm as it started slowing down. It looked like either the fuel pump or the magneto had failed. The engine was finished for the day!

"Pilot to Copilot."

"Go ahead, Paul."

"Feather number four." The propeller slowed down and ceased to spin. We were ten minutes from the enemy coast.

For a few minutes Gleichauf tried to keep up, but the formation began to pull away. If we could not keep up it would be suicide, as well as useless, to go on and get knocked off over the target area. Fighters invariably ganged up and finished off the stragglers in comparative safety before they tackled the formation. There was only one thing to do. Gleichauf pulled out of the formation and started the long flight back to England.

"Bombardier to gunners — Bombardier to gunners! Keep alert! We got a long way to go, all alone. Watch for fighters.!''

It was a long, tiresome and frustrating day, and all for nothing! No credit. We still had twenty-five missions to go.

While we were attempting our first mission, six men from the crew of Lt. William Cahow moved into the six empty bunks in our hut. Two of them were from Brooklyn, one from Texas, one from California, one from upstate New York and one from New Jersey. They would become an intimate part of our world for many months to come.

Ugo Lancia was the radio operator and a good one. He was a husky, handsome Italian — loud-speaking and excitable. He had a good singing voice and played numerous instruments, which he somehow acquired in England. The result was that we had the noisiest hut on the base.

Woodrow Pitts, from Houston, Texas, was the engineer. He had a better command of colorful profanity than anyone else in the hut. He needed such an outlet for his temper, especially when he would discover another flat tire on his cranky bicycle. That machine defied all efforts at repairs. Something was wrong everyday. Two times that I remember Woodrow picked up an infestation of "crabs" (a tiny lice-like parasite that flourished in hair). That caused a frantic trip to the infirmary and a spraying of everything in the hut. Once I picked up the lice from Pitts or from some other unknown source.

Moe Tedesco, a husky Italian from Brooklyn, was one of the gunners. He looked like Brooklyn, and he acted like Brooklyn. He knew little about life in any other environment. His thoughts and interests began and ended back there in the neighborhood where he was born and reared. He said he wanted me to come visit him someday when we got back to the States, and he would show me the real Brooklyn. He gave me his address but also the name of a pool hall. He said they would always know where to find him. Moe was about twenty-five. The Brooklyn accent, tinted with Italian speed, made his conversation interesting. Moe was the kind of man I would want along if I should suddenly end up in a brawl on some dark street in a tough neighborhood.

Hubert (Hubie) Green was the other waist gunner. He was from a city about sixty miles from New York. Like Carroll Wilson, he spent most of his spare time in bed. He had this one big habit — writing letters. That man wrote more leters than anyone I knew in the service. Hubie was tall, dark, slender — very nice looking. He had a good disposition and never gave anyone any trouble. I think he was about twenty-two years old. I didn't know what kind of gunner Hubie was. He always said he merely went along for the ride. I never heard any of his crew complain, however, about his performance not being on a par with the other gunners.

Ray Bechtel, from California, was the tail gunner. He was quiet, easygoing and cooperative. He rarely had anything to say except when a question was directed to him. Ray was so quiet I would forget he was there for hours at a time. He was a good man to have in our hut because he balanced, to some extent, the noisier characters, of which we had a surplus. I saw Ray in action many times and I know that he handled that position extremely well.

Bill Kettner was Cahow's ball gunner. He was slow-moving, steady and methodical, which was the opposite of most of his crew mates. The men in our hut were grateful to Bill because of one lucky incident. He was returning from a nearby village one day, and while walking through some woods, he saw a crosscut saw hanging on a tree limb. He immediately appropriated it. That solved our fuel problem. Those long, cold winter nights were made more livable by the fuel we scrounged with that cross-cut saw. When the war was over the Kings' forests nearby were minus a lot of trees, but we had fuel when no one else did. We kept the saw out of sight and only brought it out after dark when some choice trees had been carefully scouted in advance.

For the benefit of those readers not familiar with a B-17 Flying Fortress, five excellent detailed illustrations supplied by The Boeing Aircraft Co., will help in understanding the various sections of the airplane.

BOMBARDIER'S AND NAVIGATOR'S COMPARTMENT

AMMUNITION BOXES

COMPASS

SIGNAL LIGHT BOX

FIRE EXTINGUISHER

HEATING AND VENTILATING DUCT

DRIFT METER

AMMUNITION BOXES

BULKHEAD NO. 2

RADIO COMPASS CONTROL BOX

PORTABLE OXYGEN TANKS

OXYGEN REGULATOR

CARTRIDGE BOX

BLACKOUT CURTAINS

CHUTE

.50 CALIBER MACHINE GUN

RADIO HEAD SET

RADIO COMPASS JUNCTION BOX

BOMBARDIER'S SEAT

CARTRIDGE CHUTE

BOMBARDIER'S PANEL LIGHT

INTERPHONE JACK BOX

BULKHEAD NO. 3

BOMB SIGHT PLATFORM

NAVIGATORS TABLE

RS-2 RACK SELECTOR RELAY

OUTSIDE AIR TEMPERATURE BULB

LOOP ANTENNA

SILICA TUBE

ELECTRIC BOMB RELEASE

PITOT TUBE

BOMBARDIER'S PANEL EQUIPMENT

BOMBARDIER'S WINDOW WIPER MOTOR

BOMB RACK CONTROL AND SALVO RELEASE

BOMB DOOR RETRACTING LEVER

16

1.

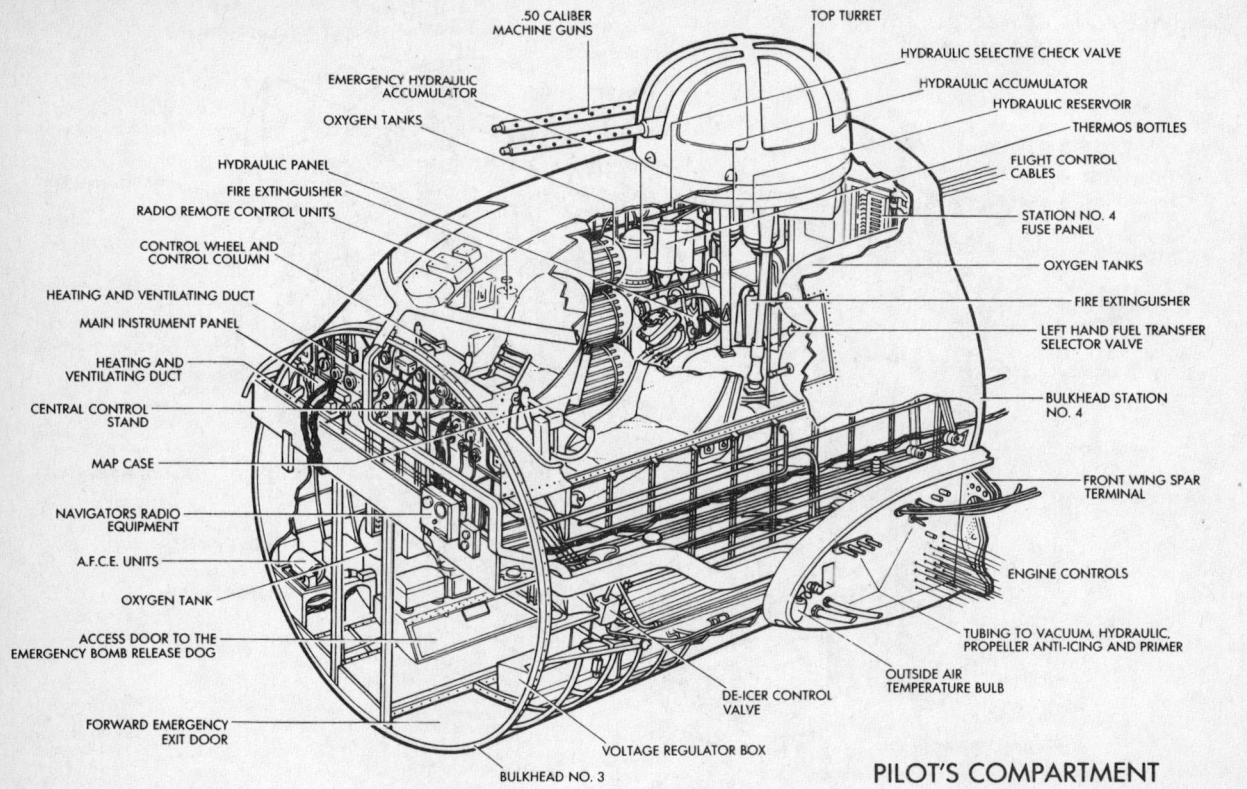

.50 CALIBER
MACHINE GUNS

TOP TURRET

HYDRAULIC SELECTIVE CHECK VALVE

EMERGENCY HYDRAULIC
ACCUMULATOR

HYDRAULIC ACCUMULATOR

OXYGEN TANKS

HYDRAULIC RESERVOIR

THERMOS BOTTLES

HYDRAULIC PANEL

FLIGHT CONTROL
CABLES

FIRE EXTINGUISHER

RADIO REMOTE CONTROL UNITS

STATION NO. 4
FUSE PANEL

CONTROL WHEEL AND
CONTROL COLUMN

OXYGEN TANKS

HEATING AND VENTILATING DUCT

FIRE EXTINGUISHER

MAIN INSTRUMENT PANEL

LEFT HAND FUEL TRANSFER
SELECTOR VALVE

HEATING AND
VENTILATING DUCT

CENTRAL CONTROL
STAND

BULKHEAD STATION
NO. 4

MAP CASE

FRONT WING SPAR
TERMINAL

NAVIGATORS RADIO
EQUIPMENT

A.F.C.E. UNITS

OXYGEN TANK

ENGINE CONTROLS

ACCESS DOOR TO THE
EMERGENCY BOMB RELEASE DOG

TUBING TO VACUUM, HYDRAULIC,
PROPELLER ANTI-ICING AND PRIMER

OUTSIDE AIR
TEMPERATURE BULB

FORWARD EMERGENCY
EXIT DOOR

DE-ICER CONTROL
VALVE

VOLTAGE REGULATOR BOX

BULKHEAD NO. 3

PILOT'S COMPARTMENT

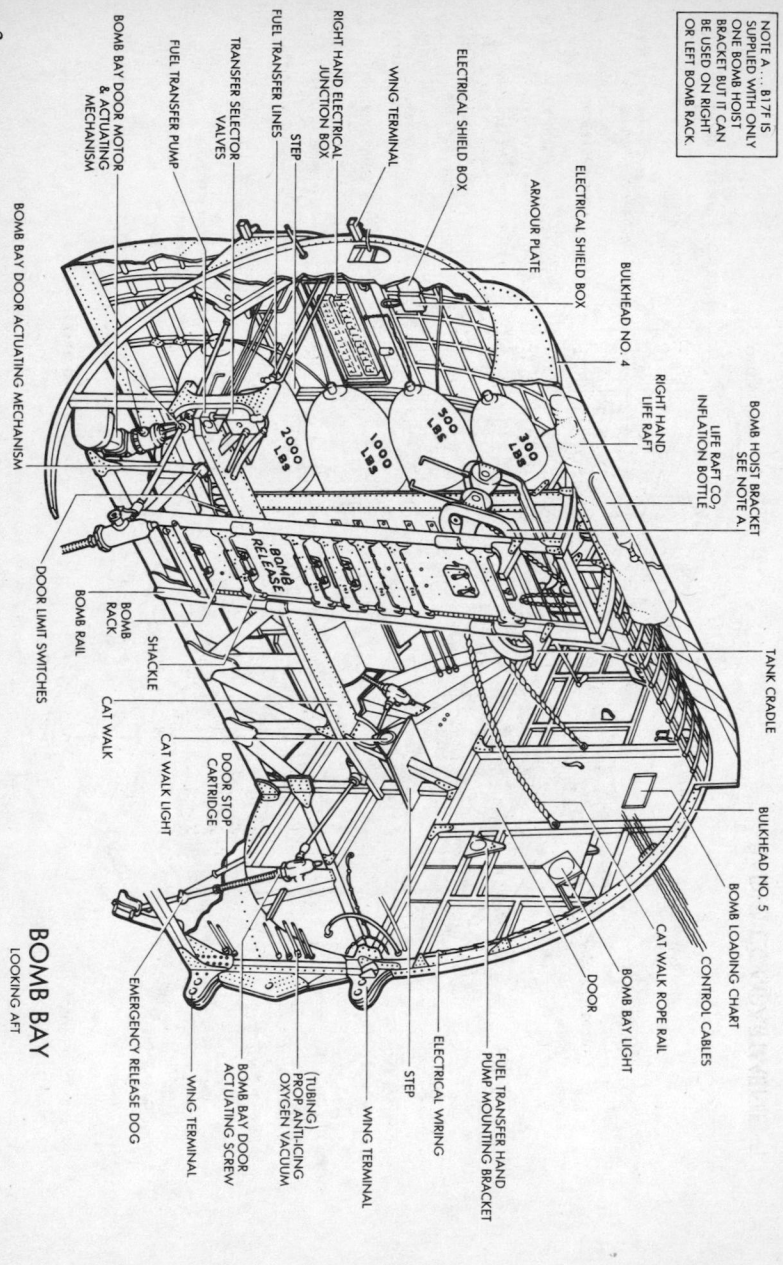

BOMB BAY
LOOKING AFT

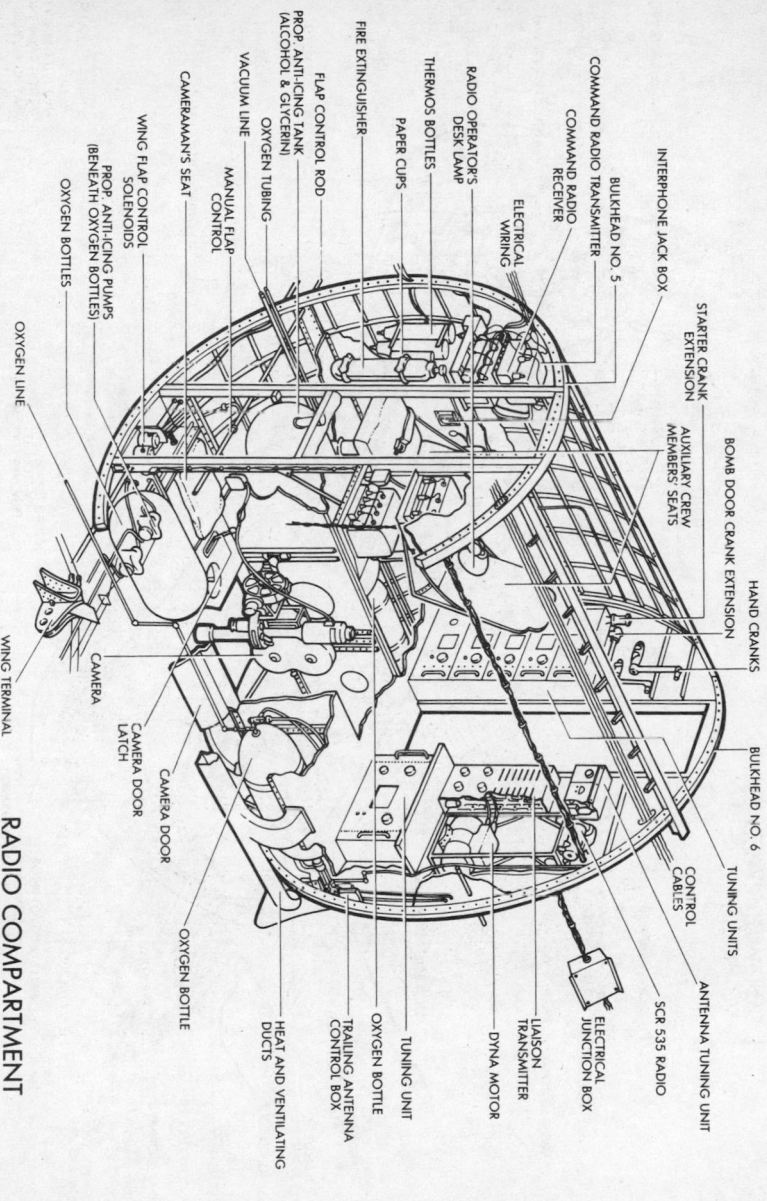

RADIO COMPARTMENT

STABILIZER DE-ICER BOOT

HAND FIRE EXTINGUISHER

EMPENNAGE DE-ICER LINE

OXYGEN TUBE

AMMUNITION BOX

.50 CALIBER MACHINE GUN

DEMAND OXYGEN REGULATORS (2 UNITS)

PORTABLE OXYGEN BOTTLE

BALL GUNNER'S OXYGEN BOTTLE

ELECTRICAL SPARE PARTS BOX

EXTRA AMMUNITION

HAND CRANKS

BOMB DOOR CRANK EXTENSION

STARTER CRANK EXTENSION

SPARE COILS LIAISON TRANSMITTER

RADIO COMPARTMENT FLOOR

NO. 6 BULKHEAD

BALL TURRET

ANTENNA LEAD IN SHIELD

FUSE PANEL

.50 CALIBER MACHINE GUNS

TRAILING ANTENNA

TRAILING ANTENNA REEL

LIAISON ANTENNA (OUT TO WING) TERMINAL

PORTABLE OXYGEN BOTTLE

.50 CALIBER MACHINE GUN

TOILET

NO. 7 BULKHEAD

ELEVATOR UP CABLE MASTS

ELEVATOR DOWN CABLE MASTS

OXYGEN REGULATOR PRESSURE AND FLOW INDICTORS

TAIL GUNNER'S ARMOUR PLATE

.50 CALIBER MACHINE GUNS

CARTRIDGE CHUTE

ADJUSTABLE SEAT

AMMUNITION BOX

RUDDER CONTROL MASTS

RUDDER LOCK QUADRANT

TAIL GUNNER'S EMERGENCY ESCAPE HATCH

ELEVATOR DE-ICER BOOT

TAIL WHEEL (RETRACTED)

MAIN ENTRANCE DOOR OPENING

AUXILIARY DIRECT CURRENT GENERATOR UNIT

SIDE GUNNER'S ARMOUR PLATE

REAR COMPARTMENTS

5.

The diagrams on the previous five pages are printed courtesy of The Boeing Company Archives.

1. The nose secton.

This drawing shows the nose section of any early B-17 E model. It does not show the gun on the other side of the nose. The navigator fired both of the side guns depending on which direction the attack was coming from. The bombardier's gun was mounted in the center of the nose although in this illustration it appears to be off center. When the later G model was introduced the two side guns were removed and a power operated turret was mounted under the nose with two guns.

The Norden Bomb Sight is not shown, but the platform on which the Sight was mounted in combat can be seen directly in front of the Bombardier's seat.

2. The cockpit (or sometimes called cabin).

This is an excellent illustration of what we called the cockpit. The seats for the two pilots and the top turret can be plainly seen. To get some idea of the discomfort caused by low temperature note the large round floor of the top turret. This was made of heavy aluminum. Now imagine how cold the feet would get standing on this metal floor for five or more hours at a time, with the temperature from twenty-five to sixty degrees below zero. The door that can be seen at the right of the picture opens into the bomb bay. Access from the cockpit to the nose was by means of a walkway under the pilots' seats.

3. The bomb bay.

The narrow catwalk, that is mentioned often in this account, can be clearly seen in this drawing. Also references will be made to the constricted space that can be seen in the center of the catwalk. It was difficult to squeeze through it with high altitude clothes and equipment on. It was not possible to get through this space with a bulky parachute snapped into place.

One of the two bomb bay doors can be seen. They were lowered of course for the bomb drop, but if a bomb should have accidently fallen free, the two doors would fall open at a weight less than a hundred pounds.

In case a bomb failed to release someone had to go back and trip the bomb shackle by hand. At high altitudes this could be quite hazardous if the time extended over three minutes. The portable oxygen bottles were good for about four minutes under average circumstances. If the crewmen lost his oxygen supply he would tumble out into space without a chute (unless he realized his predicament in time to get to the cockpit or radio room).

4. The radio room.

This illustration is of an early E model before the radio gun was added. This gun was mounted at the top in an open space called a hatch. The radio operator stood facing the rear at his gun position. The door that can be seen at the rear was removed in combat by most groups. The terrific draft created by the open space made it difficult for the operator to use his key because of the extremely low temperatures and rushing wind. (At that time the radio operator used Morse code rather than voice transmission in enemy territory).

The front door can not be seen clearly but it allowed the radio operator to look into the bomb bay and advise the bombardier that doors were either up or down, and whether any bombs failed to release.

The newer G model enclosed the open hatch area and made the radio operator's position far more comfortable.

5. The waist and tail.

This picture shows the positions of the ball turret operator, the two waist gunners and the tail gunner. Actually the two waist guns in the E and F models were mounted so that the fulcrum of the mount was slightly outside the windows to permit the gunners to fire parallel to the sides of the aircraft. The windblast caused by the enormous draft of the large open spaces was almost beyond the limits of human endurance when temperatures plunged to fifty below. Casualties from freezing and frostbite dropped seventy five percent when the G model enclosed the windows with clear plexiglass.

CHAPTER II
Mission to Brussels

August 10

I heard the Jeep stop outside a little after two A.M. I could never sleep soundly when I thought a mission was likely. I would listen to the far-off roar of aircraft engines and shiver at the thought of where we might go in the morning.

We had learned a lot from that first aborted mission, and this time we were ready when the officers arrived. Each Group had different systems. At the 381st they considered it to be more important for the gunners to go directly to the aircraft and get it ready for the mission than to sit through a briefing. Really, all we wanted to know was the kind of target it was going to be. The rest of the briefing information was of little interest to the gunners. We worked out an easy way to evaluate the target. One of us would stand outside the door of the Briefing Room. As soon as the doors were closed, the curtain covering the target map was pulled back and the reactions of the officers could be plainly heard; that told us about how rough the target was going to be. If an extra rough mission was indicated, we wanted advance notice. One thing was extra ammunition. It was against regulations, but I wanted more ammo if there was any real chance we might need it.

At the aircraft we would get our own guns ready, then prepare the nose guns so that the Navigator and Bombardier had only to make the final adjustments and slip them into receivers when they arrived. There was not enough time for them to attend briefing and get to the plane in time to do a thorough job on their guns. The guns were stored in a heavy wrap of oilsoaked cloth to prevent rusting. Before a mission the heavy oil coating had to be removed because it might absorb moisture and cause the guns to freeze at high altitude. A light oil film was rubbed on for the mission.

The target for the day was Hamburg. The R.A.F. had firebombed it during the night and we were to increase the holocaust. We were flying as spare and would fill in if any ship had to abort over the North Sea. I had mixed feelings about bombing that city. I had once spent three pleasant weeks in Hamburg. I recalled the evening I was carried along by a crowd into one of Adolf Hitler's fiery rallies — but being warned there might be street fighting, I turned away at the edge of the crowd. At that time the name Hitler meant nothing to me.

No aircraft aborted the formation, so when we reached the turn-around point, Gleichauf headed back toward England. It was a long, wearisome trip and I was concerned that fighters might spot us. But the size of the invading formation pulled all of the German interceptors inland and we saw nothing but water. Again, there was no credit for a mission.

August 15 — Brussels *Aircraft 765* *Nip and Tuck*

It was a little after three the next morning when I heard the crunch of heavy shoes on the gravel walk outside. The lights came on and Lt. Reese roused us from sleep.

"Get up, you bastards! You're flying #765 with Gleichauf: Comer, Counce, Rogers, Abramo, and Wilson . . . Wilson! — Wilson!!!"

Wilson raised up in bed.

"Come on! Let's go — and Good Luck!!"

Jim and I went on ahead of the others and got out to the ship early. We had plenty of time to get the guns ready. When Gleichauf got to the aircraft he called us for a briefing.

"We're hittin' the port docks at Brussels today — it will be a short run. S-2 (Air Force Intelligence) says they have a hundred fighters close by and moderate flak, but very accurate. Ought not to be too bad. Any questions? OK. Let's climb in and get ready to go."

Major Hendricks, our Squadron C.O., was leading and we were fly-ing as right wing in the second element of the lead squadron. As we headed out over the North Sea and the English coast faded from sight, several feints were made in fake directions and we returned to England and started over again. As early as 1943 the Allied strategy was to pro-voke Goering into putting his fighters up at the wrong time and at the wrong place. That would divide and reduce the interceptors that could attack us, and also force Germany to use up her precious fuel supply. The Germans did not have the vast oil resources of the Allies.

Surely, on our third attempt we ought to get a mission credit! How long was it going to take to get in twenty-five missions? But now clouds began to form heavily underneath the formation and halfway over the North Sea it became a solid blanket.

"Pilot to Bombardier."

"Go ahead, Paul."

"Can we drop in this soup?"

"No way — I think Hendricks will try an alternate."

"Navigator to Bombardier — I'm sure the alternate is covered, too. Don't think we're gonna drop anything today."

Oh no! Not again! Would we ever manage to get in a mission? We had what seemed to be an easy one — and now! Three attempts and all that work for nothing! The rule for a mission credit was that the formation must do one of three things: fly the course all the way and drop on the target, drop on an alternate target, or engage the enemy in combat. The latter included encountering flak, however, it was never intended to include a sporadic burst or two I am sure.

"Navigator to crew — the lead ship reported flak! We've got us credit for a mission!"

"Bombardier to crew! Did any of you see flak? I didn't see any."

"Navigator to crew! Dammit, don't argue with the Brass! They're gonna give us a mission!"

"But there wasn't any flak, Navigator."

"Pilot to Crew — if the C.O. says there was flak, you can be sure there was flak. Now don't raise any questions at interrogation." (The debriefing of the crews after a mission.)

That was the smart thing to do, of course. So — ring the bells! Beat the drums! We had a mission credit!

What a difference one mission made! We were now allowed to join in a conversation without someone saying, "What th' hell do you know about it?" I felt one hundred percent better because of that one mark on the mission tally board. We were lucky to ease into combat with sorties, because each time we had learned some valuable lessons, gained confidence, and increased the odds for surviving the first few real fights.

Only one of the eighteen crews that we trained with in the U.S. came with us to the 381st. The day after we arrived their Navigator was pressed into service, because navigators were in short supply. We were all at the hard stand to meet him on his return, and were stunned to find that our friend was dead. It hit Carl hard because the nose of the plane was so vulnerable to heavy flak fragments or fighter projectiles. The ball turret operator on that crew was so badly wounded on the Hamburg raid that he will probably never walk again. But the worst was yet to come for Carl: two days later a navigator had his testicles shot off. Shutting never fully recovered from the trauma of that shock! He lived in deadly fear that it might happen to him! He persuaded the people at Armament to cut and shape some special armor plate to fit around his genital area. Holes were drilled in the edges so that it could be tied in place with four heavy cords. It took two men to assist in tying Carl's shield in proper position, and it became the matrix of his protective armor. Shutting was the only navigator in the United States Air force with specially made genital protection armor plate. In addition, he placed two sheets of armor plate on the floor where he would stand at either gun.

The B-17 E was being replaced with the B-17 F, but a new crew could expect to be assigned one of the older, more undesirable airplanes. The main thing that bothered me was the small fuel capacity of seventeen hundred and fifty gallons, compared to the extra nine hundred gallons of the newer Forts. I hoped that whatever plane we were going to get, it would be soon. It would be better knowing what we would have to work with on a mission, than to draw a strange aircraft each trip.

On our first two sorties, I noticed that Gleichauf stayed on the Command radio frequency while Carqueville remained on the intercom to keep crew control. That freed Gleichauf to concentrate on formation flying, which used his experience to our best advantage. Paul let Herb take care of the rest. It was a good combination that worked out quite well.

August 15

Jim and I rode into Cambridge on the morning run of the supply truck, and started looking for bicycle and radio shops. There was no restriction on the sale of used items, and even new appliances could take on a used look very easily. We made our purchases and shipped the two bicycles to a nearby town by train. We carried the small radio. I doubt that any of us ever got more pleasure from a one pound investment ($4.13 each) than we received from the purchase of that radio. It made a big difference in our lives. We had the full range of the British Broadcasting Company which offered excellent music and world news. We listened regularly to the Allied Forces Network that broadcast the things Americans wanted to hear. While in England we became aware of a young singer named Frank Sinatra.

Our radio introduced us to a new type of program — very interesting, even though it was pure propaganda. We soon learned when to tune in to the German English language broadcasts. They had an announcer with an exaggerated British accent. His name was William Joyce, but he was called Lord Haw Haw. To a newly-arrived combat group at an English Airdrome, he would beam something like this: ''Welcome to the 381st Bomber Group at Ridgewell Airdrome. We wish you good luck and look forward to meeting you over the Continent very soon. By the way, please correct the clock at your Officer's Club. It is five minutes slow!'' And sure enough, on checking, the clock would be five minutes slow! That left the impression that German agents lurked everywhere.

CHAPTER III
Mission to Le Bourget

August 16 — Le Bourget Aircraft 765 — Nip and Tuck

Soon after daylight the formation was crossing the gray-green water of the English Channel. My anxiety and tension mounted, as I knew we would face the fierce German fighters, for on this clear day we would invade the lair of Goering's best. The veterans had made certain we knew what usually happened to new crews on their first meeting with Jerry. They were not expected to come back — it was as simple as that.

The intercom came on: "Tail to Copilot, Tail to Copilot."

"Go ahead, Tail."

"Fighters five o'clock low."

"Ball to Copilot. Looks like the escort."

I spotted a long line of specks closing in fast from the North. It was the escort of fifty P-47 Thunderbolts. Good! I felt better because they could keep the enemy fighters away for a little while. However, the P-47's had a short fuel range, as the disposible belly tanks available at that time only held seventy-five gallons.

"Navigator to crew — Navigator to crew! Enemy coast five minutes away."

"Bombardier to crew! Watch out for fighters!"

Scared? Where do you draw the line between fright and intense nervous anticipation? Nothing in civilian life had prepared me for the feeling of kill or be killed. Our meager gunnery training was laughable compared with the skill and experience of the veteran German fighter pilots.

The briefing on the target earlier that morning kept turning through my mind: "We're hitting an aircraft plant at the edge of Le Bourget airfield — near Paris. The figher opposition will be plenty rough! This is your first real taste of combat so ----!" The Abbeville Boys meant Goering's personal squadrons, the roughest Germany had to offer.

When I saw the French coast pass by underneath, I became more tense and keyed up. We had been warned repeatedly that German fighters liked to lurk in the area where we would have to look directly at the sun to see them. They would attempt to slip in on us undetected by most of the formation gunners. It was my responsibility not to let it happen. From my turret I had the only unobstructed view of the sky above in all directions. George Balmore, in the radio room, could see part of the area above and to the rear.

"Bombardier to crew! Bombardier to crew! Fighters twelve o'clock low! Can't make out what they are, but don't look like 47's!"

I stood up in the turret, looked down and counted twenty or more that could be seen from my position. They were German fighters, all right! The enemy pilots knew that the P-47's were at the end of their short fuel range, and were patiently waiting for them to turn back. In a few minutes the escort dipped their wings as if to say, "Good luck! See you in England tonight," and they were gone. I felt a knot in my stomach as the big Thunderbolts vanished to the North.

Immediately the enemy pulled up to our level and began circling to pick out positions for attack. Of course I was excited! It was my first time to see hostile aircraft in the sky!

"Copilot to crew! Throw the lead at those fighters if they come in!"

"Copilot to Turret."

"Go ahead."

"Keep your eye on those three fighters three o'clock high — I'll watch high and forward."

"Copilot to Tail. See anything trying to sneak in back there?"

"No, clear below and behind."

Suddenly Carqueville screamed over the intercom: "Fighter coming in twelve o'clock level — get him! Get him! Get him!"

I was tracking four suspicious fighters at nine o'clock and wheeled around just in time to get my sights on the fighter attacking us. It was headed straight for our nose spitting deadly 20mm cannon shells and 30 caliber machine gun bullets. I was so fascinated by the sight that I froze! Did not fire a shot!! Neither did the Bombardier nor the Navigator — the only other guns that could bear on a frontal attack! Light flashes from the leading edge of the fighter signalled how many cannon shells were being fired at us. I could hear some projectiles striking the airplane. It was a spectacle that drove deep into my memory. The fighter turned his belly to us and slipped into a beautiful barrel roll under our right wing and dived out of range.

Carqueville was boiling mad! He exploded over the intercom: "What th' hell's the matter with you sunnuvabitches? You're supposed to be gunners! Why didn't you shoot? That fighter could've knocked us down! You let one more come in like that and I'll personally work you over — all three of you!"

He was furious and he should have been, because there was no excuse for failure to fire. I have relived those traumatic moments many times, and I can still feel the mesmerizing power that prevented my hand from pressing that firing switch. Why didn't we fire? I will never know for sure. We were seized by the paralysis so typical of what happens to a deer hunter the first time he gets a buck in his gun sights, (or the commandment "Thou shall not kill!"')

The intercom came to life again. "Bombardier to Navigator and Turret: We blew that one! I don't know why but we did. But, believe me, it's not gonna happen again!" And it never did.

We were lucky to sustain that first attack with little damage, because the enemy had minimal opposition to divert his aim or tactics. There were three simultaneous attacks which cut down the fire that each fighter drew. The Germans were smart in choosing which way to come in, relying mainly on head-on confrontation. When several fighters attacked at one time the concentrated fire of the formation guns was divided, reducing the opposition to each fighter and disrupting the defensive tactics of the formation.

"Ball to crew — B-17 going down on fire four o'clock low!"

I looked down and it was sickening. Long streams of flame extended beyond the tail. I kept screaming to myself, "Why don't they jump? Jump! Jump, dammit! For God's sake, get out before it's too late!" But it was already too late. It was my first time to see men die in combat and it was a shattering experience. My stomach turned over at the thought of those ten men hurtling down to certain death. I wondered what flashed through their minds on that terrifying plunge to earth in their burning, spinning airplane.

Suddenly the Bombardier called out: "Flak nine o'clock low!"

"Ball to crew — flak at eleven o'clock low."

Huge puffs of black smoke began to burst around the formation. So that was flak! It was thicker than I expected, and a lot closer.

"Bombardier to Pilot — over."

"Go ahead."

"We're on the bomb run."

That meant the planes had to fly a straight and steady course for several minutes to provide a stable platform for the Bombardier and the Norden Bomb Sight.

BAM!!

The ship rocked and I saw a nearby burst of orange flame followed by boiling, black smoke. I had been told that the crew would not hear the shells burst. Well, I heard that one! Mostly I saw only black smoke explode into large globs and heard pieces of shrapnel striking the aircraft whenever a shell burst too close. Flying through the floating smoke made the field of fire seem worse than it was.

One battery of guns below began to move in closer and closer. They seemed to choose us as their special target and were firing five 88mm shells at a time. As the bursts crept ever closer I could feel the hair on my head trying to push up against my helmet. All the German gunners needed to do was make one final correction, and they would have had us bracketed dead center.

"Radio to Copilot — can't we take some evasive action?"

"Hell no! We're on the bomb run."

I prayed a little, but who knows whether it helped or not. At the time, a man with a religious background felt that it could help, and in that sense perhaps it was useful. Later, when I looked back on such moments more rationally, I wondered why I believed that through the mysterious phenomena we call prayer the Supreme Being could be induced to alter the Laws of the Universe — His Own Laws — just for me. Was I some special favorite? Was anyone praying for the protection of the innocent people who lived and worked too close to where our exploding bombs were landing? How strange and paradoxical for men to pray selfishly for their own lives, while doing everything in their power to kill other men, who in turn perhaps were praying to the same God.

I was suddenly jolted back to the urgency of the moment as I heard, "Bombs away!" The unexpected upward lurch of the aircraft, as the bomb weight fell away, startled me momentarily. As we turned left away from the target, I got a glimpse of several columns of smoke rising from the bombed area.

"Pilot to Tail."

"Go ahead."

"Did we hit the target?"

"Where we hit looks like factory buildings — don't know if that was our target."

I dropped down out of the turret just long enough to have a quick look at the fuel gauges, and got a shock when I saw that we only had a third left. After hasty calculations of probable consumption going back, with the aid of letting down from high altitude, I felt that we could make it back to Ridgewell.

"Copilot to crew — Copilot to crew. Stay alert! They may hit us goin' back. Turret!"

"Go ahead."

"Put on your sun glasses and watch that area around the sun. We don't want them slippin' in on us."

Ten minutes later: "Fighters ten o'clock low!"

'What are they doin', Ball?"

"Only two of 'em — not tryin' to come in."

"Bombardier to Navigator."

"Go ahead."

"When are the Spitfires due?"

"In about ten minutes."

Some time later: "Ball to crew — ten fighters six o'clock low — could be Spits."

"Navigator to crew: I think they're Spitfires, stayin' low to keep the Jerries from gettin' to us."

The Navigator was right because no more Bogies climbed up to our level. Before long I could see the gleam of sun on water up ahead and I began to relax because we had our mission almost made. As soon as we were over the Channel, the likelihood of another attack faded out.

At Ridgewell Airdrome, nine happy men climbed out of aircraft #765. Jerry was better than we expected, and flak was much worse. Regardless of our initial failure, we had met the enemy and returned safely . . . something many new crews failed to do.

The tenth man out of the plane was the Copilot, but he definitely was not happy. He was still fuming about our miserable performance on that first fighter attack. Carqueville glared at me, and stalked off without a word, but I got his message: "I expected more from you! Of all the people on this crew, I didn't expect you would screw up on your first combat action!"

After a plane returned the crew was not through. A truck carried the men to Operations for interrogation. Hot coffee, hot chocolate, and Spam sandwiches were waiting, one of the few times Spam ever tasted good! All of the crews gathered in the waiting room and milled about, swapping stories and checking up on other crews' versions of incidents. The Colonel was there, looking the men over:

"Nice going, Jim."

"Good formation, Lieutenant."

"Nice shooting, Sergeant."

If he spotted a man who looked shaky, he often patted him on the back with some remark to boost him up. Colonel Joseph Nazarro was a fine Commanding Officer. He had the respect of the men in his command. The Colonel was from a military family, but no typical brass hat. He was the quarterback on the 1933 West Point football team that lost only one game — 7 to 6 to Notre Dame. (He later became a four star general and succeeded Gen. Curtis LeMay as head of the Strategic Air Command.) The Colonel was my idea of what a combat commander should have been. I never heard one bitch about him from anyone in his command that made any sense.

In our Group Interrogation Room the atmosphere was loose and free from any kind of restraint. Here the complete picture of the raid was placed on paper. No one crew could see everything accurately, so the final group picture of the mission was composed from the data supplied by various crews. Often there were new items to report which set in motion the network of Air Force Intelligence (S-2) which was constantly striving to stay ahead of the enemy. A new defensive weapon or method was pounced upon as soon as it showed up, in an effort to find the best counter-method before the Germans had time to exploit a temporary success.

If a gunner thought he had shot down a fighter he made his claim at the interrogation, where the briefing officer could get confirmation from other gunners who might have seen the incident. Wilson was positive he had badly damaged a fighter.

"What kind of fighter was it, Sergeant?" asked the interrogation officer.

"F.W. 190, an' I got in three heavy bursts. I could see 'em hittin' it an' pieces flyin' off."

"Well, Sergeant, the enemy fighters who intercepted us today were all M.E. 109's with liquid cooled engines. The F.W. 190 has an air cooled engine, but the only fighters today with air cooled engines were our P-47's — did you hit one of them?"

"Oh no! I'm sure it wasn't a P-47 . . . I — uh — maybe there wasn't as much damage as I thought. I — uh — withdraw the claim."

Balmore said, "Go ahead with your claim, Wilson. Maybe you can get credit for downing a P-47."

It was after interrogation that fatigue really hit me. But the day's work still was not over. Wearily, we went back to the aircraft because the guns had to be cleaned and checked for worn parts, and stowed in oil-soaked cloths. They must be ready for another raid the next morning in case one was scheduled. It was twilight when I got back to our hut. Total exhaustion, such as I had never experienced before, so numbed me that I did not bother to go by the mess hall or take the time to wash. The long hours since the call at two-thirty A.M., the debilitating rigors of high altitude, the intense cold, and the wearying fatigue from fear and tension combined to hit me hard. I literally fell into bed, with part of my clothes on, and in two minutes was oblivious to everything, including the noise and hubbub of men coming and going.

After that first combat experience, I realized a peculiar phenomenon of the mind: it is more traumatic to listen to a factual telling of a hair-raising experience than actually to go through the same thing yourself. The difference is that when listening to such a story, one has no escape mechanism. However, when living through a harrowing experience, the mind is too occupied with defense and physical actions to provide full accommodation for fright.

Originally I had some reservations about Nick Abramo, because the ball was so important to the crew. Hanging down there all alone, cut off from the rest of the aircraft, was an unenviable position. By the time we got back from Le Bourget I was satisfied that we had a reliable man guarding the approaches to our plane from below. I guarantee that no other man in the crew would have voluntarily entered that risky, cramped, overexposed contraption. The ball required the knees to be brought upward on each side of the Sperry computing sight. Over a long flight the gunner became uncomfortable due to the inability to stretch out his legs to relieve cramped muscles. He was more exposed to the fury of bursting flak shells than anyone else on the aircraft. Almost three quarters of the ball hung suspended in space, creating a horror of exposure from which there was no protection.

Unknown to the bomber crews, the English and American Air Commands were at odds over the basic concept of how to conduct the air offense against Hitler-held Europe. In August, 1943, the skies offered the only path the Allies could use to reach the heart of Nazi territory.

The R.A.F. was certain that night saturation bombing of industrial centers was the best method. The Americans were equally convinced that for them, with the more heavily armed B-17's, daylight strategic bombing of selected targets (by virtue of their importance to the German war machine) was a better use of men and machines. True, the R.A.F. certainly had far more war experience, and had tried daylight raids early in the war with disastrous losses. Their night bombing was built around the excellent Lancaster Bomber, which was fast, long-ranged, and carried a heavier load of bombs than the B-17's. It was lightly armed, however, and not very rugged. The R.A.F. system was to send over fast target marking planes early in the night to outline the target area with incendiary bombs that would glow brightly for hours. The Lancasters followed, one at a time, avoiding German fighters under the cover of darkness. Such tactics resulted in a saturation type of destruction hoping to hit war plants, cripple the cities, and demoralize the German workers as well.

The Americans favored the use of rugged, heavily-armed bombers at high altitude because they would be above the worst flak and the effective

34

ceiling of some of the older German fighters. They thought that the highly accurate Norden Bomb Sight would permit pin-point accuracy of bombing against Germany's most vital military targets. The American view was that on night raids so many of the bombs fell outside the main target area that their effectivness was doubtful, as far as reducing the German capacity to produce war materials.

Based on their own experience with daylight bombing raids, the R.A.F. commanders were sure that when the American bombing fleet became strong enough to begin daylight raids deep into Germany, the losses would be so disastrous that they would be unacceptable. On one night of bombing, however, the R.A.F. lost ninety-six Lancasters! So what was an acceptable loss?

Gen. Ira Eaker, Commanding Officer of the 8th Bomber Command was getting ready to put the high altitude strategic bombing concept to a series of crucial tests. At a secret meeting in North Africa, President Roosevelt had given way to Prime Minister Churchill's argument that night bombing was the best use of Allied aircraft.[1] But Mr. Churchill, in a meeting with Gen. Eaker, gave him a little more time to prove the American bombers could invade heavily defended targets deep inside Germany (where we had not yet attempted to raid). The implication was that if those test raids failed, the American Air Force would begin a shift to the English night raid concept.

Our crew went on combat status ten days before the first of those really decisive missions was scheduled. In other words, we had arrived in England at the worst possible time of World War II for a bomber crew.

[1]As explained in *"Decision Over Schweinfurt"* by Thomas Coffey — David McKay Co., Inc. — New York.

The conference was in January and Gen. Eaker was anxious to make good on his promise to the P.M. But he had an unexpected blow: some of his Groups were transferred to the North African invasion. So he had to wait several months for more aircraft. Meanwhile the 270 single engined fighters available to meet the Fortresses over Europe in early April increased to over 600 by the end of July.

CHAPTER IV
Schweinfurt #1
The Ball Bearing Plants

August 17

It was to be one of the most storied air battles of this or any other war. Five or six of our men were on the mission scattered in different airplanes. Due to shortages of crewmen they were required to fill in where needed. Since this is an account of what happened to our men, I decided to tell the story of the raid in the first person, but a composite of the highlights experienced by each man. At the date this was written, it was impossible to separate the events by name and individual crews on which they were flying. The actions are true but did not take place on a single aircraft.

An ominous groan came from the Briefing Room. I knew then we were in for a rugged day. We were still groggy from the mission of the previous day, and not in the best physical condition. "The crew I was assigned to had a great deal of experience. They were all strangers to me, and I'm sure they would have preferred having a more experienced gunner. The radio operator cornered me and offered me some advice. 'We got a peculiar pilot', he said. 'He's tops when the going gets tough, but he has the habit of cursing the gunners, and raising hell over the interphones. When fighters attack he will call you every kind of sunnuvabitch he can think of. He don't mean a damn thing by it — nothing personal. It's just his way of keeping his gunners under control. After the mission he won't remember a word he said, so don't let it upset you.' (From an account by James Counce written for me the day after the raid.)"

The weather was so foggy that I doubted we would get underway, or if we did get off, it would be mid-morning. When the pilot arrived, he called us together. "All right, men. We're in for a wild one today! We're hittin' some ball bearing plants at a town called Schweinfurt in Bavaria. The route will force us to fly over the middle of Germany, goin' in and returning. Those plants make more than half of Germany's ball bearings, and if we destroy 'em, our raid will be a success — even if only a few of us get back."

There was an audible groan from the crew.

"The altitude will be 23,000 feet and we will try to divide the opposition. The Third Division will go first, hit Regensburg close by, and then fly on to North Africa. The other two divisions will hit Schweinfurt and return to England. Let's hope the plan works, 'cause if we don't fool 'em we could see three to four hundred fighters. The First Division will lead the attack on Schweinfurt and the 91st will be in front. The 381st will fly the low Group position."

The hated word "low" prompted more comments and considerable bitching because the low group always caught the worst attacks.

"Knock off the bitching! This is gonna be one hell of a raid, and I don't want to see one Goddamned round of ammunition wasted! You gunners hear me? Not one wasted round! You'll fire only when the enemy is close enough to hit, and only when they're attacking our plane! We gotta make that ammo last, and don't you forget it!"

Either Hitler's military staff, or the influential Albert Speer, had become alarmed at the continuous build-up of American bombers, and the prospect of an increasing flow of new bombers from U.S. factories. Unknown to the Allied High Command, General Adolf Galland, commanding the German fighter defense, had pulled back some of his crack fighter groups in France. He had also withdrawn some air units from the Russian Front to form a better defense system. Until then he had a fighter defense protecting Northern Germany, but little behind it. Now the Germans placed reserve forces strategically about Germany so they could battle the Fortresses coming into and going out of the Fatherland. The General felt that he could make the penalty so costly for deep daylight bombing missions that the Americans would be forced to give it up, an opinion shared by the R.A.F. Command.

The weather overcast hung doggedly on, but Col. Curtis LeMay's Third Division managed to get airborne and the mission was on. The air historians and writers emphasize the Third's ability to get off in the soupy weather. LeMay said it was because he made his pilots practice instrument takeoffs. I doubt if the Colonel could have made successful instrument takeoffs that day with the number of inexperienced pilots we had in the 381st Group. The aircraft would have been so scattered when they came out above the bad weather that too much fuel would have been used up to continue so long a flight. The distance was close to our maximum range.

When takeoff time came, the fog blanketing the area was even more dense, so we waited, and waited, and waited, and were almost sure the raid would be scrubbed. As the minutes ticked away, the hoped-for advantage in dividing the fighter interception was slowly eroding. By the time the fog decreased enough to takeoff the Third Division must have hit the target at Regensburg and no doubt was on the way to North Africa. Instead of helping, by dividing the fighters as expected, it had alerted the German Fighter Command to an all-out battle.

On the climb upward the fog began to break at about one thousand feet. By ten-thirty hours the 381st was in the air. The formation converged quickly and headed for the Continent. Little time wasted with feints, and they were up to twenty-three thousand feet altitude approaching the German border. A few minutes beyond the border an unexpected layer of heavy clouds blocked the path. A formation could not fly into clouds, so Colonel Gross, commanding the First Division, had a tough decision to make. He had three choices, none of which was desirable. One, he could pull up over the cloud cover to 27,000 to 28,000 feet, but the target might well be covered by the same clouds when he got there. Two, he could switch to an alternate target, which would upset all the planning and action already underway. Three, he could go under the cloud bank between 17,000 and 18,000 feet, giving the Germans an unusual advantage. That was the choice he decided to take. There was much criticism of his decision later, but those so quick to blame him were not up there that day, faced with an immediate choice from the hard alternatives open to him. Col. Gross was in an extremely difficult position. Based on his possible choices, I think most Commanders would likely have made the same decision.

The formation descended to 17,500 feet and plowed steadily on into German air space. For a while we had an escort of R.A.F. Spitfires, followed by 50 P-47's. They were of little help because of their limited fuel supply. The interceptors were waiting, fired up and ready. The lower altitude was very much to their advantage. The fighting characteristics of the F.W. 190 and the M.E. 109 were extra good at 17,000 feet. They had two other hefty advantages: one, they had more fuel for attacks — two, they could reach the bombers faster after takeoff.

For ten minutes after our fighters left, nothing happened. Then the Ball Turret called out: ''Ball to crew — Ball to crew! Fighters at eight o'clock low! Looks like about seventy of the devils!''

They came rushing up to intercept us and before long the low group was surrounded by a swarm of snarling fighters. They appreared from all directions and quickly showed their intention of a ''give no Quarter'' battle. They just came in and kept on coming in. The German pilots were intense in their attacks and paid little attention to their usual cautious tactics. Attacks were from all angles during the run to the target, but the high nose attack seemed to predominate. At times it looked like the entire Luftwaffe was lined up at twelve o'clock high. The outcome was very much in doubt. The Jerries gave no thought to personal safety in their zeal to teach the Fortress crews a devastating lesson. Fighter losses were high but if ten of their planes went down in flames it seemed like twenty more came up to take their places. Every time two or three fighters were knocked down, a Fortress would go too. "The plane flying on our left wing was hard hit, lost control, and went down. I did not see what happened to the crew. A little later the plane on our right caught fire and exploded. For this kind of fight we had the right pilot. He flew like he had the controls of a fighter craft. He was throwing the ship up and down and from side to side in wild lunges, as the fighters roared in for the kill. The Germans were trying to finish off this squadron before exterminating the next one. There is no question but that we were extraordinarily lucky. It was a combination of a wild pilot doing things not usually done in a formation and pure luck — whatever that is — that kept us from extinction. Evasive action helped, but I wondered what it was doing to the formation." (From the account of Jim Counce.)

Col. Hall, Operations Officer, said that one hour from the target he was not sure that any bomber would reach the objective.

Much to our surprise, enemy planes were waiting for us all along the briefed route with mathematical precision. At the time, we thought someone had talked too much, not realizing that we were encountering a new fighter defense in depth for the first time. "I remember distinctly how the pilot cursed and screamed at us over the intercom, exhorting us to stay on the ball. Counce recalled. "Left Waist! You see those bastards at ten o'clock high? Watch 'em! Here they come! Shoot the sonnuvabitches! Kill them! Blow their asses off! Knock 'em down!"

"Right Waist, you no good sonnuvabitch. I've told you a hundred times not to shoot when they can't hit us. Dammit, that fighter was rolling away from us."

"Crew! Crew! If you keep on wasting your ammunition we'll be out of ammo before we get to the target! Goddamn it, don't shoot 'til you can hit th' bastards! Don't waste one single round. You think some damn ammo truck's gonna fly up here an' give us some more bullets? Watch your ammo!"

A few minutes later: "Get those three bastards eleven o'clock high! Shoot! That's it — blow 'em out! Don't let 'em hit us!"

The pilot kept telling us, over and over, that when a fighter quit firing at us to forget about him, and concentrate on the one that was coming in next. He said. "Don't waste any Goddamn attention tryin' to confirm claims for some gunner. Keep up the fire when they come in, an' catch th' next one — hit 'em while they're comin' in — foul up their aim.''

A plane flying near us was hit and caught fire. The flame streamed beyond the tail, and down it went. Likely no one got out. About twenty minutes later, as we crossed over the Rhine River, the Squadron lead plane lost an engine. A little later a second engine began smoking. The plane dropped back, and our tail gunner reported that three fighters finished it, but he saw three parachutes.

The intercom came on, and a shaky voice said, ''I'm scared! I want my mama!''

Jim reported the following conversation from the aircraft he was in. ''Navigator to Pilot! Aren't we out of formation?''

''Out of formation? Can't you see we're the only one left in the squadron?''

Jim continued: ''The enemy fighters were trying doggedly to finish us off, and the pilot was taking heavy evasive action. It threw me all over the waist and my ammunition flew out of the ammo cans and got fouled up. Once we almost collided with a fighter, but they didn't get us. We maneuvered over to a squadron still in fair shape. One plane was throttle-jockeyin' — fallin' back, catching up, fallin' back. When it fell back too far, we sat down in its place. A few minutes later I saw that ship catch five fighters, and down it went.'' That may sound ruthless and cold-hearted, but if someone ahead of you was hit and got out of tight formation and, then began to straggle, it was accepted procedure to move right into his place.

Our route in was slightly west of Koblenz, where the Moselle River joins the Rhine. At that time the Germans probably guessed that Frankfurt was our target. By the time we had passed that city they must have realized with great anxiety that the bombers were headed for their most essential war plants — the bearings factories at Schweinfurt.

''Navigator to Pilot.''

''Go ahead.''

''You can see Wurzburg ahead and a little to your right. We'll make a ninety degree turn to the left and be on the bomb run in five minutes.''

There was another flurry of attacks, and then I saw bursts of flak nearby.

''Bombardier to Pilot, we're on the bomb run.''

''OK, Bombardier.''

The flak was moderately heavy. The fighters kept away, as always, when we went through the field of fire approaching the target.

''Bombs away!''

We breathed a sigh of relief that we were rid of that weight. The group had sixteen aircraft left at the halfway point. Suddenly, either a rocket or a flak shell made a direct hit on one of our Forts nearby, and it blew up.

Right after the target, fighter activity slacked off, and I mistakenly thought the worst was over. North of Frankfurt they hit us with one of the heaviest attacks of the day. The 381st was losing one plane after another. I thought the fighters would leave us soon and take on the incoming Second Division. There were plenty of fighters, however, to handle the Wings going in and coming back.

The pilot was listening to every burst of fire and keeping up his unending harangue: "Keep watchin' that ammo! We're gettin' closer. Make that ammo last a little longer. Dammit, we're gonna make it! The worst is over!!"

A little later we lost another B-17. Several others were in serious condition. Suddenly, I realized that the fighters were fading away. I was well aware that we didn't have much ammo left. Was it really over? Or were we due for another mauling? A great feeling of relief swept over me as the minutes ticked off.

Jim said that he looked around at the 381st and tried to count the losses, but he did not know how many ships the group put up to start the mission. From what he could see, his guess was twelve to fourteen missing, but that did not mean all of them were lost.

When the coast slipped by I felt mighty good. We definitely were going to make it! Troubles for the 381st were over, I thought — but not quite: one of our aircraft was in serious trouble and dropped down, down. Just before we reached the English coast it hit the water.

"Ball to Copilot."

"Go ahead."

"Beautiful ditching below us — I can see the crew climbin' out. I think they'll be safe this close. Air-Sea rescue oughta find 'em before dark."

Carroll Wilson said after the mission:

"The coast of England had never looked so good, and the white chalk cliffs were a welcome sight. We began to let down and those miserable oxygen masks came off. How I hated those masks!"

It was approaching dusk as we set down at Ridgewell Airdrome. A weary and beaten crew climbed out, thankful that they were privileged to get back. All of the aircraft were damaged, many quite heavily. The 381st lost eleven out of twenty-four aircraft and one plane aborted, the highest loss of any group. The leading 91st Group lost ten ships.

Interrogation was long and detailed. Official claims contended that the target was half destroyed. In truth, something like thirty-five percent of the capacity to produce bearings was destroyed.

The 8th Bomber Command had taken a frightful, shocking loss. Sixty B-17's shot down! Twenty-seven other Fortresses were damaged too severely to be repaired. Another blow dealt us at this time was the incredible failure of Air Force planning to coordinate the facilities in North Africa with a reasonable expectation of the need for repairs. Col. LeMay found, to his amazement, that the only service he could get would be refueling![1] There were no available parts, and no mechanics to repair the heavy battle damage his division suffered — which was comparable to our own.

The combined Schweinfurt-Regensburg casualties were:

    60 B-17's shot down — 16% of the total force

    27 damaged too much to be repaired

    60 B-17's left in North Africa due to no facilities for immediate repairs (what eventually happened to them

    ____ I do not know)

   147 Total Aircraft

Morning brought a severe letdown in morale. At breakfast very few men showed up. The long rows of empty tables took away my appetite. Only yesterday men were crowding in line waiting for seats. That day there were too many unoccupied seats. The usual chatter and banter was absent. Men ate in silence and left quickly. I found myself looking around for faces that I knew I would never see again. What about the future? Was yesterday a preview of what we could expect? That question hung heavily over Ridgewell Airdrome on the morning of August 18th.

It seemed to me that it would be a week before we could get enough replacements to make up the minimum requirements of a Combat Group. Nevertheless, that evening I made a trip to the base canteen to check out the faces. The people I looked for were there, so that meant nothing was shaping up for the next day, as I read the signs. The men who loaded the bombs were called Armorers. If none of them were at the canteen we knew that bombs were being loaded and made mental preparations for the next morning. Many times last minute weather changes would make raids possible. Three favorable conditions had to exist simultaneously: visibility over the target had to be fair, local conditions had to be favorable for takeoff, and visibility had to be assured for landing a large group of planes on the return.

[1]The only account I have seen about this incident was in *"Decision Over Schweinfurt"* by Thomas Coffey.

The Americans and British had a decided advantage over the German weather forecasters, because of the Allied weather stations in Greenland and Iceland. The weather forces that determined what conditions would prevail over Europe developed in the Arctic regions. It was helpful to be able to tie in the long-range forecasts with on-the-scene reports from Allied weather planes sent out over the target areas. Also of great value was the Turing electronic machine. It quickly unscrambled the German military and diplomatic code, and could read the German weather reports broadcast to their military and air units each day.

The 8th Air Force officially claimed 288 German fighters were shot down on the August 17th Schweinfurt-Regensburg mission. The R.A.F. throughout the war was positive that American claims were grossly inflated. I certainly agreed. There was really no reliable way to determine accurately the number of aircraft shot down. Probably one-third would have been closer to being correct.

The problem in claiming fighters shot down was that it was rare when only one position fired at a fighter. Sometimes twenty guns were involved and in a few cases as many as fifty. At times several gunners thought they shot down the same fighter and put in claims for it, so the claims ballooned. Also, enemy fighters were so heavily armored that they could shake off heavy hits and keep coming.

At the command headquarters General Eaker's staff that morning pondered deep and searching questions. What was the lesson learned at Schweinfurt? Had the R.A.F. been correct in their predictions about daylight Fortress raids deep into Germany? The General, very likely, reached two conclusions: one, the Fortresses could battle their way to any target in Europe regardless of German all-out opposition; two, the Bombers must have long-range escort fighters to hold the losses to an acceptable figure when making deep thrusts to well protected targets.

The questions were: What fighters did we have that could go with the B-17's to distant targets? When could we get such fighters delivered to England? The proposed new modified P-51, with Merlin Rolls Royce engines, was not released yet for full production. As far as we knew, the only other fighter with enough range was the P-38 Lightning. Was the P-38 a match for the excellent M.E. 109's and F.W. 190's? The P-38 was a good fighter, but not great, and I'm sure the General wanted something better. We, the bomber crews, knew nothing of Bomber Command's urgent appeal for long-range escort. We would have slept better had we known how strenuously they were pleading with Gen. Arnold, in Washington, for immediate help.

After the Schweinfurt showdown the Colonel no longer had to exhort his experienced pilots to stay in tight formation. Those who got back had learned a lesson they would never forget. They saw what the Jerry fighters did to "throttle jocks." There were a number of reasons why a tight formation was so essential to standing off German fighter attacks. A bomber could not concentrate much fire power against a fighter except on tail attacks. The Germans knew that, so they mainly hit with a frontal charge. A single Fortress could bring to bear only three guns on a head on attack (the nose gun and the two top turret guns). The navigator could fire only if the attack was approaching at an angle to the nose. The top turret guns could not be brought down quite level, so a German fighter charging straight in at the nose could sometimes get under the trajectory of the turret, leaving only the Bombardier's single gun to oppose him. (When the B-17G model was brought out in October of 1943 the single nose gun was replaced with two guns in a chin turret and the navigator side guns were eliminated.) That meant three 50 caliber machine guns versus four 20mm cannon and two to four 30 caliber machine guns — quite an unequal match-up if the fighter was opposed by only one B-17. (German fighters varied in the kind and amount of armament). So the chief defense factor was a large number of guns from adjoining aircraft, exceeding the fire power of the attacker. The tighter the formation was, the more fire it could bring to bear against the enemy. Even so, the Bogies had armor plating protection around the engine and cockpit, which cut the chances of our fifty caliber projectiles getting to the pilot and the most vulnerable parts of the aircraft.

Attacks from the rear were infrequent because very early the Jerries learned that to attack a B-17 from the rear was not the way to remain alive and healthy. First, the lethal tail guns were assisted by the top turret, the ball turret, and sometimes the radio gun. Second, the fighters overtaking the bombers had a slow rate of closure. That meant the B-17 guns could begin firing at one thousand yards and do a lot of damage before the Germans got close enough to fire their cannon, which had a shorter range of six hundred yards. Thus, a tight formation was the ultimate defensive tactic of a bomber force beyond the range of fighter escort.

That night Jim said to me, "Do you remember that time when we were flying alone over the mountains and number one engine burst into flame?"

"Sure, I remember it. We didn't know enough to realize it was highly dangerous. We know now."

"If it happened tomorrow the whole crew would be rushing to the nearest escape hatch."

That incident did not disturb us a bit. Herb calmly retarded the throttle then opened it up and sucked out the blaze as if it were an everyday occurrence. But I would never again remain calm with an engine fire. I had seen what happened, and how fast, after engines caught on fire.

August 18

For the first month at Ridgewell the mental strain of not knowing what to expect with the dawn of each new day was severe. No amount of training, and especially the kind we had, could prepare one to step from a sheltered civilian life to the chance he would face death, or an injury even worse, in the next twenty hours. All of a sudden my priorities had undergone a traumatic shift. The small anxieties I used to worry about seemed so trivial. Did I once worry about making my sales quota? Or about paying the monthly bills? How absurd! It boiled down to revising my mental priorities to accept a new way of looking at things — a new mental attitude that would have been alien and totally unacceptable six months ago.

I turned to Balmore: "George, I've begun to study the men with the most missions, and I can see some common characteristics among them."

"Like what?" asked Wilson, who came awake long enough to hear part of the conversation.

"Well, the best way I can explain it, they act like they don't give a damn what happens! Haven't any of you noticed that?"

"Now that you mention it, yes. Some of 'em do act that way," replied Nick.

"Is it an act? Or do they really feel that way?" asked George.

"My guess is it starts out as an act — a sort of front to mask their real feelings — then they work themselves into a mental state where they really don't worry much about tomorrow. It's the old philosophy that you can make yourself be what you think you are. I guess that's what we need to copy. I remember that General Pershing once said that when he wanted his best troops he went to the guardhouse and let them out."

"The men who raise enough hell do let the tension work off," said Rogers.

"Well, I know for sure, cautious civilian thinking isn't going to work over here. I don't know how much I can change my mental outlook — or how fast — but I am starting to try right now."

After making my decision, I began consciously to try to drive out contrary thinking. "Why worry about tomorrow? There is no tomorrow — there is only today. Quit thinking about tomorrow or next week or next month. You can't control what will happen tomorrow, so why spend the precious time you have today worrying about it? The only time you have for sure is now. Today is real. So forget what the future may bring and learn to enjoy to the fullest extent what you have now. When life is threatened each hour becomes more irreplaceable. Today you are alive and well, so be grateful. For all you know this may be your last day! Don't ruin it by morbid forebodings of burning airplanes and horrifying plunges out of the sky. To hell with tomorrow!''

I began to grope my way slowly, with twists and turns, and a few detours, to controlled thinking. I went a good way toward that objective during my stay in England but it was during another tour of combat duty, in a different area of the conflict, before the process matured, and a combat raid for me became just another day at the office (15th Air Force, Foggia, Italy — 50 missions.)

I think the best soldiers in combat develop a mystic feeling of immunity to death. Sure enough ''others all around me may get it, but the bullets and shrapnel will miss me! I've got this special thing going for me. What special thing? I have a strong feeling I'm going to make it, no matter how hopeless it seems, or how rough it gets.''

On days we weren't flying, we tried to find things to do to fill the idle hours. I began keeping a record of the things we did, and included some of our conversations. I kept detailed accounts of our raids, gathering together eight or ten men — some of them from different aircraft — and going over what happened after each mission. I gradually began to record not only the combat raids, but what went through the minds of men under combat stress. There also developed for me a new pleasure in simple things. When the continuity of life was threatened the reality of what life was became clearer. After all, one achieves an exalted state of existence only at rare moments. The rest of life is the daily sequence of one small insignificant thing followed by another. If one stands aloof waiting for another mountaintop experience, and fails to find zest in the small matters that comprise most of life, he or she will miss a majority of the best life has to offer.

CHAPTER V
Mission to Gilze-Rijen

August 19 - Gilze-Rijen   *#003*

I heard the Jeep stop outside and that surprised me, because I was so sure we could not mount a mission with our recent heavy loss of aircraft and our damaged planes.

Counce bounced out of bed. "I thought you said we wouldn't go out for another week."

"I didn't think we could! How many ships can we put up?"

"Not more than one squadron 'til they get some more patched up," Nick Abramo answered.

"I'll bet they're puttin' together a force from two or three groups," said Wilson.

An annoying sensation plagued me some mornings. I shook and shivered while dressing. Was it the early morning cold, or just my nerves? By the time I was on my way to the mess hall the shakes were gone.

I saw Gleichauf at Operations before briefing. "We're goin' to have an extra passenger along today," he said.

"Who we takin'?"

"Lt. Cohler, one of the Flight Surgeons, will be riding with us in the nose."

"Good idea! They need to know what it's like."

Jim and I got to the plane early. Only the loud stutter of the small engine operating the electric generator broke the silence. The crew chief had finished his daily inspection and was asleep in the cockpit. Soon other men arrived and the sounds of clanging metal and hand charging reverberated through the aircraft.

Buck Rogers was not with us. He was badly shaken up on the Schweinfurt raid, and was now in the hospital. He suffered internal injuries from the severe bouncing he took in the tail of the plane during heavy evasive action. Buck was probably a little too old for combat gunnery, although he was a tough guy. A new man, Raymond F. Legg, from Anderson, Indiana, had replaced Rogers for the time being on the tail guns.

Legg came from a rural area. He was twenty-one years old — quiet, good-natured, steady, and a nice looking young man. I liked him on first sight, but how he would do on the tail guns was yet to be seen. That day was an ideal mission to break in a new man.

Balmore was grounded again with frostbite, and an operator named Brophy was with us in the radio room. It was almost time for the officers to arrive, when it suddenly occurred to me that Wilson was missing.

"Has anyone seen Wilson since we left the hut?"

"I thought he was gettin' up when I went out the front door," Counce said.

About that time a truck stopped and out climbed Wilson, not overly concerned about being late. He arrived just ahead of Shutting.

Paul gathered us into a circle to hear the briefing. "The target today is Gilze-Rijen, in Holland. Not too bad! We will put up three composite squadrons made from two groups. We will have fighter escort all the way in and out. Flak will be moderate to heavy. We could see some fighters, so don't get the idea that this is gonna be a milk run! The Germans have two hundred fighters close enough to intercept. This is Lt. Bernard Cohler, one of our Group Flight Surgeons. Lieutenant, you'll fire the right side nose gun. Jim, show the Lieutenant what he needs to know about the gun."

Shutting turned to Cohler. "If you have any trouble with the gun, let me know quick, an' we'll switch guns."

What a contrast to our last raid! This one showed promise of being a snap. The 381st furnished one squadron, and the other two came from the 91st Group. I did regret that I had to participate in a raid against the Dutch and their lovely country. Years before I had spent some pleasant days in Holland. How unfortunate that it happened to be located between Germany and the North Sea!

The formation got underway after a long, drawn out flight across England in an attempt to confuse the Germans. The fighter escort was to meet us a little short of the Dutch coast. Not much fighter action was expected in view of the escort protection, and the short time over enemy territory.

"Radio to Turret. Radio to Turret."

"Go ahead."

"Something wrong with my oxygen regulator."

"What th' hell is it this time? You radio jocks always think you got oxygen trouble!"

"The gauge wiggles."

"Wiggles? Are you sure you're sobered up from last night?"

"I'm perfectly sober — the thing flutters — wiggles."

"I think you're imagining things. How do you feel?"

"I feel OK."

"If you feel good, don't worry about the gauge. You're gettin' enough oxygen, or you'd know it."

"Turret to Waist."

"Go ahead."

"Keep an eye on Brophy. Can you see him from where you are?"

"I can see him."

"If he shows any sign of trouble go take a look, quick."

"OK. We won't be on oxygen very long today, anyway."

When it was fairly certain that the mission would not be cancelled, I called Purus. "Turret to Bombardier."

"Go ahead."

"Are you ready for me to pull the bomb fuse pins?"

"Yes, I think so — go ahead."

So I took a walk-around oxygen bottle and went back to the bomb bay, and pulled the pins out of the bomb fuses. That meant that when the bombs fell out, an impellor would quickly spin off (caused by the wind), leaving the striker pins free to hit on impact with the ground and trigger the explosion.

"Turret to Bombardier."

"Go ahead."

"The bombs are armed. Rack switches are on."

"OK, Turret."

The flak started coming up as we approached the coast. Lt. Cohler had a ringside seat for some close-up views. I knew how he was feeling, seeing it for the first time. That plexiglass sure looked agonizingly thin when the shells exploded.

"Bombardier to Pilot."

"Go ahead."

"We're on the bomb run."

It soon became obvious that the bomb run was too long.

"Pilot to Bombardier."

"Go ahead."

"Why the hell didn't we drop?"

"Don't know, Paul. Either his position was off or the Sight wouldn't line up. We're starting a three sixty."

"We'll be twenty minutes coming around for another run. If we fool around over this target they'll get some fighters up here."

A few fighters had been reported flying low and to the left. I suppose that some silly new gunners became confused and cut loose at the 47's thinking they were 190's. The escort immediately retreated to an altitude well above our fifty caliber range. Twelve to fourteen 190's saw the opportunity and slipped in under the escort and raced toward the formation.

"Copilot to crew! Copilot to crew! Fighters eleven o'clock high — comin' in! Blast 'em! Shoot th' hell out of 'em!!''

I could see my tracers hitting the first one but he kept right on coming. Lt. Cohler had the excitement of a head-on attack, and one fighter whizzed by him so close that the pilot's bright red scarf could be plainly seen. The formation leader was shot down, and I saw two more Fortresses explode and go hurtling toward the ground far below. Lt. Alexander, one of our squadron pilots, was a lucky man that day. A 20mm cannon shell ripped through the cockpit side window, brushed him lightly on the head, and zoomed out through the other side without exploding. Unbelievable!

I could hear Legg firing from the tail, and twice I zipped around to see what the action was back there. He looked like he was doing all right from what I could see.

"Bombardier to Pilot.''

"Go ahead.''

"We're on the bomb run again.''

"Hope we drop this time!''

Three or four minutes later: "Bombs away! Let's go home!'' from Purus.

I felt the load release, and the formation made a left turn and was soon back over the North Sea.

The next morning Balmore was at the station hospital and overheard the men kidding Lt. Cohler about his "mission.'' One of the orderlies said, "Lieutenant, how was it yesterday? Rough?''

The reply was, "Yeah, it was rough all right, but you sonnuvabitches will never know how rough!''

The opposition on our last mission was the Fock Wolfe 190. Most B-17 men considered it Germany's finest fighter at that time. It performed well between twenty and thirty thousand feet. On balance I thought the P-47 and F.W. 190 were evenly matched on a plane-to-plane basis. The 47 was superior above thirty thousand feet, and I thought the 190 was better from about twenty-two thousand and lower. The advantage the 47 had as an escort aircraft was in tactics. It could fly high above the formation and swoop down with an altitude and dive advantage when the 190's attacked the Forts. The way it worked out, the F.W.'s had to become the aggressor and run the risk of being attacked, while the P-47's became the defensive force and could choose their time to attack when they had a height advantage.

On August 20th, the loud speaker on the base came on in the middle of the morning. "All combat personnel report to Operations — all combat personnel report to Operations." It continued at intervals — every fifteen minutes.

On the way to Operations there was much bitching among the crowd.

"Why can't those Operations nitwits leave us alone?"

"Another one of those aircraft recognition classes! I know what a 190 and 109 look like!"

"They keep us on alert all th' time, an' on a day we don't have to go out they gotta dream up some horse shit to look good on their reports to headquarters."

At Operations there was gloomy silence until we were all assembled, and then we didn't really believe what we heard. "This is goin' to be a real surprise! We're giving every combat man a four-day pass, and we'll have personnel trucks ready to leave at 1:30. We'll take you right to the outskirts of London where you can catch a tube into the city." When the cheering died down, the voice continued: "You men need some free time — now is our chance to give you four days off while we get our damaged planes repaired. This pass will be mandatory unless excused by the Flight Surgeons."

Someone in the crowd said, "But some of us are broke! Hell, we can't take off for London with no money!"

"We thought of that. The Finance Officer is standing by to issue an advance on your next pay, for all those who need it."

The whole thing was organized superbly. The Command obviously wanted all of us away from the base, away from the empty tables at the combat mess, away from the empty bunks in the huts. They wanted us to rid ourselves of whatever tensions had built up inside. Someone at headquarters was smart enough to know that the best therapy was a big blast — a wild weekend that would let it all come out. Those in charge were concerned about the morose attitudes and glum faces after Schweinfurt.

There was a scramble to get ready, but no man in the 381st was going to be left behind when those trucks took off. We were in London before dark, and the celebrating got off to an early start. We took full advantage of our good fortune for we might not get another four-day pass for a long time.

London was an exciting place to be in 1943. Throngs of men, far from home, were seeking pleasures of various kinds, trying to find some escape from the stifling military confinement. The area along the Strand and near Trafalgar Square was especially crowded. There is a statue of Admiral Horatio Nelson on the square, along with two huge stone lions, one on each side of the Admiral. According to legend, the lions roar whenever a virgin passes, which is not often.

When the drinking establishments opened to provide the stage for the evening festivities, downtown London was crowded with men in many kinds of uniforms. From open doorways one could hear snatches of lusty songs from groups well along with their drinking. Although the nightly blackout was strictly enforced, up and down the streets there would be the flare of a cigarette lighter so some soldier could get a look at a girl standing in a darkened doorway. From those doorways there was a lingering odor of cheap perfume that attempted to camouflage the need for a bath. Soap and warm water were rare luxuries in wartime England. There were swarms of men walking arm in arm, sometimes fifteen abreast, headed for some bistro. Here and there one could see a soldier and a girl walking along, perhaps toward her room in some shabby hotel or flat. Would the soldier discipline himself to hunt up a pro station at three A.M. or run the risk of a venereal disease?

By 10 P.M. the favorite bars of the soldiers were crowded and getting wound up. The noise was deafening but no one minded. There was camaraderie and loud talk, but seldom any brawls. Soldiers swapped favorite tales and enjoyed a few hours away from military confinement. Then someone with a commanding voice would get up and pound for attention, and start singing:

"Roll me over, in the clover,
Roll me over, lay me down,
And do it again."

And the favorite barroom song of wartime England would roll on and on. There were endless stanzas, and each participant could make up his own. The singing would go on until the singers grew tired.

During the war years drinking establishments in England were rigidly regulated. At the night time closing hour, soldiers were just getting started. To circumvent the restrictive hours, private clubs opened up. One of those was the Bazooka Club, near the Strand, and patronized mainly by the R.A.F. An English friend sponsored Jim, George and me and I do not recall any other American members. That place became a favorite and convenient hang-out for us when we were in London. The club was a lively place. The members were mainly connected with Allied Air Forces. There were Australians, South Africans, Canadians, and a small number of men from the Free French and Free Polish Air Forces.

Those nationalities mixed surprisingly well, and many pleasant evenings were spent swapping tales with the men who manned the Lancaster Bombers or flew the Spitfires. One night I was with three R.A.F. men at the Club. One of them asked me, ''You Yanks really think you tagged out two hundred and eighty-eight Jerries on your ball bearing raid?''

''No,'' I replied. ''We probably got a hundred, for certain, and maybe a few more. The claims get duplicated.''

''Those Jerry chaps don't scratch out easy, ya know.''

''You're damned right they don't! All that armor plate! Say, what's it like up there all alone over a German city at night? I think it would scare the hell out of me.''

''Some nights it's a piece of cake — some nights it's a rough show!'' said one.

''The worst time is when we get caught in those searchlights! We are stone blind until we get clear of those bloody lights.''

One man turned to a handsome young chap, with blonde hair and a curling mustache. ''Bill, tell him about that night you fell out of the open hatch.''

Bill wasn't eager to talk about it, but after some persuasion, he began: ''We were in a Wellington Bomber, ya know. The rear entry hatch cover becomes part of the walk-way through the waist. I was operating the wireless when we flew through some flak and took a bit of a hit mid-ship. It banged the craft around, ya know, and the pilot called me to take my torch and see if the control cables were OK back there. I picked up my torch, but the thing wouldn't light up. I stepped back into the waist, flicking the switch, and dropped out into bloody space. The flak had knocked off the hatch cover! I grabbed the rim of the hatch with one hand and hung on — no parachute, you know.''

''You mean you were hanging out in space with one hand?''

''I couldn't get a good grip with my other hand, and I knew I couldn't hang on very long. The wind blast was terrific. My mike was still snapped on 'cause we have a long cord, but I couldn't talk, just gurgled and made choking sounds. The pilot heard those funny noices and rushed someone back to see what was wrong. He followed my mike cord back to the hatch, and grabbed me just before I was slipping off. It took two blokes to pull me back into the aircraft. A bit of a show, ya know!''

The temperature in the room that night was about fifty degrees, but Bill's forehead was dotted with big beads of perspiration as he recounted, for my benefit, his frightening experience. I never heard a more hair-raising tale throughout the war.

The last night of our four-day pass was a real bash! It must have been four A.M. when we hit the sack. By the time we got up the next morning it was too late to find any place open that served breakfast.

"Why don't we go back to the club?" George asked. "Maybe they'll have some doughnuts or pastries left over."

There was no intention to start drinking so early in the day, especially on an empty stomach, but one round wouldn't hurt. That was how it began and before long we were off on a super bender until it was time to leave for Waterloo Station and get a train back to Ridgewell. I did not recognize my condition until I took a few steps, and everything went blank. George and Jim had matched me drink for drink all day, but those were the only men I have ever known who never showed any visible signs of intoxication. Big George picked me up and staggered down the stairs and got us into a cab. At the huge Waterloo Station, he managed to get me through the crowd and aboard the train, avoiding the Military Police.

August 21

George had a good friend, a radio operator named Feigenbaum, who came from New York, not far from where the Balmores lived. "Feig" spent a lot of time in our hut because of Balmore. He had a companion we called "Brooklyn," and the two were always together. They paired off well: Feig was the comic, and Brooklyn was his straight man. Together, those two could entertain a barracks for hours, with just normal conversation. Feig had an unusually husky voice with an inclination to stammer. He loved to stumble in at two in the morning and wake up the entire hut to tell about his date. Anyone else would have had pratically everything in the hut thrown at him, but Feig was in a class by himself.

The day after our last sortie, Balmore came back from Operations, visibly shaken.

"What's wrong, George.?"

"I can't believe it — I just can't believe . . ."

"What can't you believe? What is it?"

"They say Feig got a direct hit in the chest with a twenty millimeter — gone instantly!"

"Oh, my God! Not Feig! His first mission?"

"Yep, his first lousy mission! John, I can't believe a man like Feig will never be around any more. Just last night he was here in the hut with us!"

George was low for several days and we all had Feig on our minds, for he was an unforgettable man.

August 22

That morning Gleichauf and Carqueville came by our hut shortly before noon and gave us the latest news. "We've been assigned #765. It's not too bad as B-17's go," Carqueville said.

"For an E model, it's OK. It's about as good as we can expect," I answered.

"That's right. New crews don't get the choice aircraft, John," Gleichauf added.

Herb suggested that we take a good, hard look at the aircraft and see what we could do to improve it.

"OK, Jim and I'll get to work on it right away."

The E Models held only seventeen hundred and fifty gallons of fuel, while the newer planes could take on nine hundred more gallons with the addition of the Tokyo tanks added at the far ends of each wing. On long missions we would have to sweat out the fuel consumption, knowing that the leaders would have another nine hundred gallons to play with and might forget about us jokers dragging up the rear.

August 23

That damp night at the hut we were talking about combat crews and how they got together at the various training centers in the States.

Tedesco asked, "You and Jim been together since gunnery school?"

"Longer than that," Counce answered. "We first met at the Boeing Aircraft Engineering school at Seattle."

"But how did you get assigned to the same crew? That's a hundred to one chance," Tedesco insisted.

Jim said, "It wasn't chance. It was an unusual situation. We were at Gowen Field at Boise, Idaho, for assignment to combat crews. One day Comer and I got to wondering if they had made up crew lists yet and we decided to find the chief clerk and see what he would tell us. The chief was a decent guy, so I asked him, 'How they go about assigning engineers to combat crews?' "

" 'Oh, the Head Engineering Instructor does that — two of you to a crew.' "

" 'You mean there will be two engineers on every crew?' "

" 'That's right — a first engineer and a second engineer.' "

" 'What's the difference?' "

" 'The first fires the top turret and gets another stripe. The second fires a waist gun.' "

" 'When will they start assigning us?' "

" 'Maybe the engineers are already paired off. What are your names?' "

" 'Comer and Counce.' "

" 'He looked through the pile of papers and pulled out a sheet.' "

" 'All right, here you are. Both of you are on this list. Go ahead and look at it.' "

"John and I were both listed as first engineers."

" 'Well, what do you think about your second engineer?' I asked John."

"He said, 'He won't be worth a damn. I don't want to be on any crew with him — what about you?' "

"Look who they put with me! The lousiest gunner in the class at Vegas, and a screw up along with it!"

I turned to the chief clerk. "Could you — uh — accidently switch names and put both of us on the same crew?"

"I guess I could — I doubt if anyone would notice it — but if I did . . ."

"If anyone did notice, it was only a typing error — right?" I cut in, and we both took out a five dollar bill.

"Sure. Just a typing error. These new clerks we got here are always goofing things up. Which one of you is going to be first engineer?"

Jim said, "Want to flip for it?" "John won the toss and we slipped the chief the two fives."

CHAPTER VI
Mission to Villacoublay

August 24 - Villacoublay   Aircraft #765 - Nip and Tuck

I was awake when I heard the Jeep outside. As usual, it took some effort to get Wilson out of bed, but the others were up quickly. At Operations, the sounds from the Briefing Room were mixed, so I had no clear idea what to expect until the pilot arrived.

"Here's the deal for today. We're hittin' an aircraft Work Shop Factory at Villacoublay, which is south of Paris. The altitude will be twenty-five thousand and the temperature forty below. An escort of P-47's will go half way to the target. You know that Jerry has his best fighter groups protecting the Paris area, so we can expect a hot reception. Keep a sharp lookout and start firing as soon as you can reach 'em — hammer at 'em all the way in — louse up their aim."

I turned to Jim. "It's gonna be a balmy day in th' waist — only forty below. Imagine that!"

"Damn, I forgot my shorts!"

"I hope those red and yellow nose bastards don't show today."

"If they do, start prayin'," Nick said.

"They're no meaner than those checker-nose devils," added Balmore.

No words could adequately express our admiration and appreciation for the American escort pilots. Few of us in the 8th Bomber Command would have escaped either oblivion or a prison camp in 1943 without their help. Bad news about crews we knew at Boise and Casper kept seeping through, which highlighted the fact that we had been lucky so far. So when I saw those escort fighters approaching, I said to myself, "Thanks for your help — I hope I see you at the pub tonight and can buy you a drink."

George was back with us in the radio room and I felt better, because he was the best I knew at that position. Balmore had two phobias: one, aircraft fires; two, oxygen troubles — some of it purely imaginary. I knew in advance that on every mission he would find something wrong with his oxygen system.

Soon after takeoff Gleichauf went on intercom: "Pilot to crew — I forgot to tell you that we are the spare today. We will trail the formation at high left. If no one aborts before we reach the coast of France, we turn around and come home."

The bomb load was thousand pounders, which I liked better than the five hundred pounders. They were heavy enough to fall out if the release shackles operated at all. Sometimes during that period bombs remained hung up in the racks. Bomb rack malfunctions were common with the E and F models but were rare with the later G models. When there was a hung up bomb or two it was my signal to go into the highwire bomb releasing act on the ten inch catwalk between the radio room and the rear cockpit door. Two vertical supporting beams halfway between the two doors restricted the walk-through space so severely that it was almost impossible to get through it wearing a parachute. So I had to work on the narrow walk without a chute; it was like a high wire performer with no safety net. Oxygen supply was from an unreliable walk-around bottle good for four minutes with no bodily exertion or excitement that could double the need for oxygen. An oxygen failure on that open walk, with nothing below but five miles of air, was something I tried not to think about.

The formation came together on time and turned toward the English Channel. We were flying parallel to a higher group that was behind the 381st, so we could spot an abortion quickly. Suddenly I caught a glimpse of something white floating by. I whirled around too late to see what had happened. There was a parachute with no one in it. Pieces of wings, tails, and fuselages littered the sky. Where there had been several aircraft a moment before, there was nothing but empty space and falling debris. I caught a brief glimpse of one ship going down. The fuselage had torn off flush with the trailing edge of the wing. All four engines were still running and the ship was revolving rapidly, like the way a rectangular piece of paper will do when released in the air. It was a nauseating sight. Forty or fifty men were wiped out in a matter of seconds. I saw another ship emerge below in one of those flat, Flying Fortress spins. A B-17 when out of control often went into a shallow circling descent that was neither a dive nor a spin, as we normally use those terms. I saw it so often that I coined the word "flat spin" to describe it. My first reaction was that fighters had slipped across the Channel and jumped us from out of the sun when we weren't expecting them. I searched the sky wildly for some sign of enemy aircraft, and noted other turrets doing the same thing.

"Copilot to Turret — do you see any fighters?"

"No — nothing above us. It must have been an explosion."

"Copilot to Navigator, did you see what happened?"

"No, I was looking to my left — didn't see a thing 'til it was all over."

"Copilot to Ball. Nick, what's happening down below? How many planes were lost? See any chutes?"

"Air's full of pieces and parts of planes! There were four or five that got it! All but one broke up. I see three chutes."

"Oh, Lord! Five ships and only three chutes?"

"That's all I see. They're goin' to land in the water, an' the rescue boats are already headin' out to pick 'em up."

"Copilot to crew — Copilot to crew. Four or five ships were torn up, we don't know why. Either an explosion or collision. Stay calm! It wasn't caused by fighters."

Whatever caused the tragedy, I wondered if it could have been avoided with better disciplinary control of the Group. The puzzling part of the catastrophe was that we were flying very close to the planes that were lost, yet we had felt no concussion or unusual air currents. In a few minutes the remainder of that Group aborted and returned to their base.

Ten minutes from the French coast, Shutting called the Pilot, "Paul, Paul!"

"OK — go ahead."

"There's a wing ship at three o'clock in the second element pullin' out!"

"I see it."

A few minutes later we dropped down into that vacant position.

"Bombardier to crew — Flak, nine o'clock low."

"Flak, eleven o'clock high."

The fire was moderate and caused no damage.

"Radio to Turret — Radio to Turret."

"Go ahead."

"Something's wrong with my oxygen!"

"What's th' problem?"

"I don't feel good."

"Turret to Waist — Jim, go take a look at Radio's regulator."

Counce was back on intercom quickly. "Nothing wrong with your regulator, Radio. I think you imagine you're not getting enough oxygen and are breathin' too heavy. Relax! Breathe normally an' you'll be OK."

"Tail to crew — escort catching up with us — high at six o'clock."

"This is the Navigator — they sure look good to me!"

"Bombardier to crew! We're gonna need 'em real quick. Bogies at eleven o'clock low, comin' up!"

The P-47's had numerous clashes with F.W. 190's trying to get to the formation. I counted ten enemy craft that might have been shot down. I didn't know for sure unless I saw a fighter explode or the pilot bail out. If any of them crashed, we were too far from the scene by that time to see the impact.

I wonder if there has ever been a sight — show or drama — as thrilling as watching a series of dog fights between good pilots, with all of them aware that death awaited the losers. It was such a fascinating sight I sometimes forgot briefly that I was a part of the drama. At times I almost felt like it was a highly realistic war movie in which I was a bit player.

"Navigator to Pilot . . . over."

"Navigator to Pilot."

"Navigator to Copilot."

"Motion Paul to get on intercom."

"Go ahead, Navigator, this is Paul."

"Five minutes to the I.P."

"OK."

Several minutes later Shutting called the pilot again. "There's the I.P. down on the right, about one o'clock." (Initial point).

"I see it — hard to miss the Eiffel Tower."

"Navigator to Bombardier."

"Go ahead."

"On the bomb run in three minutes."

"Ball to Copilot."

"Go ahead."

"Flak — six o'clock low."

The Tail called, "Flak — five o'clock level."

WHAM!!

That burst was mighty close! Then four more bursts — all close. The aircraft was now on the bomb run, and had to fly straight and level. Another four bursts were so nearby I could hear the shell fragments strike the aircraft hard!

"Copilot to Waist."

"Go ahead."

"Anybody hurt back there? Any serious damage?"

"Some good sized holes behind me — not serious — so far."

That flak battery of four guns had us in their sights and were bursting salvos all around us. Each salvo crept closer.

BANG!!

The ship rocked and pitched from the concussion of the nearby shell explosion. They weren't far off target — that was certain! I grudgingly acknowledged and admired the accuracy of those German gunners so far below. When I could hear the ''whoosh'' sounds of the shell bursts and see the orange flame in the center of the explosions, that told me they were getting much too close! For the second time German flak gunners had us so well targeted that they needed only one more very small correction to lay that salvo right on us.

''Bombs away!''

That was always sweet music to my ears.

''Radio to Bombardier.''

''Go ahead.''

''One bomb's hung up in the bomb bay.''

''Turret to Bombardier — I'm goin' back and try to release it.''

''Hold your position, Turret. We can't drop that bomb 'til we get clear of French territory,'' said the Copilot.

Recently a new ruling had been posted forbidding any plane to jettison bombs or equipment over occupied Europe. There was a left turn and a wide circle and we were heading back toward England.

''Ball to crew — three fighters four o'clock low — 190's, I think.''

''Copilot to Tail.''

''Go ahead.''

''Can you see the fighters?''

''No, they're outa my view.''

''Can Waist see the fighters?''

''Left Waist to Copilot — can not see them.''

''Ball to Copilot — they're comin' up from underneath.''

I heard the ball guns open up with one heavy burst after another. In a little while the firing stopped.

''Tail to Copilot — I see those fighters now — they're droppin' down an' away.''

''Tail, this is Nick. They changed their minds when four Balls opened up. I hit one of 'em real good. One broke off without firing.''

I expected a sharp clash with the red and yellow nose meanies near the target, but they failed to show. I knew we would meet them somewhere before long.

''Bombardier to Copilot.''

''Go ahead.''

''Fighters one o'clock high.''

''Navigator to crew — could be Spitfires — they're due right away. Be careful!'' The Spits looked like 109's at a distance.

As soon as we identified those sleek R.A.F. beauties, the ones mainly responsible for saving England from Goering's bombers in the Battle of

Britain, I felt certain we had no more worries about fighters for the day. The Spitfires were beautiful airplanes in the sky and deadly to tangle with. Their R.A.F. pilots were veterans of countless sky battles. The Spitfire was designed to meet German bomber attacks over England. They could land, rearm and refuel, and get back in the air rapidly for the next wave of bombers. Large fuel tanks were not needed and would have been a handicap for the fighting over Britain. The small fuel tanks, however, reduced their effectiveness as escort aircraft.

"Ball to crew — flak ten o'clock low."

"Tail to crew — flak six o'clock level."

It turned out to be light and inaccurate. The formation began a gradual let-down as soon as we neared the English Channel.

"Turret to Bombardier — I'm goin' back and release that bomb."

"OK — need any help?"

"No, don't think so."

On the cat walk I discovered with relief that the stuck bomb was in an easy position to reach. With a long screw driver I tripped the shackle that held the bomb and it tumbled out. I watched until it struck the water with a gigantic splash, then returned to the cockpit.

"Turret to Bombardier. Bomb bay clear, you can raise doors."

"Thanks, Turret — Bombardier to Radio."

"Go ahead."

"Are doors comin' up?"

"Doors are up."

The 381st didn't lose a ship that day, but some other groups behind us caught it much rougher.

There was a famous B-17 that took part in the raid on Villacoublay. The "Memphis Belle" was the first American aircraft to survive twenty-five missions. Its crew was the first combat crew on a B-17 to fly twenty-five missions over Europe. The World War II movie, *Memphis Belle*, was filmed partly in England. It played up the Villacoublay mission, and one scene showed wounded men being lifted from B-17's at the end of that raid. The movie helped to sell war bonds and became popular during the war period. The "Memphis Belle" and her crew flew back to the U.S. and toured the country in support of the War Bond Drive.

At interrogation many questions were asked about the horrible tragedy that wiped out four or five planes. The next day the official version was released. Two B-17's were caught in a propeller blast, due to a sudden shift of position of a lead ship. That meant the air turbulence, created by that unfortunate move, caused two pilots momentarily to lose control of their aircraft. I could visualize their frantic efforts to avoid a collision, and the helpless feeling they had as the wind blast forced them together. When they collided there was a violent explosion that wiped out two other aircraft close by.

On August 25th new B-17F's with their crews arrived and were assigned to the 533rd Squadron. They were indeed welcome because the squadron was under strength, which kept all crews on constant battle call status. We were happy to see the new men, but even more delighted to get the new Fortresses, with their increased fuel capacity and better performance.

August 28

Carroll Wilson was the number one goldbricker I knew in the Service, and I knew a lot of accomplished ones. But he had a redeeming quality to balance it. He had the natural ability to con people into things the rest of us could never have managed. In the States we would send him to the Orderly Room for passes because he rarely failed to talk them into it. But there was one incident in which Wilson was the principal actor that topped all of the ludicrous stunts I saw in my Air Force years.

The Bomb Sight incident began one morning when we were in crew training at Casper, Wyoming. We took off to let the Bombardier do some practice drops with a Norden Bomb Sight. Soon after takeoff the oil pressure on one engine dropped off too much and we returned to the base to have a relief valve replaced. Now the Norden Bomb Sight was guarded with elaborate security. The Sight was the cornerstone of the high altitude concept and elaborate means were taken to insure that it did not fall into the hands of the enemy in time for it to be duplicated and used against us. Bombardiers were held responsible. When Purus checked out a Norden Sight for a practice flight he was required to wear a .45 automatic and keep that Sight under surveillance at all times.

When Herb landed the aircraft and pulled into the hardstand I saw right off that the crew chief was alone. I told him the bad news. "I'm afraid we're gonna have to replace a relief valve on number three engine. You want me to start taking it out while you go get a new one?"

"That would speed things up. I oughta be back in twenty to thirty minutes."

When the crew chief took off for Aircraft Supply, Herb asked, "How long we going to be tied up?"

"Forty minutes to an hour," I answered. "We'll have to run up the engine and check out the pressure after the valve is changed."

Herb turned to the other men. "Come on, let's go to the club for coffee. We have plenty of time and we don't need to hang around here."

Purus shook his head. "I can't go, Herb. I've got to guard this damn Bomb Sight."

"Aren't you a commissioned officer? Well, order one of these sergeants to guard the Sight while we're gone."

Purus hesitated. "I don't know . . . well, I guess it would be all right. Here, Wilson, buckle on my forty-five and stand where you can see the Sight up in the nose at all times. Don't let it out of your vision — and NO ONE is to enter this aircraft 'til we get back. And remember, this gun is loaded! Be careful!"

I was working high on an engine repair stand with my head up behind the engine most of the time. A few minutes later I looked down and saw Wilson practicing fast draw with that forty-five.

"Wilson! Put that gun back in the holster! You know better than to play with a loaded gun!"

He meekly agreed to do so. Five minutes went by and I glanced down. He was at it again.!

"Wilson, you're gonna kill someone! Put that gun where it belongs.!"

I felt someone tap my foot and looked down. There was one of the Sight technicians I had seen at the bomb sight vault several times when Purus checked out a Norden Sight.

"Sergeant, we got an inspection due today on the Sight you're carrying. How long will you be here?"

"Another thirty minutes, I guess."

"Good! I'll have the Sight back in less than thirty minutes."

"Don't talk to me! See that Sergeant with the gun? He's in charge of the Sight. Talk to him about it."

I went back to work and assumed he cleared it with Wilson. In a few minutes I had to come down for a tool and could see the technician in the nose of the plane, removing the Sight. He was clearly visible through the plexiglass, and I saw him leave the aircraft carrying the Bomb Sight and walk off close enough to Wilson that I thought sure he saw him.

I heard the rest of the crew returning. When Purus looked up at the nose of the plane his face went white.

"Wilson!" he screamed. "Where's the Bomb Sight?"

Carroll whirled around and stared in utter disbelief at the gaping, empty space in the nose, where the Sight should have been. His mouth popped open and he went into shock. He couldn't say a word — just blabbered incoherent sounds. That was when I realized that Wilson didn't know where the Sight was.

Carqueville ran over to me. "John! You must have seen something! Where's the Bomb Sight?"

"No idea," I said, "I was busy and had my head up in the engine nacelle. How could I see anything?"

Stark tragedy had suddenly struck Purus and Carqueville! They had succeeded in losing the Air Force's top secret device. A prison sentence was altogether possible. The crew chief returned just in time to catch the last of the act. He glanced at me, saw that the Sight was in safe hands, and said nothing.

Purus turned his fury on Wilson. "You stood there and let someone walk off with the Norden Sight!" He was almost hysterical. "Don't you know what that means? The Germans would pay a million dollars for that Norden Bomb Sight!"

Carqueville sat down on a box and buried his face in his hands. I heard him muttering, "Why couldn't I get nine sane men like the other pilots do?"

Wilson finally recovered his voice. "I only looked away for five seconds — whoever got it had to work mighty fast!"

Balmore yelled, "Hey! Isn't that someone carrying a Bomb Sight?" He had spotted the technician who was now about forty yards from the bomb sight vault.

"That's him! Catch the Sonnuvabitch! Don't let him get away! Catch him!"

All nine of them took off like the Keystone Cops after Charlie Chaplin. It was a scream to watch! Wilson was leading the way, determined to redeem himself, waving the forty-five and yelling, "Stop, you Sonnuvabitch! Stop! Or I'll drill ya!" Even Carqueville put on a burst of speed that amazed me.

When the unfortunate man heard all the commotion he turned, and was astonished to see a madman flourishing a lethal forty-five and eight more hostile men bearing down on him. He started to make a run for the safety of the vault, but realized he couldn't make it carrying the heavy Sight.

"Hands up! Hands up!" screamed Wilson, and he leveled the gun as if to shoot. The technician quickly put the Sight down and raised his hands. They swarmed over him and pinned him to the ground and held him there.

"We got him! We got him!"

Our brave men had captured the dastardly spy! Attracted by the noise, five or six men from the vault ran quickly to the scene, and from the distance I saw the man get up and several men help brush the dirt off of his clothes. There was a short conference and nine sheepish, subdued men headed back to the aircraft. That rukus over the Bomb Sight was funnier than anything I had ever seen on a movie screen. The crew chief went into such hysterics that he lost his balance and fell off the engine stand. Fortunately I was there to break his fall. The returning heroes did not appreciate the uncontrolled mirth of the crew chief and me.

"What's so damned funny?" growled Counce.

Balmore was inordinately sensitive about anything that made him look silly. I could see that he was getting angry, and about ready to take a swing at me, so I quickly got out of range. "Go ahead and laugh," George fumed. "We were trying our best to get the Bomb Sight back, and you guys think it's a joke."

Carqueville had regained his composure and turned on Wilson. "You had only one thing to do," he said, "and that was to guard the Bomb Sight, yet you let a man walk off with it!"

"Honest, Sir, I never took my eyes off that Sight," Wilson insisted, "except for a few seconds when I lighted a cigarette."

The truth was that Wilson never once glanced at the Bomb Sight. With his glib tongue, however, Carroll could get out of anything! I listened to his spiel, still laughing, but said nothing about his Billy the Kid act. I owed him something for his lead role in a real-life comedy so memorable that it still lingers in my memory as one of the funniest things I have ever seen.

Carroll had another characteristic that was not so funny. On training flights he would find a comfortable spot in the waist or radio room and sleep for two or three hours at a time. He would wake up and get bored with the long flight and wander around the airplane trying to find something to do. One night he wandered into the cockpit while Jim and I were running down an open circuit. Jim was holding the large cover of the main fuse box and I was trying to locate a burned-out fuse. Wilson decided we needed help so he turned to Jim. "Here, let me hold that while you help John." In his awkward movements he jammed the cover against the open fuses and shorted out almost every electrical circuit on the airplane. A ball of blue fire rolled out of the fuse box, between the Pilot and Copilot, and against the windshield before it burned out. The only lights left in the cockpit were a few luminescent instrument figures. Carqueville was so infuriated that if he could have reached Wilson at that moment he would have inflicted physical damage. Fortunately, we had two flashlights.

August 30

By the end of August the crew had settled down into a routine that was predictable. Carl Shutting was the clown, and every crew needed one. The ground crew was always grumpy in the cold, pre-dawn hours when the combat personnel arrived at the aircraft. But when Shutting dumped out his gear at the hardstand the mechanics gathered around him to chuckle at his antics and wisecracks. He always had something missing from his equipment bag. It might be a mike or an electric glove he had neglected to replace from the last mission. Some mornings I would have a spare of what he needed. Other mornings it was not unusual for Carl to have one of the ground crew rushing to get something. He refused to enter the nose of an aircraft without his special armor plate on the floor. When he donned his testical protective armor he had no problem getting two volunteers to assist in tying it in place. The mechanics followed him around until time to enter the ship. It was the only show on the base at that hour. Shutting set out to create a character behind which the real Carl Shutting could hide. He was never as slap happy as he often appeared to be. All of us built up a wartime pose which made us appear different from what we were in civilian life. Carl carried it two levels beyond the norm. He adopted a homespun manner of talking similar to Bob Burns, an early-day Bing Crosby radio character (who coined the word ''Bazooka'' to describe the odd musical instrument he played). Gleichauf told me Carl had a special cap that he wore at night to keep his bald head warm that created mirth and kidding.

CHAPTER VII
Missions to Amiens-Glizy and Romilly

August 31

Woodrow Pitts made an early trip to the Grog Shop and was back within a couple of hours. "They're loadin' those damn bombs."

"Are you sure?" Green asked.

"Hell, yes — twelve five hundred G.P.'s" (General purpose bombs).

I turned to Balmore, "Where did Abramo and Wilson go? Anybody know?"

"They took off for the pubs two hours ago."

"You know Nick never leaves 'til they close the pub — somebody has to go find them an' tell them to break it off."

Counce spoke up. "I'll do it. Anyone want to go along? We don't want Nick to piss in his pants tomorrow."

They were back in time to listen to the late news from B.B.C. There was no point in going to bed until the newscast was over and the noise and lights died down. I lay in the sack a long time before sleep would come, wondering where we would go in the morning and how rough it would be. I could never resist the question before a mission: "Which of us will not be here this time tomorrow night?"

August 31 - Amiens-Glizy   *Aircraft 765*

The next morning I stood outside the Briefing Room with Counce until we heard the reaction to the target when the map curtain was pulled back.

Jim said, "About average — probably somewhere in France."

"That's how it sounds to me."

The weather looked questionable, but there was always the chance it would break before sunup. We were happy to have George back with us in the radio room after a layoff to recover from frostbite again. Raymond Legg was doing well as a replacement for Rogers, whose future status was unknown.

Gleichauf called us into a circle for the crew briefing. 'We're hittin' Amiens-Glizy in France. There are two hundred and fifty fighters that can intercept. Flak will be moderate, and fifty P-47's will pick us up at the

Coast. Colonel Nazzaro will lead the Wing flyin' with Colonel Gross, the Wing Commander.''

The Group got off on time and the climb and assembly was flawless. It seemed to me that things always went smoother when Nazarro was leading. By the time the three Groups were assembled into Wing formation we were over heavy clouds with ground visibility zero.

''Bombardier to crew, Bombardier to crew — oxygen check.''

''Turret OK.''

''Radio OK.''

''Ball OK.''

''Tail OK.''

''Pilot and Copilot OK.'

'Waist OK.''

''Bombardier to crew, test fire guns.''

One by one I listened to the positions rattle off a short burst. For ten minutes the formation droned on toward the Continent.

''Pilot to Navigator.''

''Go ahead.''

''Is this cloud cover goin' to foul up the drop?''

''If it stays like this it will — got two alternates but they may be covered, too.''

''Turret to crew, flak three o'clock high.''

The anti-aircraft fire was light and inaccurate.

''Waist to crew, Waist to crew — fighters four o'clock high. Looks like the escort.''

The cloud cover held on but there were a few breaks in it.

''Navigator to Copilot. Tell Paul if these clouds don't open up real soon, we won't hit the primary target — we're gettin' close to the I.P. now.''

Gleichauf switched from Command to intercom at the Copilot's signal.

''Navigator says it don't look good for the main target.''

As we approached the drop area, visibility was nil and there was no possibility of executing the primary plan. I suppose most leaders would have turned around and headed for England. But with plenty of fuel Nazarro intended to use all possible means to inflict damage to Germany's ability to wage war. We flew around for a long hour with the lead Navigator searching for an alternate or a suitable target of opportunity. Our 47 escort was excellent until they had to turn North toward England. Suddenly there was a break in the clouds and an enemy airfield loomed straight ahead. I do not know if the Lead Bombardier recognized it or not.

"Bombardier to Pilot."

"Go ahead."

"There's an airfield and we're going to drop on it."

"Radio — watch the doors down."

"This is Radio — doors are down."

After a short run I felt the bombs drop away.

"Navigator from Pilot — what did we hit?"

"Don't know — didn't recognize it."

'Bombardier to Tail, how did the strike look?'

"Looked good to me — covered the field."

We were lucky to get a quick bomb run and an excellent strike pattern. The mission was an example of good leadership turning a failure into a success. The return flight was uneventful until we neared the home base. Visibility was far too poor for a sizable force of planes to attempt to land at the same time. So each ship was on its own to feel the way down and hunt holes in the mist, at the same time avoiding a collision with other aircraft.

September 2

Lt. Purus never changed from the way he was the first day I met him. Quiet and soft spoken, mild in manner and disposition, he was a solid man to have on the crew. What I remember best about Purus was that he managed always to look neat and clean even in the English mud. The Bombardier was responsible for the bomb load as soon as the aircraft moved away from the hard stand. Those bombs had three safety devices to insure against an accidental explosion: (1) a cotter key had to be removed by hand from the fuse mechanism of each bomb; (2) an arming wire had to pull out of the fuse assembly when the bomb fell from the aircraft; and (3) an impellor had to spin off of the fuse assembly from the action of the wind on the drop. As long as any of those three safety measures were in place, the bomb was supposed to be inert and no more dangerous than a block of concrete of the same weight. Any of those devices would restrict the striker pin from igniting the explosion at the moment of impact with the ground.

Our practice was to remove the cotter pins as soon as we were reasonably sure the mission was going as planned and a few minutes from the enemy coast. Since I was nearer to the bomb bay than Purus, I performed the pin pulling assignment. If the mission had to be cancelled later, the pins had to be reinserted before the ship could land, a much harder task than removing them.

Balmore worked at a table adjacent to the bomb bay door. He could open the door and see into the bay. So he reported doors up or down and when the bomb load released. If one or more bombs failed to release, the radio operator immediately called the Bombardier. By arrangement with Purus I took over the task of working the stuck bombs free, because I was closer to the bombs and had the only tools on the aircraft. Ordinarily I could trip the bomb shackle with a long screw driver and quickly get rid of it. But if we had an unusual situation, with several bombs in difficult hang-ups to reach, we kept the bomb bay doors open until we were at sixteen-thousand feet, letting down on the return. At that point Purus and I went back and did whatever was necessary to get those bombs out of the ship. Once a bomb failed to release from a rack the aircraft was not permitted to land until that bomb was ejected one way or another. Believe me, it was not a fun thing to work out on that narrow cat walk with the doors open below.

While the bomb was theoretically supposed to be inert with any of the safeties in place, I would not have wanted to wager any money on it. But one night a guard was sitting in the cockpit of a B-17 that was loaded with bombs for a mission the next morning, and somehow in fooling around with the switches and controls he accidently dropped all twelve bombs out of the airplane. They knocked down the bomb bay doors and hit the pavement of the hardstand and rolled in every direction. None of them exploded, but we had a white-faced guard who thought for a few seconds it was his last moment on earth. The strange thing was that he should not have been able to do this without pulling the salvo ring, which was an emergency release for the bombs in case the electrical system should fail.

September 3

In early September our gunners began to get the foolish notion that we were a hot crew. Our slight combat experience did not justify such arrogance, but as silly as it sounds, we began to get cocky. It was like a boxer who has won his first two fights and thinks he is ready to take on the champ. So when Jim Counce found a can of red paint, Nick came up with a great idea: ''Why don't we paint the engine cowlings red? It'll give our ship a special look.''

The suggestion was quickly OK'd. Didn't a hot crew need a hot airplane? Something a little different from the other crews? We borrowed a paint brush and without checking it with the Pilot spent the afternoon changing the appearance of Aircraft 765. Standing at a distance to admire our work, we thought it looked sharp.

I listened to the Briefing Room noise and judged it medium tough, and decided to put aboard an extra thousand rounds of ammunition. The standard load was seven thousand rounds, and it was against regulations to add more. But we had a special friend, Vernon Chamberlain, who was the armorer for 765 (as well as a number of other aircraft). He could always get more ammunition when I wanted it, which was every time a mission sounded like it could turn out extra mean. Vernon was from a small town in Arkansas, and our relations with him were unusual, to say the least. He did extra things for us over and beyond his assigned duties.

I listened intensely as Gleichauf spelled out the hazards for the day: "The target is Romilly, an ammunition factory, about fifty miles east of Paris. One Group of P-47's will meet us ten minutes inside the coast. Now watch your fire! Don't let me see any of you shooting at the 47's! We need them close to us. If you fellows keep shooting at them, they are gonna stay the hell away from us. Altitude will be twenty-eight thousand five hundred feet and the temperature will be forty-five to fifty below. Watch out for frostbite. OK, let's go."

Some of the P-47 pilots had visited our base three days earlier, and we had a discussion about the difficulties in distinguishing between P-47's and German F.W. 190's. At a distance they did look alike. Sometimes the 190's painted their engine cowlings white to look more like 47's. The main distinguishing difference was a bulge of the nose of the 190's and the shape of the wings in silhouette. We told the 47 pilots they must never, never point the nose of their fighter at the Fortress unless in an obvious turn, because the Fortress gunners became extremely nervous when they saw the lethal guns of a fighter pointed directly at them.

Purus distributed the "bail out kits" and we climbed in and closed the hatches. The kits contained a tiny compass, a rubber map of the area we would fly over on that mission, a rubber water container, and water purification tablets. There were also concentrated chocolates and benzedrine tablets to help overcome the shock of bailout and the long glide down in the chute. After each raid the kits were turned in. The thinking was that if a man did bail out and avoided capture upon landing, the kits would be helpful for the first week of flight from the area toward the nearest locations that would provide some chance to make contact with the Underground. We knew the parts of France where the population was sympathetic to underground resistance, and also the Balkans presented an opportunity to tie up with resistance forces.

The temperature was unusually bitter and my feet were numb for hours. Most gunners wore the thin felt electrically-heated moccasin and pulled on fleece-lined flying boots over them. Then they tied their regular shoes to the parachute harness. It was a precaution in case they should have to suddenly bail out. No one wanted to land on the Continent minus shoes! That would have been a disaster, captured by the enemy or not. It was impossible for me to tie my shoes to the chute harness because there was not enough room in the turret, so I passed up the electric shoes and wore my heavy leather shoes with the flying boots on top of them. I had to suffer through many hours of agony when temperatures were extra low and often had to keep exercising my feet for extended periods to avoid freezing.

Major Hendricks did a good job of guiding the formation arourd flak areas as we crossed the French Coast. Soon after entering enemy territory the intercom came on.

"Ball to Copilot — another Fort aborting! That's three of them in the last five minutes."

"Dangerous this far inland, Ball."

Meanwhile Cahow's crew was in trouble. This is the way Lt. Cahow told it: "We lost an engine at the worst possible time. We were too far into enemy territory to abort. The big worry was that we had to pull out the stops and draw full emergency power on the three engines that were left to try to stay up with the formation. All the engineering data said this kind of power could only be used for five minutes, but we had to pull that excessive power for hours. Both my co-pilot, Stanley Parsons, and I kept hearing all of those strange noises that straining engines make — and a lot of other noises that we imagined. We kept the bomb-bay doors up until the last minute. Even then the drag was too much but we caught up with the formation soon after bombs were away. The three remaining engines kept getting noisier and rougher. We could see the engine cowlings shaking from the strain. I didn't know whether we would make it back to our base or not."

"Tail to crew — escort five o'clock high."

"Copilot to crew, they are stayin' high to keep out of your range, an' I don't blame them."

"Ball to Copilot."

"Go ahead."

"Can you see that Fort trailin' us by about a thousand yards?"

"No. Can't see it from the cockpit."

"The markings look odd."

"Keep your eye on it. Call me if it does anything strange."

"Bombardier to crew — oxygen check."

All positions checked in except the Tail.

"Bombardier to Tail — Bombardier to Tail — come in."

"Bombardier to Right Waist."

"Go ahead."

"Can you see the tail gunner?"

"Yes. Looks OK to me."

"Go back an' signal him to get on intercom."

"Three minutes later: "Tail to Bombardier, my phones got unhooked. Sorry."

"Navigator to crew — fighters at ten o'clock low."

"Bombardier to crew — they're 109's."

"Waist to Copilot."

"Go ahead, Wilson."

"Two fighters flyin' like an escort for that trailing Fort. They're not 47's but could be Spits helpin' us out on their way back from a sortie."

"Navigator to crew — get ready for the fighters — the 47's are at the end of their range."

"Waist to Copilot — I can see those two fighters better now — they are 109's. Hey! That Fort is shootin' at us!" (Germany had some captured B-17s).

"Copilot to crew — those sonnuvabitches are throwin' twenty millimeter shells at us."

"Turret to crew, P-47's are diving on that Fort. Hope they shoot the bastards down."

That was the only time I watched a B-17 shot down with glee. I saw brown Jerry chutes pop out and the Fort went ito one of those typical flat spins that told me it was out of control.

"Waist to Copilot — the 109's are comin' up to mix it with the 47's. They must feel mean today."

The German pilots usually waited until the escort turned back. I knew that was going to happen any time. Perhaps the enemy pilots were inexperienced and too eager for action. It was a hell of a fight. I saw two P-47's shot down for certain, and another possible. It was hard to tell when a Jerry fighter was knocked down unless it was seen to explode or the pilot bail out. I saw five that might have been knocked down, although some of them could have recovered. Most of the heaviest action took place four to eight hundred yards from us at various levels. It was some show! The 47's hung in there longer than I expected and when they finally had to break off and head for England, the German ships had used up too much of their fuel to hit us hard with direct attacks. Some parts of the formation did get some fighter action, but we escaped most of it.

I kept watching Cahow and he was holding in tight. There was no sign that any of his remaining engines were developing trouble, in spite of the continuous high power he was drawing.

"Navigator to Pilot."

"Navigator to Copilot — tell Paul the I.P. comin' up in five minutes."

There was silence on the intercom for a few minutes. Then Purus called, "Be on the bomb run in three minutes."

"OK, Bombardier."

"Copilot to crew, flak twelve o'clock level."

The anti-aircraft fire turned out to be mild — off just enough to miss our elevation. Did I love that! Flak, while not nearly as dangerous as fighters, scared the hell out of me. When it was bursting around us I stood in my turret and cringed and shivered. I never did get used to it. If I had been occupied with necessary activities, lining up a Sight or flying the aircraft, perhaps I could have ignored it. But with nothing to do, unless we were facing attacks, I could not help watching the bursts explode, and I became somewhat of a coward. I could visualize those white-hot pieces of jagged cast iron zipping by my unprotected rear! I don't know what thoughts the other men had during those agonizing moments, but I may not have been the only coward on board when the burst came heavy and accurate.

A new swarm of enemy interceptors approached from the south.

"Bombardier to crew — Bogies at twelve o'clock high — get ready!"

The fighters showed us some new tactics by adopting a peculiar pattern from five o'clock high. Wilson got in some excellent bursts; I saw him strike two of them hard. I had some dandy shots but at longer range. I thought I was reaching them but, if so, the fighters showed no signs of it and came roaring in. The M.E. 109 was a super rugged airplane with ability to shrug off punishment that would down most airplanes. The attackers eventually ran low on fuel and were replaced by a fresh group. They annoyed us with pecking attacks most of the way to the coast, but were not the hot pilots we usually saw near Paris.

"Navigator to Copilot.'

"Go ahead.'

"Fighters coming up from below. They look like Spitfires — we're not supposed to have any escort on the return."

"This is the Pilot — I don't give a damn why they're here -- just glad to have them."

And so was I! Those Spits must have been on the way home from a mission and saw us up above surrounded by fighters. That finished the attacks for the day, and soon I could see the coast ahead. The formation began a slow letdown.

"Turret to Copilot — looks like Cahow has it made now."

"Right! I was worried back there when he had to feather that engine so early."

We were half way across the Channel: "Tail to Copilot."

"Go ahead."

"A B-17 turning back towards France."

"You mean we had one of those bastards in our formation?"

"I guess we did. Where else could it come from?"

"No wonder the fighters kept finding us so easy. Those bastards were right in the middle of us radioing our position all day."

"Pilot to crew. Pilot to crew. I want all of that damn red paint off of this airplane before you hit the sack tonight. It was drawin' fighters in on us today! We don't want anything on this airplane to attract the attention of enemy fighters."

Now let's switch back to Cahow's crew:

"I thought we had it made when we approached our base, but the tower ordered us to proceed to a repair base not too far away. When I banked the plane to turn on the downward leg number one and number two engines both quit, either out of gas or worn out with that heavy power for so many hours. I never found out which. I kept the plane in a steep bank and landed more than one half way down a very short runway, and had to ground loop it when we ran off the end. The tower officer came screaming out to the plane, hardly before the dust had settled, wanting to know who in the hell the dumb SOB was that would make a landing like that! He really backed off and became quite nice when my crew came tumbling out, all in combat gear, looking like gorillas. Moe Tedesco, Ugo Lancia, Hubert Green, Ray Bechtal, and my bombardier, Jim Leverett, were all heavy weights, and over 6 feet tall."

September 6

If someone was looking for the Gleichauf or Cahow crew, they listened for a cacophony of discordant sounds and located the noise center. If they heard no load reverberations disturbing the airwaves, they knew that both crews were either on a pass or flying a mission. Let me describe a typical evening at ten P.M. Lancia was blasting away on his trumpet, accompanied by another instrument handled by a man from a nearby hut. In his off-key voice, Tedesco was trying to sing the Italian song they are playing. Across the room from this bedlam, Carroll was sleeping as soundly as if at home in a quiet bedroom. Under his cot was a pile of dirty socks and underwear.

Balmore was doing a tap dance to the rhythm of the music and looking around for an aproving audience like he was a young George M. Cohan. No one paid any attention to him, because it was the only routine he knew and we had seen it before. Hubie chose this moment to leap out of bed and start penning another letter, probably sixth or seventh of the day. Who in the hell did he write all of those letters to? Did he have that many girl friends back home?

Rogers was trying to read but, distracted by the noise, he beat against the metal wall in protest, then gave up. In disgust he turned up the volume of the radio to attempt to compete with the sound from the other end of the hut. Bill Kettner got up and added a piece of green wood to the struggling fire in the small metal stove, wood recently purloined from the King's forest under cover of night. An outsider strolled in and picked up one of Lancia's idle instruments and superimposed his unwanted contribution onto the sounds already shaking the hut. The metal walls vibrated from the pulsating sound waves and in turn amplified the volume.

Outside the weather was cold even though winter had not yet arrived. Jim stepped out to study the weather and forecast what we can expect by morning. His meteorological discourse attracted scant attention. Woodrow Pitts was absent, which meant he had not returned from his nightly scouting trip to the canteen. I was writing in my notebook, trying hard to capture on paper the feel and pulse of this odd hut and describe the assortment of characters.

There was a loud banging on the metal wall from outside, and two men from an adjoining hut opened the door and demanded that the noise level be lowered by several decibels. They were ignored because who cared what they wanted? It was getting late, but going to bed was out of the question until the occupants wore themselves down.

The sound of a heavy crash against the wall overpowered the music volume. Jim said to me (the only one who was close enough to hear him), "Pitts hit the hut with his bicycle. Must have tanked up pretty good."

"I wonder what he found out."

An explosion of classic profanity — not the ordinary timeworn barracks expletives — but a flow of words with expressive character. The door opened and Pitts entered.

"Hey, Pitts!" said Counce, "did ya step in the big mud hole in the dark?"

"Or do you have the crabs again?" asked Kettner.

'Hell, no. I don't have the crabs! I went over my boot top in the stinkin' mud. And my bicycle has another flat.'' That triggered one more outburst of colorful adjectives.

"All right. All right. Knock off the noise. Let's hear what Pitts found out," says Tedesco.

The sounds faded out and we looked at Woodrow. "Well, I talked to three armorers. They're loadin' thousand pounders. All the signs say go in the morning.''

"In that case," I said hopefully, "let's hit the sack an' get some sleep."

Such a silly suggestion was unworthy of consideration. Lancia turned to Pitts. "New Jersey raises more vegetables than your whole state of Texas."

"Bullshit!" Pitts roars in rebuttal. "The Rio Grande Valley grows more in a week than your two-bit New Jersey farmers grow in a month!"

We are off on one of the nightly arguments. Ray Bechtel said, "California grows more than Texas and New Jersey put together."

Pitts and Lancia turned on Bechtel, and Pitts looked to me for support of the Lone Star State. I declined to join the fray because none of us knew anything about growing statistics. Barracks arguments are won by the loudest voice.

Wilson stirred and opened one eye. "What time is it?" he asked.

"About midnight," someone answers.

"Why didn't somebody wake me up for chow?"

"I got an extra Hershey Bar if that will help," I volunteered.

Kettner interrupted, "Hold it! Hold it! It's time for the late news."

He switched the radio to B.B.C. "This is the news: Royal Air Force Lancasters are out in force over the Continent tonight. Flight Officer Leahigh-Smith, flying a Mosquito, reported he could see a huge column of fire sixty kilometers from Cologne. The sounds of heavy gunfire in the Channel could be heard today east of Southampton. . . The Admiralty admitted the loss of a freighter from a convoy south of Iceland. . . Air raid sirens are wailing over the Midlands tonight. . . Continued mopping up actions in Italy against slight opposition. There are unconfirmed reports that the Italian Military Forces are on the verge of surrender. . . The Prime Minister said in Parliament today that we will drive the Hun from France and the soil of Belgium and Holland, but let the Hun guess when and where our forces will strike."

CHAPTER VIII
Mission to Stuttgart

September 6, 1943
Stuttgart, Germany   *Aircraft: Tinker Toy*

The noise of the Jeep outside woke me up. I flipped on a flashlight and looked at my watch: it was 0230 hours . . . an early start! What did that mean — an extra long mission? As I heard the familiar footsteps on the gravel walk, going from hut to hut, I was half-way hoping it wasn't my morning to go. When I heard the steps go on past our door, however, I became resentful that they were passing me up. Now what did I really want? That sound of crunching feet on gravel put me in an ambivalent mental state: the dread of going versus the prospect of excitement. The door opened, and I listened with little enthusiasm to the reading of the battle roster.

On the way to the mess hall George said, "I wonder how the Operations Officer feels when he reads out our names — he knows some of us won't make it back."

"Someone has to do it, George. Which would you rather do? Take the risks yourself? Or have to choose which men may die?"

"I could never send men out to fight, John, and maybe to die . . . I would feel responsible for those who didn't get back."

At Operations I waited with Jim and George for some signal from the Briefing Room.

"I wish they'd start the Briefing — Oh! Oh! Listen to that!" Jim grimaced.

There was a deep and prolonged groan followed by silence! My insides constricted because the pilots thought we had a super mean one coming up.

Balmore said, "I hope it's not Schweinfurt again — or somewhere worse."

"Where th' hell could that be?" asked Counce.

An hour later I had the extra ammo on board and was about finished with the guns. Someone stuck his head up in the hatch under the nose and called, "Put the guns away, leave 'em right where they are. Grab your equipment — hurry!"

"What's wrong with those knuckle-heads at Operations? Don't they know we can't change planes this late and get ready on time?"

Then I realized it was Gleichauf down below. "The Operations people aren't knuckle-heads!" he said. "I made the aircraft change! Where we're goin', 765 can't make it on gas."

"I'm sorry . . ."

"Forget it. Grab your stuff, and let's go! Hurry up!"

In the back of the speeding truck Gleichauf gave us the story. "We're hittin' Stuttgart, in South Germany — another ball-bearing plant. It's the longest raid B-17's have attempted. Some aircraft will have twenty seven hundred gallons of fuel, but we will have only seventeen hundred and fifty. It is gonna be close on fuel. No way 765 could make it on gas. P-47's will be with us a little way, then we go it alone. We'll be over enemy territory five hours."

It was the big league for sure. When the truck stopped, and I saw the aircraft we would fly, I was stunned! Of all the planes, we got Tinker Toy. No one wanted to fly that plane. It was the jinx ship of the 381st. The tales of her raids read like a book of horror stories. No crew had ever flown her on a routine mission. Invariably it was a life and death struggle to get back. Most people would say there's no such thing as a jinx, but they weren't there to witness the dead men pulled from Tinker Toy, or to observe the heavy damage she suffered, raid after raid.

Jim saw the name and gasped, "We're in for it today! A mean raid to begin with, and on top of that, look at the ship we draw."

Balmore looked like he had suddenly become ill. "Somethin' bad is bound to happen today."

"Oh now, George, an airplane couldn't really be a jinx — that would be like believing in ghosts," I countered.

Gleichauf walked by. "Cut this talk about a jinx and get this airplane ready! We only have ten minutes until time to start engines!"

We were running woefully short of time, and I was shocked at the poor condition of the guns. All we could do was to keep working on them, mainly to remove the rust from the working parts, after the plane got into the air. We were almost across the Channel before my two guns were ready.

There were no bail out oxygen bottles in the aircraft, but I had six that I always carried in my equipment bag for emergencies. They were steel cylinders wrapped in piano wire and filled with oxygen compressed to eighteen hundred pounds pressure.

Gleichauf knew Purus had picked up a case of diarrhoea during the night. Johnny made a hurried exit into the darkness, and when he returned Paul asked, "Are you gonna be able to make it?"

"That was the third crap since midnight," he answered.

"If you feel you shouldn't go, I'll call Operations to try to get another Bombardier."

"Not enough time for that," Purus replied. "I'll go — but I may get more calls."

Shutting had a suggestion. "Take along one of those metal ammunition cans. If you have to crap you can throw it overboard on the Krauts!"

Carl was to regret that advice a few hours later.

The formation came together quickly, to save fuel, and then set out over the cold waters of the English Channel.

"Radio to Turret."

"Go ahead, Radio."

"My oxygen is leaking."

"Here we go again! What's th' problem this time?"

"I already told you," Balmore replied testily. "My oxygen's leakin'."

"How do you know that?"

"Because the right system is goin' down too damn fast!"

Before I could leave the turret to go to the radio room the pilot came on intercom: "Turret, stay where you are! We're too close to the French Coast."

"Pilot to Right Waist."

"Go ahead."

"Jim, take a look at the Radio oxygen system."

"OK, Pilot."

Five minutes later Jim called, "Waist to Pilot! Waist to Pilot! There's a slow leak in the right aft oxygen system — no telling where it is."

"Copilot to crew — Copilot to crew! All positions in the rear switch to the right oxygen system — use it up first."

That was all we could do for the moment. The route was over France to the Rhine River. We crossed the coast at a lower level than usual and were still climbing.

"Waist to crew — B-17 pullin' outa th' formation — can't see anythin' wrong with his engines. What the hell is he trying to do?"

The escort had already turned back to England and it was still a long way to the target.

"Waist to crew. Fighters — six o'clock low, comin' up fast! May be 190's."

For a few minutes the B-17 trailing us flew along unmolested. I think the Jerries were puzzled and may have suspected a trick.

"Tail to crew! Three 190's are jumpin' that Fort behind us."

"Waist to crew! Th' wing's on fire — why don't they jump? Oh, I see some chutes now!"

There was heavy smoke and another Fortress was on its way down.

"Bombardier to Copilot."

"Go ahead."

"That was stupid! Why do you think he pulled out of the formation?"

"Some new pilot, nervous and inexperienced — thought it would be easier to fly all by himself."

As we approached the Rhine River, George called again.

"Radio to Turret — pressure's down to a hundred pounds."

"Even so you should have enough . . . your left system is OK and you can kick off of oxygen at sixteen thousand feet coming back."

Tinker Toy was an old ship, an "E" model. It had small oxygen tanks in each turret that had to be refilled from the main system tanks on long flights. We were used to that, as aircraft 765 was an E model.

"Ball to Waist — my oxygen tank's gettin' low. Be ready to fill it in a few minutes."

"OK, Nick. Let me know when you're ready," Counce answered.

"Bombardier to Navigator."

"Go ahead, Johnny."

"I got another call — got to use that damn ammo can! Take over my gun until I'm through."

The forward nose gun was much more vital to our defense than either of the side guns in the Nose.

"OK," Shutting said. "I'll take over your gun, but you're gonna freeze your butt at 35 degrees below!"

"I know that but it's better than lettin' it go in my pants."

"Copilot to Nose — keep the intercom clear!"

"Waist to Ball. Ready for me to fill your tank?"

"Yeah — soon as I swing around. I'll hold steady 'til you tell me it's clear."

My ear phones were not the best and the higher we climbed, the worse they were. I could make out only fragments of the intercom conversation.

Jim finished filling the ball turret tank from the left rear system pressure. When he removed the filler hose there was a loud spewing noise, and Jim realized that there was moisture in the oxygen system, no doubt caused by the condensation of moisture during those prolonged periods when that aircraft was out of action for repairs from battle damage. Hard ice had formed to hold both valves open, letting the precious oxygen pour out of both the ball and the left rear system tanks. He frantically tried to re-engage the ball valve but the ice was too hard. In desperation, he ran to the waist for the nearest walk-around bottle and quickly hammered it onto the system valve. But he could do nothing to stop the drain of the ball pressure and it dropped to zero. Most of the system pressure in the rear of the aircraft was now gone.

"Waist to Copilot . . . ''

I could not make out what Jim was saying.

'Copilot to Ball — Copilot to Ball, come in.''

"Go ahead.''

"Get outa that Ball quick, Nick. Jim says your oxygen pressure is gone.''

"I'm comin' out of the Ball.''

"Copilot to Radio.''

"Go ahead.''

"Help Nick out of that ball and hook him up on your spare hose.''

"Paul — Paul!'' Herb motioned for Gleichauf to switch over to intercom. ''Got a bad problem in the back. Th' ball oxygen is gone an' not much left for the other men. How about sending Nick to the nose? He's in the radio room now.''

"Nick, can you hear me?''

"Go ahead, Pilot.''

"Move to th' nose right away. Got to save what oxygen we have back there.''

"Copilot to Abramo — don't forget your chute!''

Meanwhile Purus had completed his uncomfortable session with the ammo can, but the Navigator did not hear the order for Abramo to hasten to the nose, because his ear phones were disconnected as he changed back to his regular gun position.

"Copilot to Turret — watch Nick through the bomb bay.''

It was very easy to get hung up in the center of the bomb bay. A stocky man like Nick, in heavy flying clothes, had trouble squeezing through the narrow part of the cat walk where two vertical beams supported the weight of the bomb load. I got out of the turret and looked into the bombay to see Abramo struggling valiantly to break through. With a violent lurch he broke free, but dropped his parachute. He made a grab for it, but accidently caught the rip cord! A cloud of white silk flooded the lower bomb bay. His chute was finished, so he stumbled groggily into the cockpit and on down to the nose, ignoring the oxygen hose I held out to revive him. He was too far gone for his mind to function normally, and was struggling against collapse. Shutting, unaware that Nick was coming, had the entrance to the nose blocked. Nick crashed into him and down went the Navigator, knocking over the Bombardier's recently used ammunition can before the contents had time to freeze. The smelly mess spilled liberally about his clothes.

"Navigator to Pilot."

"Go ahead."

"I've got Johnny's shit all over my clothes!"

"What! You say Johnny shit on you?"

"No! No! His ammo can turned over on me! What we gonna do about my clothes?"

"What you're gonna do is get back on those guns. Right now! Worry about your damn clothes when we get back to Ridgewell."

"Navigator to Nick."

"Go ahead."

"You all right now?"

"Yeah, I'm OK."

"Look at what you did to my clothes."

"Copilot to Nose! Cut the talk an' keep that intercom clear!"

"Turret to Waist — my ear phones are real bad. Tell me what the situation is back there. Talk very slow."

"We — got — oxygen — for — one — hour."

"One hour?"

"Right! — One — hour."

We had just crossed the Rhine River and that meant real trouble if all we had was an hour of oxygen left in the rear at twenty-six thousand feet.

"Copilot to Bombardier — the Jerries are sendin' up everything that can fly — even some M.E. 187's."

"First 187's I've ever seen — and they're using JU 88's, too." Purus answered.

The 381st was flying a tight formation and that saved us some attacks. The enemy fighters were not as aggressive as I had anticipated over that part of Germany. I suspected that most of those fighters were trained for night fighting against the R.A.F.

"Navigator to Pilot."

"Go ahead."

"Ten minutes to the I.P."

Two M.E. 109's hit us but they were caught with a heavy converging fire, and I thought both were badly damaged. Cahow's crew was in serious trouble. Their aircraft had sustained some heavy hits, and the ball turret door had blown off. But down in that ball Bill Kettner obstinately refused to leave his gun position. Despite the enormous wind blast at thirty five to forty degrees below zero, he hung in there for the next three hours! It was bad enough to be in that ball on any mission, but that terrific force of wind, when he had to face directly into it to meet an attack, was an ordeal beyond the call of duty. I do not know how he survived it.

"Bombardier to Copilot — Herb, motion Paul to switch to intercom."

"This is Paul."

"Bomb run is coming up. I hope those clouds floatin' over th' target don't mess up the drop."

Unfortunately for us, one small cumulus cloud did obscure the target from the direction of our approach. The lead Bombardier could not line up his sight.

"Pilot to Bombardier — are we goin' to drop?"

"No. I think we're goin' to come around on a three sixty." (circle)

"Oh, hell! That will ruin us on fuel!"

The formation executed a slow, costly circle and came back over the target. Again the cloud obscured the main objective. The situation was so confused that I'm not sure what target we hit. It may have been an alternate. One good thing: I was greatly relieved to get rid of that bomb load!

"Radio to Bombardier."

"Go ahead."

"Three bombs hung up in the racks — don't raise doors."

"Turret to Bombardier — I'll go back and get rid of 'em."

"Pilot to Turret — stay on your guns — too many fighters around us now."

"Turret to Copilot. How do your fuel gauges read?"

"Between a third and a quarter — closer to a quarter. Not good!"

"It's gonna be damn close on gas!" I answered.

"We're on auto lean — th' flaps are pulled down. Not much else we can do 'till we can drop out of formation and slow down," Carqueville explained.

"We have about five hundred gallons — three hours using our altitude." I answered.

"Navigator to Copilot. We're three and a half hours to Ridgewell. We might make it to some air field on the coast."

"Doubt we can make it to England if we stay at this high altitude all the way to the Channel," I answered.

I felt that if there was moisture in the aft oxygen tanks we probably had the same in the forward system. I made a test by filling a walk-around bottle. Sure enough, when I unhooked the bottle the filler valve was frozen wide open. I hammered the bottle back onto it and stopped the drain. Being forewarned by Jim's earlier problem, I was ready and knew what to do.

"Radio to Pilot."

"Go ahead."

"Oxygen pressure about gone back here. What we gonna do?"

"Turret to Pilot — I got six bail out bottles — should be good for thirty minutes each, if they're careful."

"Rush 'em back real quick. Herb will take over the turret 'til you get back." It required some time to distribute the bottles and coming back to the cockpit I got hung up in the bomb bay racks. There was no oxygen left in the walk-around bottle I was using, so I knew that I had to break free quickly. I could feel myself slipping. With a final effort I tore loose and barely made it to the rear door of the cockpit. I fell partly in, with my legs dangling into the open bomb bay, and passed out. When I came to, I was plugged into the spare oxygen hose. I got back into the turret and called the Copilot.

"Turret to Copilot — thanks for pluggin' me in — I was lucky to make it to the cockpit."

"You're wrong, John. You plugged yourself in," Carqueville replied.

"No way I could do it! I was completely out when I fell into the cockpit door.'

"Well, no one helped you."[1]

"Then we got Gremlins aboard! Hey, Gremlins — thanks for pluggin' me in."

"I wish your Gremlins would help us out on oxygen and gasoline!"

How I got connected to the cockpit hose still remains a mystery.

Wilson, Counce and Balmore took two bail out bottles each. That left the remainder of the system oxygen, plus one bail out bottle they found in the waist for the Tail Gunner.

"Pilot to Copilot. Three things we can do. We can make a run for Switzerland. We can try to dive down to a lower Group. Or, we can bring one more man to the cockpit and let the other three bail out when they use

[1] I was actually beyond walking down the catwalk. I lurched toward the cabin door like a drunk on a diving board. It was a very close thing! Carqueville insisted then and later that no one helped me. But I have seen too many men in that same state of anoxia, and none of them could have made such a connection after they became unconscious. Either the copilot or the navigator had to help me, but neither would admit it.

up their oxygen . . . Switzerland sounds like the best bet to me.''

''I think so, too,'' answered Carqueville.

''Tail to Pilot — there are fifty to sixty M.E. 187's between us and Switzerland.''

''Then forget about Switzerland.''

A few minutes later: ''Pilot to crew. We're goin' to try to drop down to the lowest Group. Ought to help on oxygen — watch out for fighters.''

For the very first time being in a low Group sounded good. Gleichauf dropped the plane down and pulled into an opening in the formation, barely in time to avoid a swarm of fighters that tried to cut us off.

''Turret to Copilot.''

''Go ahead.''

''Got to refill the turret oxygen tank. It may freeze like the ball did. If so, I can't save it, but I can keep the main pressure from leaking out.''

''Any options?''

''Well, I could try to operate the turret from the cabin oxygen hose . . . I couldn't turn the turret much without unhooking the hose.''

''Try filling the turret tank.''

The same situation existed as had happened earlier. I jammed on a walk-around bottle and pounded it into position which saved the forward system pressure, but I could do nothing to keep the turret oxygen from spewing out. I quickly switched to the spare cockpit hose, but I could not turn the turret very much unless I dropped the hose. So when I had to meet fighter attacks I cut loose from the oxygen hose. When the attack was over, I dropped to the deck and re-engaged the oxygen hose before I lost consciousness. The supply of oxygen was barely adequate. I vaguely remember once when the intercom was blasting: ''Get him, John! Top Turret! Top Turret! He's comin' in at twelve o'clock high. Shoot th' sonnuvabitch!'' With all that going on I was half conscious and strangely undisturbed. I didn't give a damn if half the Luftwaffe was coming in as a unit! Lack of oxygen (partial anoxia) causes a curious mental sensation. The ability of the body to execute commands from the brain drops in proportion to the drop in the oxygen supply. Example: when off of oxygen one could not place the hand on the nose as directed; it might touch the left shoulder.

''Copilot to crew — over France now, so we can't get rid of those three hung-up bombs 'til we get to the Channel.''

That meant carrying some extra weight we did not need, and to make matters worse, the bomb bay doors had to be left down, causing an extra drag and higher fuel consumption.

Bail out bottles were never intended for any use other than bailing out at very high altitudes. I usually carried five or six in my equipment bag for oxygen use if they should be needed. That day the extra bail out bottles saved several men. Three of them would have had to bail out or risk dying or suffering brain damage. The mission to Stuttgart was the only instance I know of where men at twenty-six thousand feet were able to retain consciousness with such crude equipment for an extended period. A valve had to be opened with each intake of breath and closed while exhaling. George made one bottle last for forty-five minutes.

I got out of the turret long enough to look at the fuel gauges, then refigured our estimated consumption. "Turret to Copilot — it looks like we're gonna shave it extra close on fuel. Depends on how much we got left when those gauges show empty."

"And that won't be long!"

"Pilot to Navigator."

"Go ahead, Paul."

"Why we swingin' so far west?"

"Don't know — makes no sense to me . . . this headin' will take us close to Paris," Shutting answered.

"Isn't Paris out of our way?"

"Hell, yes — it's not the shortest route," fumed Shutting. "They're sittin' up there in the lead plane with plenty of fuel, forgettin' about us in these old planes with small tanks. Paul — my uniform stinks!"

"I don't give a damn about your uniform, Navigator. We got real problems — don't they know some of us won't make it if we go a hundred miles out of the way?"

Wilson finished his last oxygen bottle and refused to leave his gun position. In a few minutes he collapsed. George brought him to and moved him forward to the radio room. It must be remembered to Wilson's credit that in a very bad spot he was determined to do his job to the end.

"Radio to Copilot — we're down to th' last of our oxygen — if you want us to bail out we got to do it before we all pass out."

"Hold it, George! I think the formation is going to let down to twenty-one thousand feet to save fuel," Carqueville answered.

At that altitude men would live, even if they passed out. Soon it was twenty- then nineteen, and at sixteen thousand the formation leveled off. The men were perfectly safe now. Jim had been off oxygen since he gave up his bottle to revive Wilson.

"Copilot to Turret."

"Go ahead."

"Pilots are calling the leader about runnin' out of gas. We're not the only one in trouble."

The intercom was silent for a while, then the Copilot called, "The fuel warning light for number two engine just flashed on."

'And that's Paris far off to our left," the Navigator added.

A fuel warning light meant that the engine tank had less than fifty gallons left. The normal cruising consumption of gasoline was about fifty gallons per hour for one engine. When holding in a formation the consumption increased due to some jockeying that was inevitable, but as soon as the formation began a gradual let down the rate would drop considerably.

"Copilot from Turret, when will they start to let down?"

"Not much 'till we approach the Channel."

Ten minutes later: "There goes the last warning light!"

"Pilot to Turret, you think we can make it over the Channel?"

"Not unless we got a little more fuel than those gauges show. Some of the older E models have a slight reserve when they read empty. Let's hope Tinker Toy is one of them. That's our only chance of making it over the water."

"I think I can see the coast ahead about five minutes. All of our gauges are reading empty," Carqueville interposed.

"Ask the crew if any of them want to bail out now over land. We got some altitude to play with — our chances are about fifty-fifty of making it to an airfield on the English coast," replied Gleichauf.

All crew members elected to stay with the aircraft and take the risk; they knew that if we ran out of fuel and had to ditch without power, the chances of being able to set down on the water successfully were poor.

As luck would have it that day, we could do nothing right and crossed where it was a wide stretch of water. Now Gleichauf could drop out of the formation and slow down. Three other B-17's pulled out and fell in behind us. They must have thought we had a definite English air field in mind. We cut far back on power, using our 10,000 feet of altitude to drop slowly downward.

"Pilot to crew — Pilot to crew. Jettison everything heavy — get those bombs out quick so we can raise the doors."

The ammunition was the first to go because it was heavy. Jim Counce picked up full boxes of fifty caliber ammo and tossed them out of the window like they were match boxes. He was that strong. Carqueville released the three bombs while I removed the turret guns and heaved them out. At last we could raise the bomb bay doors that had been down since the bomb drop.

"Pilot to Radio."

"Go ahead."

"Stay in contact with Air Sea Rescue frequency 'til we're over land. Don't know when these engines will quit."

"Radio to Copilot — lots of Forts calling Air Sea Rescue — sounds like eight or ten will have to ditch." (Land on the water).

"Tail to Navigator — those three B-17's are still tailin' us."

"Pilot to Navigator."

"Go ahead."

"Pick the nearest English air strip you can find on your chart."

"Can't pinpoint where we are exactly — but there should be some small air fields anywhere we hit the coast."

"Pilot to Bombardier. Soon as you can see the coast, watch for a place to land."

We were still letting down, drawing so little power that the engines were barely above idling R.P.M., and I expected them to quit at any moment.

"Bombardier to Pilot — I can see the coast ahead, very faintly."

"Pilot to Navigator. Do you see an air strip? Which way?"

"Navigator to Pilot — don't see any air field. Never crossed the coast before without seeing two or three!"

We had inadvertently picked out the only spot on the English Coast, or so it seemed, that did not have a number of landing fields. It could not go on much longer. My mind was in turmoil: "These engines have to have gasoline to keep running and the tanks are down to fumes! Where are all of those landing strips I see every time we come over the English Coast? Either we find one in a matter of minutes or we put this big airplane down in some farmer's back yard! We are too low to bail out! I hope all of us survive the crash landing, but that is not likely! Come on engines! Hang in there a little longer. There's got to be a landing strip nearby. Where? There are a thousand air fields in England. Well, one way or another we're going down in the next few minutes. There is no way this can go on!"

"Navigator to Pilot! Look over to your left at ten o'clock. Isn't that a small air field?"

"I see it! Thank God! We're gonna make it! John, fire the emergency flare when we get close enough that they can see us comin' in."

By that time I was at my usual low altitude position — between and slightly behind the pilot and copilot. The flare would alert the air field that we were landing without normal landing procedures. The copilot turned to me, "Pump any fuel we have left from number two and number three engines to number one and number four engines. We got to have at least two engines on the approach.''

I sucked the remnants in the inboard tanks to the outboard engines. As we slowly dropped down to the small runway I ''ceased breathing,'' hoping those two engines would not quit until we got near the short landing strip. ''Keep going, engines! Just another thirty seconds! That's all I ask — another thirty seconds. We almost got it made.''

The wheels touched down and I resumed breathing. Gleichauf quickly braked the speed and pulled off the runway to let the trailing B-17's land. Then one of our two remaining engines quit! It was that close!

We had landed at a small R.A.F. Spitfire Base. Nick's parachute silk was partially streaming out of the bomb bay and that drew a crowd right away. They probably thought someone was hanging on the end of the chute!

I could not bounce back to normal all at once; far too much had happened in a short period of time. The hazardous experiences of the day had brought us perilously close to disaster. And now to be safe again was almost too much to take in. Slowly the tensions evaporated and my sense of well being returned.

Some R.A.F Officers came out to invite Paul and his officers to their club. Gleichauf asked me, ''Have you seen Shutting?''

''No,'' I said, ''not since right after we landed.''

It was odd that Carl could have vanished so quickly. I found him hiding in the tail. ''Go on, John,'' he said. ''Act like you don't see me.''

''No, Gleichauf's lookin' for you — might as well come on out.''

Carl had peeled off his outer coveralls, but it didn't help much. He was right about one thing: HE DID STINK! Off he went to where I presume he had a table to himself. True, his charisma that day left something to be desired, but he had lived through unbelievable hours in the most cantankerous Flying Fortress of World War II, known as Tinker Toy. Nothing had gone smoothly or as planned that frantic September day for Carl R. Shutting. Yet there he was, alive and uninjured, and back on friendly soil. So what else really mattered? He could have his clothes cleaned.

I never knew a mug of ale could taste so good! The English were very hospitable and wouldn't let us pay for a thing. Meanwhile the ground crew found enough gas in five gallons cans to get us back to our base. A little before sunset we took off for Ridgewell. At the 381st the men were surprised to see us, because we had been reported lost over France. A few more hours and all of our clothes and personal things would have been gone.

We lost forty-five Fortresses and four hundred and fifty men (except those men who were picked up before dark by the Air Sea Rescue people), on that poorly planned, poorly executed mission to Stuttgart. In addition to the heavy loss of lives and planes, a half million gallons of fuel (uselessly consumed) transported at high cost in men and materials across perilous sea routes, bristling with submarines. All for nothing! That was the worst waste of Air Force power that I saw in World War II. Far too much was risked on a paper-thin margin of fuel consumption. Seventeen B-17's went down in the Channel from lack of fuel, and we barely escaped being one of them. The excellent Air Sea Rescue Service saved many of the downed men, but no figures were released on the exact number picked up from the water. I doubt if I will ever completely forget the anxieties and frustrations that besieged us during the raid on Stuttgart. The only thing we did right all day was to get back to England. The amount of damage to that weird aircraft was far below what Tinker Toy usually suffered on a combat mission. Was she a jinx plane? I don't know. What we call a jinx must surely be a state of mind, when studied objectively. But Tinker Toy gave me a feeling that she had a malevolent dispositon, as if she were determined to punish the men who forced her to endure the tortures of combat. I had a strange impression that she would always come back from a mission, no matter how torn and bleeding, as long as she wanted to. Somehow she was not like other airplanes.

I have read no explanation of the unnecessary longer return route from Stuttgart, when so many of the aircraft were desperately short of fuel. It seemed to me that someone in command made an error in judgement, but then we were not privy to all the facts. There may have been good reasons, such as a large fighter force waiting for us on the more direct return route. The story of war is a mixture of good command decisions versus poor ones. On the whole, Bomber Command provided good leadership. Once in a while, like September 6, 1943, nothing went right. It must have been the bleakest day in Gen. Eaker's life. Fortunately for us, such days were rare in the air offensive over the Continent.

It was on the Stuttgart raid that Carroll Wilson came of age. When the chips were down, he showed me special qualities that were impressive. He proved that he had courage beyond the ordinary. I had always felt that it was not a question of ability with Carroll — that he could do whatever he set his mind to do. After all, he was only twenty when he came with our crew, and he had some growing up to do.

That night when the lights were out my mind slipped back to that frantic day in Nevada when I fired a gun from an airplane for the first time. Each gunner had to have at least eight percent hits on the tow target sleeve to qualify. Even on perfect shooting most of the projectiles will miss a small target when fired from a distance because of the spread out shot pattern. The aircraft was a single engine craft with two open cockpits. Before takeoff the pilot gave me his instructions:

"When we get near the firing range I'll give you five commands: One, hoist the ammunition can over the side an' secure the gun — don't drop that can! Two, feed the ammunition into the receiver. Three, hand charge. Four, fire until finished or I tell you to stop. Five, clear the gun and stow it. One more thing: keep your gunner's safety belt fastened at all times 'cause it's going to be real rough up there today."

All the way to the firing range I struggled feverishly with the safety belt. It was so tight that I couldn't budge it, and was a foot and a half too short for me to stand up in the cockpit to fire. I had no microphone to tell the pilot, so it boiled down to working in that super rough air without a safety belt, as risky as that would be. The intercom was impossible! All I could hear was loud babbles of static.

"Squawk—awk—eek—ug—."

I supposed that was command number one. I lifted the heavy can of ammunition out into the slipstream and at that moment the aircraft lurched upward and I came close to dropping my ammunition. I hooked the can onto the gun and relaxed for a moment. That was a mistake! When I looked back at the can I was horrified to see the ammunition belt streaming rapidly out into the air! With a desperate lunge I caught the end of the belt, — it was whipping and gyrating in the slipstream like a long, angry snake. I dragged it slowly back into the can and asked myself a question: "What in the Hell ever made you think you wanted to be an aerial gunner?" I looked at the pilot's mirror and he was shaking his head and frowning.

Loud intercom static blasted my ears: "Squawk — eek — awk —."

I could not make out one word so I hooked the ammo belt into the receiver of the gun. It was one of the few things I did right all day — that is, it would have been right with the safety belt on. I was leaning out over the gun when the aircraft pitched violently downward and I was thrown up and almost out of the open cockpit. I could feel myself going overboard. I reached down frantically but was too high by that time to grab anything. At the last second one foot caught a projecting edge down below, and it was enough, but just barely, to make the difference. At that low altitude I wouldn't have had time to find the rip cord of the parachute. Before my breathing returned to normal the intercom exploded again. I caught the word "charge" so I hand charged a round into the gun chamber ready for firing.

More static: "Gurk — gook —awk—."

That meant fire, — but at what? More loud squawking and the wings shook violently! Where was the damn target? More static! Then I saw it — so far away it looked like a postage stamp. Did they expect me to hit anything that small and that far away, out of a bouncing airplane?

My first burst was too high. Then the gun stopped! My mind went blank about gun stoppages. In the excitement I automatically hand charged and the gun resumed firing. That told me it was either a short round or a badly worn gun. In all, I had seventeen stoppages, and seriously doubted I had ever touched the target sleeve. Finally I stowed the gun in disgust! Instantly there was a furious babble of static. What was the pilot trying to tell me? Then I remembered! I had forgotten to clear the gun, and there was one live round left that could have killed someone on the ground! Pilots had the authority and the obligation to ground gunner candidates who were not suitable to handle weapons in the air. After my inept performance that day I thought he was likely going to wash me out on the spot. When we landed he took his time getting out of the front cockpit, and I cringed as he approached me.

"You almost lost your ammunition two times! Your cockpit procedure was the worst I ever saw! You failed to clear the guns and could have killed someone! But, in spite of all that, I think you got some good hits on the target. Now tomorrow, calm down and you'll be all right."

He started off, then turned back. "Sergeant, one time I saw you bounce too high. Your safety belt was much too long. That's dangerous in rough air."

"Yes sir, it was — uh — too long. I'll watch that next time."

Waiting for the scores to be posted was agony. I hoped that I hit the target sleeve at least once. When nineteen percent was posted by my name, — one of the highest scores that day, I was stunned. I had lost seventeen percent of my ammunition because of rounds that wouldn't fire, and still hit nineteen percent???? That score triggered a transformation. I imagined myself an aerial Doc Holiday and swaggered a little on my way to the barracks, — like I thought Doc would do.

September 7

The next morning it was great to awake at a reasonable hour and look forward to a day of unruffled simplicity. The morning after a rough raid I always felt in tune with the universe. I had once again thumbed my nose at the odds and was still there. Even the small, everyday tasks that might otherwise seem menial were pleasant to contemplate. It was good to polish shoes or do some routine repair on flying equipment. When one lives on the brink of extinction, his outlook on life undergoes a change, for he realizes that life is a fragile and precious gift. I had a full day at my disposal and I intended to enjoy every moment of it. Nothing was going to louse up my day!

Counce looked haggard when he got up and started dressing.

"How you feel?"

"Terrible! Got a bad headache."

"You were off oxygen far too long yesterday."

Surprisingly, at this early hour of the day, Wilson stirred and sat up. "Anybody got some aspirin? I've had an awful headache for hours."

I handed him an aspirin bottle and a cup of water.

"It will probably take three or four aspirin to knock this one," he said.

"No, don't take more than two, Wilson. If that won't do it, go see the Flight Surgeon."

Jim said "I hope this headache is the only damage I got from yesterday.

"Have you noticed any dizziness?"

"No, just this blasted headache. Being out of oxygen was my fault . . . I should have had a bottle on hand and somethin' to hammer it on with."

"That's ridiculous," insisted Wilson. "How could you have known there was water in the oxygen system?"

"Well, I should've been ready for an emergency like that, and I wasn't."

"If it makes you feel any better, Jim, go ahead and blame yourself, but no one else does," I answered.

Counce and Wilson took off for the base hospital, and I pedalled to Operations to do some work on my electric suit. I felt so good I was even glad to see Lt. Franek. To my surprise Carqueville was there, in animated conversation with Reese and Franek. I could tell he was pleased about something and wondered what was goin' on.

"John, guess what?"

I waited for him to continue.

"I've been made first pilot again."

"Hey! That's great! When will you take over your crew?"

"Today! Believe me, I hope they give me some good men. I'm so used to all of you, but I can't expect to get men like Gleichauf has. I'll get whatever is available from the spare gunners, navigators, and bombardiers . . . I'm gonna miss you, John, and Balmore and Jim."

I deeply regretted that the relationship with Herb would be broken, but I was happy for him because I knew how much he wanted to get back to first pilot status. That evening we pedalled into Great Yeldham to celebrate Carqueville's sudden elevation to first pilot position. Nearly all the crew went along. Balmore joined some villagers in a dart game. He was very good and could beat any of the crew with no effort. In fact, he could hold his own with the English who had played the game since childhood. Some of them were real experts. They arrived at the pub with their special dart cases, and had a great time competing with their friends and engaging in village gossip.

September 10

On a mission, the navigator in the lead plane did the Group navigating. But if the formation broke up on the return, or we had to fall out of it to conserve fuel, Carl had to quickly pinpoint our position. With only an occasional glance at his charts, he wasn't always able to recognize our exact position instantly. That's where Balmore entered the picture. A good radio operator was priceless to a navigator. George could attempt either a position fix or a Q.D.M. A fix[2] would provide Shutting with our latitude and longitude at a given time. A Q.D.M. would give him a compass heading directly to the radio station Balmore contacted. Either one would put the navigator in excellent position to bring us over Ridgewell Airdrome even if the weather was foul.

[2] A fix was a matter of triangulation — a known distance (between two radio stations) and two angles (created by the angles of the radio beams reaching the two stations).

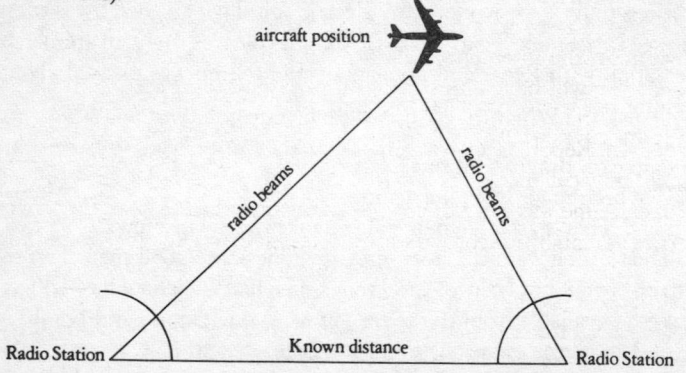

aircraft position

radio beams

radio beams

Radio Station

Known distance

Radio Station

CHAPTER IX
Mission: Airfield in Belgium[1]

September 9 - Airfield in Belgium   *Aircraft 765*
Nip and Tuck

Buck Rogers was back with us again and that made me feel better. I felt safer with Rogers in the tail than any tail gunner in the 381st. Raymond Legg, who had been flying in the tail while Buck was recuperating, was a nice kid. I liked Raymond, but Buck was the best I had seen in that position at that point.

Now that Carqueville was a first pilot with his own crew, Lt. John M. Kels, from Berkeley, California, was assigned as our copilot. He was easy going and relaxed, quite a contrast to Gleichauf's tense concentration. Kels was twenty-three years old, a large, well-proportioned man who made a good appearance. We could not expect him to be another Carqueville right off. It would take a while for him to know the crew, and what he could expect from each man. Kels was an excellent replacement and I had no doubts about him from the first mission with us.

There was an atmosphere of excitment at Operations. No one actually said what was about to happen, but it was hinted that something big — real big — was about to break. Gleichauf was visibly excited when he arrived at the aircraft. ''The long-awaited Invasion may be on this morning. They don't say so for sure, but all crews are warned to make no comments on the intercom about anything they may see crossing the Channel. We will have an escort all the way in and out. The mission should be short. When we get back, leave your gun positions set up for another raid. Report to interrogation quickly and be ready for a second mission if they call it.''

Takeoff time was early. Before dawn the planes were lined up on the taxi strips. A night takeoff was a fascinating sight. The darkness was

[1]The official roster of missions shows Lille-Nord on this date. My diary shows an airfield in Belguim. Perhaps different formations hit both targets that date.

spotted with moving lights as the aircraft moved steadily into position. There were sudden stabs of bright illumination as pilots hit a landing light to help outline a tricky turn. The aircraft pulled up close together near the end of the runway and the throb of engines dwindled to a steady rumble. The lead ship was in place. One minute . . . two minutes . . . three minutes . . . there was the signal flare. Four engines opened up with a deafening roar. The ship trembled. Brakes were released and the aircraft sped down the runway appearing as a series of fast moving lights, the turbo superchargers gleaming blue-white from the heat, an eerie glow under the wings. The next plane followed, then another. Eventually our turn came. When we pulled into place Kels put the cowl flaps in trailing position. On takeoff I stood between and slightly behind the pilot and copilot where I could see the instruments clearly. I did not get into the turret until we were nearing the Channel or North Sea.

"Tail wheel locked — light is out," said the copilot.

Gleichauf glanced at me and I nodded. A last look at the controls and the four engines opened up. Paul held hard brakes until the engines reached full takeoff power of twenty five hundred R.P.M.s.

"Brakes off."

The ship lurched forward as the four engines grabbed the air — Paul jockeyed the throttles momentarily for control, then commanded, "Lock throttles!"

"Throttles locked," replied the copilot moments later.

My eyes were glued to the engine instruments. They jumped rapidly from one engine to another until I was satisfied they were going to hold. Then a hasty look out of the right and left side windows at the gas tank vents. Sometimes they siphoned out fuel into the air on takeoff. Back to the instruments: still OK. I had time now for a fleeting look at the runway. By this time speed was coming up and I started calling out the air speed, "Sixty . . . sixty-five . . . seventy . . . seventy five . . . eighty . . . eighty-five . . . ninety . . " so the pilots would not have to look at the air speed indicator.

Gleichauf pulled back the wheel and released it, starting a series of gentle bounces, that would tell him when there was enough lift on the wings to pull the plane into the air.

"Ninety-five . . . one hundred . . . one-oh-five. . . ''

The aircraft lifted smoothly from the runway. "Wheels up."

"Wheels coming up," responded the copilot.

"Hundred and ten . . . hundred and fifteen . . . '

The aircraft was gathering speed. We hit some propellor wash from a preceding aircraft and there was a risky moment or two. Kels said,

"Wheels are up — lights out."

"Hundred twenty . . . hundred twenty-five . . .". I relaxed because there was nothing to worry about for the present. It was still dark but in the East there was a faint hint of dawn. Far ahead were lights we must follow carefully. Gradually darkness gave way to pre-dawn light. The Squadron formed in proper order, ready for Group rendezvous. I was keyed up for this raid, expecting big things to open up. After the climb to high altitude we headed out to sea toward the target. I suspected that the object of the raid was not so much bombing damage to a target as a diversionary action to draw off enemy air interference with the naval craft if indeed the invasion was underway.

"Navigator to Bombardier."

"Go ahead."

"Look at all those ships."

"Pilot to crew — Pilot to crew, make no comments about anything you see below. Sometimes intercom talk leaks through to Jerry." (By freak electronics).

Sure enough, ships were strung out in a long line from the British Coast half way across the Channel. It looked like the invasion was on, but I could hardly believe we were strong enough then for an all-out attempt against the Continent. It was an exhilarating view, but I had to cease sightseeing and turn my attention to the business at hand.

"Navigator to Pilot! Navigator to Pilot!"

Kels motioned to Gleichauf to switch to intercom.

"This is the Pilot."

"Enemy Coast in five minutes."

"Pilot to crew — keep alert."

"Bombardier to crew, oxygen check."

"Tail, rajah."

"Ball, OK."

"Radio, rajah."

"Turret, OK."

"Cockpit, OK."

"Ball to Copilot — Ball to Copilot."

"Go ahead, Ball."

"Flak, eleven o'clock low."

Boom! A real close one! I heard fragments strike the aircraft hard, but could see no damage from my position.

"Copilot from Ball."

"Go ahead Ball."

"Sir, I am wounded."

There was a momentary lag on the intercom. I was not certain I had heard Nick correctly.

"Copilot to Ball, will you repeat that?"

"Sir, I am wounded."

We never used the word "Sir" on the intercom and Nick seldom used it on the ground unless a high ranking officer was present. What induced Nick to become so formal when he was wounded?

Kels motioned Gleichauf to get on intercom. "Nick was hit by that heavy burst of flak."

"Pilot to Ball — Pilot to Ball! Where were you hit? How bad is it?"

"Got me in the leg an' foot. Goin' numb, but hurting some."

"Can you move your foot?"

"I can move it OK."

"We are just now enterin' enemy territory. Think you can stay on the guns until we get back over water? It won't be long."

"Yeah, I think so."

"Good! We'll get you out of the ball as soon as we're back over water."

"OK, Pilot — I can make it."

"Radio to Ball, turn your heated suit up high to hold down shock."

"OK."

"Bombardier to Ball, use pure oxygen Nick. We got plenty today."

"OK, Bombardier."

"Pilot to Ball, if you start feeling dizzy let us know an' we'll get you out of there quick."

"OK — I'll make it."

"Navigator to Bombardier. There is the I.P. — be on the bomb run in five minutes."

"Waist to Turret."

"Go ahead, Waist."

"Number three engine is throwin' a little smoke."

"OK, Jim."

"Turret to Copilot — is number three on autolean?"

"No, it was runnin' a little hot, so I put it on autorich."

"Suggest put it back on autolean and open cowl flaps enough to keep it about two fifteen." (215 degrees cylinder head temperature.)

"OK, John."

A few minutes later the Waist called, "Number three has quit smoking."

"Good! Remind me to tell the crew chief when we get back."

"Bombardier to Pilot — we're on the bomb run."

"Tail to crew. Flak five o'clock low."

"Waist to crew, flak three o'clock low."

The flak was mild and not very accurate which was welcome to me, and no fighters were in sight, which was unusual.

"Bombs away."

I felt the load drop off and the aircraft surge slightly upward.

"Radio to Bombardier, bomb bay clear."

"OK, Radio, doors coming up."

"Doors are up."

"Pilot to Ball — Pilot to Ball."

"Go ahead."

"How are you feeling?"

"Foot's hurtin' worse. Get me out soon as you can."

"We'll have you out in a few minutes now."

"Bombardier to Radio, get the blanket ready to wrap up Nick when we get him in the radio room."

"Bombardier to Ball, I'll be back as soon as we leave the Coast and help you out of the ball. I can see the Coast up ahead now."

The fighter escort was perfect. No enemy planes were sighted. Flak was meager. Nick was unfortunate to catch a flak fragment from the only burst that was close to us. The formation began letting down and Purus went back to help Nick, who was in pain but not enough to justify a morphine shot. Purus decided it would be best to leave the foot and leg wrapped in blankets and not try to bind the wound. The bleeding seemed to have stopped. It was much too cold to expose the foot to outside air temperature. All they could do for Nick was keep him warm and as comfortable as possible. Gleichauf broke from the formation to get fast medical help for Nick. At lower altitudes the intercom was unneeded in the cockpit. Paul turned to me. "Fire a red red flare on the approach."

When I was sure they could see it, I fired the flare that signalled wounded man aboard. Shortly afterward I saw an ambulance head for the taxi strip we were expected to use.

As soon as the aircraft stopped Nick was lifted gently onto a stretcher and into the ambulance. As it pulled away I had a depressed feeling. I had come to admire Nick. He was a brash young man, but he had been a mainstay down in that ball, where none of the rest of us would have ventured by choice. It took a special kind of man, with a tough mental attitude, to handle the anxieties of that position amid the bursting flak. Herb Carqueville was waiting when we climbed out of the ship and very much upset about Nick. Capt. Ralston, the Flight Surgeon, was also there. I knew Nick would get the best of care and treatment.

At interrogation we learned nothing more about the ships we saw in the Channel. Orders were to leave the guns mounted in the aircraft and stand by for the possibility of another mission. It never came. All afternoon we stayed close to the radio waiting for a news flash. Not a thing was said about an invasion. The next morning newspapers carried a story of an invasion rehearsal — no doubt a part of the continous effort to confuse the enemy as to when and where the invasion would come. The code name for the exercise was "Starkey."

I had serious reservations about the ethics of dropping bombs on the Occupied Countries. All of us understood the necessity of destroying submarine pens, harbor facilities and war plants. But the civilian population of Belgium and Holland were caught between the grinding forces of two ruthless military machines. Make no mistake about it — the Allies were ruthless and had no hesitation to sacrifice innocent people to achieve military objectives. Did the bomber crews have any accountability for raining death from the skies on helpless populations who had nothing to do with starting the war? Edward Cayce, the noted psychic reader, is reputed to have been able to describe the events of previous lifetimes by some psychic ability to read directly from the pages of what he called the "Akashas Records." I prefer to think that no such celestial archive exists. Nevertheless, I was bothered by my part, as insignificant as it was, in the impersonal fury of destruction poured down on Europe from above. And I think that most of the men who manned the bomber crews were uneasy whether they admitted it or not.

Across Europe the portraits and statues of military commanders look down from positions of honor. Their names and deeds have been encased in a mantle of glory. But war is not glorious — or noble. War is incredible brutality and inhumanity beyond description. Too soon the cruelty and terror of the campaigns are forgotten. The faces of the conquerors hang alongside the portraits of saints and only a little less honored.

September 11

During the early part of September the 8th Air Force was reorganized. General Carl Spaatz assumed command of all American Air Force Operations in Europe. Major General Ira Eaker moved up to command the 8th Air Force. The 8th Bomber Command was put under General Frederick Anderson. The rest of the command shaped up as follows:

First Division	Brig. Gen. Robert Williams
Second Division	Brig. Gen. James Hodges
Third Division	Brig. Gen. Curtis LeMay

Divisions were increased on paper to four wings, each composed of three combat Groups. The combined strength was to be built up to that structure in the immediate future. Such plans would mean larger formations and improvement in the odds for survival for each man. Whether the build up would take place soon enough to be of any help to me was yet to be determined. The casualty rate was so high at that period that even large numbers of new crews and aircraft would build up the force less rapidly than expected.

When I began to feel sorry for myself in reference to the heavy odds I remembered that I could have been assigned to the 100th Group — the hard luck Group of the 8th Bomber Command. That unfortunate outfit had earned the undying hatred of the German Luftwaffe. Whenever their group insignia was recognized the Jerry pilots were instantly infuriated. One story explaining the circumstances that brought this on kept circulating so persistently that it must have had the elements of truth. According to that story, the 100th was under intense attack over the Continent and in desperation one Fortress lowered its landing gear. That is the internationally recognized signal for surrender. When the German fighter pilots pulled in close to escort the surrendering craft down, some of the Fortress gunners suddenly opened fire at the unsuspecting fighters while they were out of position to return the fire. Several fighters were shot down and some pilots lost. From that moment on the 100th was a marked Group and the sight of that hated insignia inflamed the German pilots to turn full attention to the 100th.

September 13

Sam Spivak was one of the early crew chiefs in the 381st and a good one. He was the brother of Charlie Spivak, a well-known orchestra leader of that period. When Sam and Gleichauf got together it was old friends meeting again. It was reassuring to have that kind of man in charge of keeping our aircraft in top condition.

One bitterly cold day Sam was working alone, high up on an engine stand with his head in the nacelle space behind the engine. Electricians, armorers, and other specialists were coming and going. Sam heard another vehicle stop but paid no attention to it. An English voice said, "Yank, how do you like our English weather?"

No American liked the miserable winter-spring weather of 1943 in England and Sam thought he was talking to one of the English runway workers. His reply was a volley of profanity that clearly expressed what he thought of English weather in very definite and colorful terms. When he did not hear any reply, Sam stooped down to where he could see to whom he was talking. He got the shock of his life: there stood King George VI, flanked by British and American military brass! Sam tried to stutter an apology but the King cut him short. George VI was laughing heartily and said, "Forget it, Yank. I had it coming. And I've heard better profanity than that many times. I'm an old navy man, you know."

CHAPTER X
Mission to Nantes

September 16 - Nantes, France   *Aircraft 765*

Carqueville was flying his initial mission as a first pilot with a crew newly put together. He would be on the right wing and we would be on the left wing of the second element of the squadron.

✦ ✦ ✦ First element
✦ ✦ ✦ Second element

I saw Carqueville at Operations early that morning and he said, "John, my men are nervous and scared, as all of us are on our first raid. We may need some help if fighters hit us hard. Keep your eye on us."

Jim cut in, "Keep tight formation and the fighters won't pick you out as a green crew."

The target was submarine installations at Nantes, on the Loire River, a few miles from the Bay of Biscay, on the West Coast of France. Takeoff and wing assembly was smooth and on schedule. A short time before we reached the enemy coast Purus called me.

"Bombardier to Turret — pull the bomb fuse pins."

"OK, Bombardier."

"Ball to crew, fighters six o'clock low — can't make out what they are."

"Tail to crew, they are P-47's."

The escort flew criss-cross patterns above us and for an hour nothing happened. Then the Navigator spotted trouble.

"Navigator to crew, 109's eleven o'clock low — looks like about fifty of them."

Reliable Jerry had timed the range of the escort perfectly and approached the formation at the time when the 47's would have to turn back. When the Thunderbolts were gone the enemy interceptors pulled up to our altitude and began the usual circling tactic to pick out the best angles for attack. We could never be certain what they looked for, but a ship with signs of mechanical trouble or a straggler was sure to be high on the hit list. We also knew they looked for the weakest formations and suspected that they tried to spot green crews. Perhaps certain groups had earned a reputation of being rough to attack. Other groups may have been easy targets in the past and when they recognized the opposition by the insignias, they may have changed their tactics.

"Bombardier to crew, fighters are hitting the high squadron."

The attack screamed by us at about two hundred yards and we let go with burst after burst. There were seven fighters attacking in a single file.

"Tail to crew — 109 comin' in six o'clock high."

I whirled around to help Legg and we hammered hard at the 109 and another right behind him.

"Ball to Turret."

"Go ahead."

"I think you an' Tail got one — I can see it going down smoking."

I saw us hit it with a dozen bursts, but I think Legg did the most damage. That was the kind of fight I liked. We were never swarmed by fighters but there were enough attacks to keep us busy. By that date I had enough combat experience to be keyed up to maximum performance by fighter action.

The fight slowed down, but ten or twelve interceptors were still buzzing around the formation. A fighter was leading three other Bogies and circling us at about twelve hundred yards.

"Navigator to Turret."

"Go ahead."

"Hey, John, think we could hit that sonnuvabitch at four o'clock high?"

"He's a little out of our range, but we might fire high an' lob a few rounds into him if we're lucky."

"Let's dust him off for the hell of it."

"OK — fire away."

I set my elevation several degrees above his flight path and took a long lead. Both of us squeezed off three or four bursts. We picked the wrong man to mess with. He was not bothering us and we should have left him alone. His wings wiggled as if out of control for a few seconds then he went into a dive and came straight at us with the other three fighters following his lead. We had a full thousand yards to fire and the nose and turret guns poured a deadly hail of lead and steel all of the way. We were assisted by other gun positions in adjoining ships. One after another those fighters barrel-rolled under our right wing, and I heard Jim open up as they flashed by his position. Then Legg cut loose as they dived down out of range. The 109's were so rugged they could absorb a lot of punishment and keep right on coming in. Well, one of us did hit the lead ship with an improbable shot.

"Navigator! This is the pilot. That was damned stupid! That fighter wasn't botherin' us an' you and John made him mad. Those four 109's could've knocked us down. Don't either of you ever pull a stunt like that again.''

Gleichauf was really hot and he had a right to be. We should not have instigated that attack. Fortunately, he did take effective evasive action while the four of them were coming in on us. That was probably why we did not take any damage.

As soon as the fighters dived past us I whirled around to see how Herb was doing. Two fighters were zooming by his aircraft and severe damage was clearly evident.

''Turret to crew, Herb's been badly damaged. His ship is riddled from the waist back an' looks to me like the Copilot and Top Turret are wounded.''

''Waist to crew, Herb is all right as far as I can see.''

It was typical of Jerry tactics to mount two or three simultaneous attacks to divide the defensive fire. In this case it worked well because we were tied up with our own problems. When Herb needed some help we could not give it to him.

''Navigator to Pilot.''

''Go ahead.''

''The I.P. is just ahead of us.''

''Bombardier to crew, flak twelve o'clock high.''

The fire was light and inaccurate, which was great with me. I hated that damn flak. The bombs released on time and the formation made a right swing out over the Bay of Biscay. Two aircraft had release problems but they got rid of their bombs as we passed over a harbor nearby. I watched the boats making frantic movements in an attempt to avoid the bombs they could see falling directly on the harbor.

''Bombardier to Pilot. I think Herb is goin' to be able to hang on. His Copilot is sitting up in his seat now.''

The flight back to England was long and tiresome. When we landed Major Hendricks, the Squadron Commanding Officer, sent for Shutting and me. The Major was usually a mild mannered man, but when we reported he was steaming.

''I've seen some asinine things in my day, but you two men drawing four fighters in on our squadron for no sensible reason takes the prize for stupidity. Don't you have sense enough to leave fighters alone who are not bothering us? If I ever hear of any such irresponsible action from either one of you again there will be severe disciplinary measures!''

When we were out of range of the Major's hearing Shutting whispered, ''I never knew Hendricks had such a temper. Good thing we both kept our big mouths shut.''

"Damn right! If we were not so short on combat personnel he would have thrown the book at us."

Well, it did sound like a good idea at the time. The action was getting a bit dull and we thought dusting off that fighter would liven things up. And that is exactly what happened, but not the way we anticipated. I still wonder, when I think of that day, which of us hit that fighter. It was one hell of a shot.

A gunner who wore size thirty-eight did not make it back from the mission and my blouse problem was solved. It was an excellent fit and I had a full uniform again. I hoped the unfortunate man got out of the ship in time.

September 18

When the combat action slowed down, the 381st resumed their endless classes, not only because the information might be useful, but also to fill the vacuum between raids. The aircraft recognition classes were a matter of repetition. Pictures showing the silhouettes from different angles of vision of all the enemy aircraft we were expected to see would be flashed on and off of the screen. In time we came to recognize an aircraft at a distance the same way we recognized a Ford or Chevrolet without conscious thought.

The prisoner of war classes made a lasting impression on my mind. I can recall the lecturer saying something like the following: ". . . Never resist an armed soldier because he is looking for an excuse to kill you after what you are doing to the cities of his country. German civilians are worse than the soldiers. They have been known to shoot men parachuting down. German soldiers will follow the Prisoner of war rules of the Geneva Convention. So if you have a choice, surrender to soldiers rather than to civilians. If you are captured, your orders are to tell the captors your name, rank, and serial number and nothing else. Give the enemy no other information no matter how trivial it may sound to you. Your second order is to attempt to escape if you can. Don't do anything foolish. Remember that as a prisoner of war you are costing the enemy food, housing, materials and manpower. Dead, you cost the Germans nothing. You will be questioned to extract whatever information they can get out of you. The Germans are skillful at interrogation. You might be ushered into a comfortable office where a smiling officer offers you a cigarette and a chair. He might have a glass of beer brought in. There could be small talk about the U.S. Perhaps the officer has visited our country. This could go on until he thinks you are disarmed. Then the questions will get closer and closer to what he is probing for. If you are not careful, you will spill information the enemy can use to put together a better picture of what we are doing and how we are doing it . . .''

Sometimes the lecturer was an escapee from a prison camp and we listened with intense interest. ''Your third order is to obey the orders of the enemy as long as they do not aid the enemy war effort. You will refuse to work in a war plant or to do anything that will work against your country. You have little to fear from the German soldiers in the way of physical abuse. No matter what you have heard, we have no confirmed cases of torture of American or English soldiers. Herr Hitler still feels he is going to win this war, and hopes to create a working relationship with the U.S. and England after the war.''

''Your fourth order is that you will be under the command of the senior Allied officer in your prison camp. The enemy will issue most of their directions through him. Never wear or carry anything in clothes or equipment that is not definitely a military issue. If the enemy finds any- thing on your person other than military or aircraft paraphernalia, you might be considered a spy or a saboteur. If they suspected you were an agent, you would be turned over to the Gestapo, and rest assured that the Geneva rules would not apply. They would put you through torture to extract useful information . . .''

September 21

When a four-day pass was available we always made a strenuous effort to get into London early enough to find a hotel room. My favorite place was ''Prince's Garden,'' the site of the Eagle Squadron Club of Ameri- cans who served with the R.A.F. before the U.S. was drawn into the struggle. It was located far enough away from the beaten path of soldiers on leave that rooms were usually available up to mid-afternoon.

One night in London I bumped into Johnny Graves in a bar near Trafalgar Square. He joined me at Sheppard Field that day when a few of us were conned into volunteering for aerial gunnery. We were together at the Boeing Aircraft Engineering School, at the Las Vegas Gunnery School and the various training bases where combat crews were put to- gether and developed. I was struck immediately by the change that had taken place in Johnny since I had last seen him. The look in his eyes and the lines tightly drawn across a face too young for such lines told me he had been through some harrowing experiences. This is what he told me: ''We were badly damaged and had no chance to make it across the North Sea. The radio operator got in touch with Air-Sea Rescue, and as we headed down to ditch, there was enough power left to control the ship. We hit hard and bounced some before settling. Two of us were out real fast and got the rafts launched, and managed to cut loose before the ship sank. Right quick I saw we were in trouble 'cause the raft I was in began to deflate. There was a leak, either a defect in the raft or some battle damage. I got the hand pump going and me and one of the waist gunners kept that raft inflated. It was almost dark when we hit the water and we knew our chances of being rescued before the next morning were almost nil. The other raft drifted away in the dark and was never found. In a very short time we were soaking wet from the wind blowin' spray on us and so cold — so cold. I was worried the hand pump would wear out before morning, but the two of us stayed with it all night. When dawn came the other three men were dead of cold and wet exposure. The exercise of pumpin' was just enough to keep two of us alive all that awful night. . .'' Graves paused, unable to go on and tears welled up in his eyes. In a few minutes he recovered. ''You'll never know what it was like. Looking at them cold and lifeless was terrible. They were almost like brothers. That morning a patrol boat spotted us and the ordeal was finally over. I'm OK now, John, on another crew, but it won't ever be the same for me again. I'll keep remembering how they looked. . .''

There may have been other overnight survivors in the North Sea, but Johnny Graves and his crewmate were the only two I heard about. That leak in the raft turned out to be the difference between life and death.

There were not nearly as many air raids against London in late 1943, but one had to be prepared for an air raid any night. If an air raid warning sounded, I followed the crowds to the nearest shelter and waited it out. But one night I was opposite Hyde Park when the sirens began to shriek. That eerie, baleful sound always made shivers ripple through me. There was an anti-aircraft battery in the Park, so on impulse I decided to forget the shelter and watch the show, reasoning that I might not get another opportunity to watch anti-aircraft fire close by at ground level. I gazed with intense fascination as the huge searchlights stabbed the sky with brilliant beams of light. It was awesome to see those batteries fire and the orange-red bursts high in the sky. A bomber got caught momentarily in the converging beams of two searchlights and gleamed bright in the sky like a lighted billboard. I tried to visualize the blinding terror of the men in the bomber, knowing as they did that they were a perfectly outlined target for the R.A.F. night fighters.

Suddenly pieces began dropping around me and I realized that jagged chunks of cast iron shell fragments could strike me any second. Quickly I ran into the shelter of a large overhanging doorway until the sirens sounded all clear.

''Good show?'' came a voice out of the darkness.

"Yes, indeed," I replied, "quite fascinating to watch the batteries fire."

"It might be so to me if I hadn't seen it so many times, you know."

"Do you often stand here rather than go to the shelters?" I asked.

"Oh, no, tonight I was going to visit friends. When the sirens opened up I was not near a shelter I knew about and I saw this big doorway," was the answer.

We stood talking for a while, then he asked, "Were you headed somewhere special when the raid started?"

"Just back to Picadilly to see if I can find any of my friends."

"Would you like to go with me to visit my friends for a little while? And see how some of us Englishmen live in wartime London?"

"That would be interesting. I can go to the club later."

The friends were a couple with two children living in a nearby flat. They talked at length about the difficulties and trauma encountered in rearing a family surrounded by the terror of war. Both of the men were ex-soldiers who had sustained wounds and were now working in war plants. I felt a warm glow of comradeship with those people who were so hospitable to a man they had never seen before. On my next trip to London I used all my rations at the P.X. and carried numerous scarce items to this fine family. The children were delirious with excitment over the candy and the mother was delighted with several bars of soap and some sugar I conned the Mess Sergeant out of.

September 22

When an air crew had been in heavy combat action, and appeared to be shaken up, they became eligible for one of the rest homes maintained in England. It was not a matter of the number of raids, but the mental condition of the crew. The Flight Surgeon kept a watchful eye on the men before and after missions. He alone decided when a crew needed a week or two of respite from the war.

Carl Shutting organized a campaign of odd behavior by the crew for the benefit of the Flight Surgeon, Capt. Ralston. He had it worked out well, carefully orchestrating the act to catch Ralston's attention, but I had no confidence it would work. The elated Navigator came to our hut in fine spirits that afternoon: "We did it! Ralston thinks we are on the edge of bad nerves. We're leaving for the rest home in the morning for a whole week away from this rat race."

"Where are we going?" asked Jim.

"Some village on the Upper Thames River — that's all I know. Maybe we can get out of this mud for a week anyway."

"We got you to thank for this. I didn't think our little act would work. You know there isn't a damned thing wrong with any of us."

"We know that, John — but Ralston don't — and that is what counts."

"It sounds great."

We left for Cholsey in fine spirits. The day was clear and cold, which was exceptional for the time of the year. It was too bad that Wilson was in the hospital for frostbite, and Rogers was not included because it was evident that he was not going back on combat duty. George, Jim, Shutting, Purus, Gleichauf and I were the lucky ones.

At Cholsey Station a personnel truck met us. It was a short ride to our destination. When we pulled into the long driveway, I was surprised at the layout. It was a magnificent old manor house, beautifully covered with ivy. The house was four stories high and the lovely grounds were spacious and well kept. Green lawns, attractive hedges and bright flowers were a welcome sight.

The staff met us at the door. "Welcome to Buckeley's Manor! We hope you will have a pleasant stay here. Each man will be assigned a room to himself. The schedule for meals is posted on the bulletin board, and you can dine any time during the hours listed."

We went upstairs and were shown our rooms. Imagine having a room all to myself.

"Here are your sheets."

Sheets? I had forgotten about such things.

The bathrooms were down the hall.

"What time of the day do you have hot water?" I asked hopefully.

"Oh, it's always hot until ten P.M. Then we turn it on again each morning at seven o'clock."

Unbelievable! How long had it been since I had a hot bath?

"Let's go downstairs and fit you men with tweed trousers and pullover sweaters," said one of the staff members. "You are free to wear these clothes instead of your uniform while at Buckeley's."

After dinner that evening all of us were issued passes for the week.

"You are free to do what you wish with your time while here. We have tennis courts, a trap or skeet range, badminton courts and there are golf courses nearby. Or you may enjoy archery and horseback riding. You will be issued a bicycle so you can ride into the villages or explore the countryside. The beautiful Thames River is close by and we suggest you take a boat trip up the Thames. A boat runs a regular schedule every day. Enjoy yourselves while here. Forget about the war. If you have any other requests, please let us know."

The Thames River upstream is quite different from the muddy, commercial estuary a traveler sees at London. The Thames I saw was a beautiful river, clean and sparkling. Fine old estates bordered each bank, and their well kept grounds sloped to the edge of the estuary. Most of the homes had private piers and boats; it was England at her finest. The stream wound between inviting lawns and over-hanging trees for mile after mile, becoming more picturesque as the boat moved further upstream.

At Buckeley's there were men from many groups in the Air Force, and some recently from North Africa. I noticed that most of the latter were recovering from wounds or nervous shock. Late at night we sat around huge open fireplaces and swapped experiences — experiences that no doubt were expanded in the act of retelling. Each morning our routine included some fast tennis to limber up, then a bicycle ride around the back roads until lunch time. In the afternoon we would shoot skeet for a while, then take off for another ride through unspoiled rural byways. We were lucky to find a pleasant pub at Wallingford, a village remote from major cities. Uniforms were non-existent except for us — too rural for soldiers. That pub gave me an insight as to how the villagers lived. I listened to intimate political discussions, and learned for the first time that England had a fast-growing movement toward socialism and some tendency toward mild communism. I learned that, although the English strongly supported Churchill, many of them were opposed to the Tory Party. They wanted him for the war, because strong leadership was required, but I listened in amazement to what they wanted in the future. They did not want a Churchill government after the war. They were determined that England was not going back to a government dominated by the aristocracy. (After the war when Americans were shocked that Churchill was turned out of office, I remembered Wallingford and knew why.)

The time spent at Buckeley's Manor was one of the most pleasant weeks I have ever experienced, because it was such a contrast to Ridgewell Airdrome. It was a week's interlude of tranquility in the midst of war.

At the Cholsey Station Shutting said, "We won't have another week like this one in England — it has been great! I hate like hell to go back to the war."

"Same here," Gleichauf replied.

Late that afternoon we reached the village station and rode the rest of the way on our bikes that had been checked in at the station when we departed a week earlier. It was almost dark but we could see the Fortresses returning from a mission.

Back at the hut Jim asked Lancia, "What's gone on since we left?"

"We made a run on Emden — got in an easy one."

"And we used a new radar gadget that let's you see through the clouds," Pitts added.

"Wait a minute," I said, "there's no such thing."[1]

"No bullshit! The navigator sees right through the fog," Pitts insisted.

"How did the drop come out?"

"Not too good, but this was our first time to use it. Give them a chance to work the bugs out of it. Sounds good to me," Lancia replied.

"What do they call this new thing?" George asked.

"The Limeys call it Pathfinder."

That was one of the early American attempts to use the radar device that we later called Mickey.

"There's a rumor that one of the Squadron Commanders tried to quit flying this week," said Kettner.

"Who was it?" I asked. "Not our C.O., I hope."

"The story is this Squadron Commander got fouled up mentally — broke down — said he couldn't take it any more. We don't know who it is."

"They're tryin' to keep it hush-hush," Tedesco added. "I heard they won't let him quit flyin' — would be bad for the morale of the men."

"How would you like to fly a raid with that commander leading it?" Jim asked.

CHAPTER XI
Mission to Emden

The temperature was warmer, so Balmore joined me for the long bike ride into Ridgewell. The White Horse Tavern was a favorite watering station for soldiers and civilians. Three men from the base came in and took over a table next to us. After a while I could not help overhearing their conversation, perhaps because it dealt with a common subject high among the gripes of combat personnel.

"Why can't we get better flyin' equipment?" one man asked. "They keep improvin' the goddam airplanes, but they screw us with lousy equipment."

"The bastards who designed it don't never have to wear it in combat — that's one reason," said another.

"Wonder why they can't copy the R.A.F.? They been improvin' their stuff for years. Some of it is damn good."

"Harry Houdini couldn't get out of one of our chutes if he landed on water! He'd drown like a rat caught in a fish net," added a third voice.

"But the R.A.F. has a quick release so they can cut loose the chute just as they hit the water."

"Or in a high wind."

"OK! Why can't we copy them?"

"But my big bitch is that lousy oxygen mask. I think the Gestapo must have designed it."

"I know what you mean. How did they manage to get that extra thing in it that makes your nose start to run as soon as you put it on?"

"I don't know, but after a couple of hours in that wind back in the waist, the Copilot calls me up an' says 'What's the matter with you? I can't unnerstan' what you are sayin'.' How the hell can I talk plain with a mouthful of snot?"

"Where did they dredge up those bastards they call engineers who design this stuff?"

"Some 4F draft dodger not worth a shit for anythin' else. But even those no-goods should've come up with better electric gloves. Why in the hell did they put the heat in the palm of the hand? Don't need it there! It's the fingers that freeze holdin' metal at fifty below. But no, the bastards never thought of that.''

''If one of them had to fly a few missions in the waist or radio room, he would come up with some electric overshoes real quick instead of those silly electric shoes we have to wear. If we had to bail out we would be on the Continent without any shoes! How would you like that?''

I turned to Balmore. ''Electric overshoes! That's exactly what I need. You know what, I think I could make a pair of them. The idea of how to do it just hit me. I'm glad we came here tonight. I'm going to start huntin' up the materials first thing in the morning if we don't get a call.''

George looked at me but said nothing. I could tell by his look that he thought I was hallucinating. The possibility of making something like that out of scraps with crude tools was not in the realm of his understanding.

October 2 - Emden   *Aircraft 765 - Nip and Tuck.*

Two weeks had gone by since we had last been out on a mission and I did not expect one that morning. I was groggy when Reese turned on the lights.

''Wake up! You guys been loafin' long enough.''

The combat mess hall was getting crowded again with the influx of new men. One real rough raid would take care of that! It was easy to pick out the recent arrivals. I could see the anxiety written on their faces and in their gestures. After a while, if they lasted long enough, they would be able to mask their fears. Only a few men, who were born with less than the normal sensations of fear, could quickly become accustomed to the frightening proximity of death, which was a companion one had to accept on every mission. As men became more experienced in combat action, their confidence increased along with each successful raid, but twenty-five missions was insufficient to form a protective mental armor against constant danger. If they sustained enough combat time it would eventually become a way of life, overcoming most of the fear and anxiety. For me this happened in the 15th Air Force when I had about sixty missions. A man learned to hide his thoughts behind a facade of cocky bravado — an image often displayed at the mess hall before a mission. A veteran looked like it was a breeze, not a care in the world, but inside his stomach was churning. The main difference between beginners and experienced men was that the latter knew they could take it, and the new men did not yet have that mental shelter. I studied the faces with an ambivalent mixture of amusement and compassion.

At Operations the Briefing Room reaction was moderate. Jim said,

"Doesn't sound too bad."

We threw our heavy bags of equipment into the personnel truck. On the ride out to the aircraft, Legg said, "You don't think this one will be another Stuttgart?"

"From the sounds I heard we are not goin' that deep today," I answered.

Wilson came awake. "John, do you think Tinker Toy is really a jinx ship?"

"I don't know. What is a jinx anyway?"

Someone from the dark interposed, "You're damn right she's a jinx! Think of all the men killed in her an' all that damage raid after raid."

"Maybe so, but how can metal, wire, and plexiglass take on a personality? Yet I have to admit there is somethin' different about that plane," I replied.

There was plenty of time to get ready. When Gleichauf arrived he gathered the crew into a circle out of the hearing range of the ground men. "Not too bad today. It's Emden — a short run over the North Sea. We may see a hundred fighters, if the Germans figure out where we're goin' fast enough. We'll have a P-47 escort over the target. The flak will be mild and the temperature about thirty-eight degrees below."

The weather over England was favorable for takeoff and the Wing formed on schedule. The flight over the North Sea was tiresome; the formation was loose and erratic, reflecting the large number of new crews. We were ripe for a heavy fighter attack. The route was parallel to the enemy coast for a while. I saw the Island of Heligoland to our right.

"Bombardier to crew, oxygen check."

Each position chattered away with the routine procedure that assured that no one was in trouble out of sight of the others.

"Navigator to Pilot."

"Go ahead."

"We're going to swing right in five minutes, then make a ninety degree turn to come over the target downwind."

"Turret to crew — Turret to crew — the escort five o'clock high."

"Tail to Copilot, those 47's look good up there. I bet we don't see any Bogies today."

"This is Ball, flak four o'clock low." It was scattered and ineffective.

"Tail to crew, I was wrong — fighters at six o'clock low — look like 190's."

The formation pulled in a little tighter. The Jerries made some quick passes close by, but I saw no B-17's sustain damage. The 47's dived into them and that was the end of the attacks for a while.

"Bombardier to Pilot, we're on the bomb run." That meant the aircraft had to be level and steady for the bomb drop. At this point the bombardier in the lead aircraft took charge. The other bombardiers watched his bomb bay and the moment they saw the first bomb fall from the lead ship they released their loads. On the bomb run the lead bombardier was in control of the ship through the Norden Bomb Sight. It connected into the automatic pilot. When the moving indices of the sight lined up properly, the bombs were released. The Norden Sight computed air speed, altitude, wind drift, and all other factors that could influence the accuracy of the bomb strike.

Immediately after the bombs were released on the shipping docks and submarine pens, the Wing made a long, slow left turn and headed for the North Sea.

"Turret to Navigator."

"Go ahead."

"How would you like some more easy raids like this one?"

"Suit me fine except it has been a little dull."

"Not too dull for me," Gleichauf cut in, "I like 'em dull."

Bomber Command announced we had lost twenty-eight ships on that easy mission to Emden. To me it was almost a milk run. Why? There was only one answer: too many pilots throttle jockeying back and forth lousing up the formations so that they were vulnerable to fighter attacks. Who do you think the fighters would choose to hit: the tight, well-disciplined formations or the loose ones signalling green crews? The Wing was a sorry looking operation on the Emden mission, and if we put that kind of show against a tough target, I shuddered to think what whould happen.

October 3

I was eager to put my idea of electric overshoes to work. Fortunately I found everything I needed in the discarded equipment bins. In two or three days I had the design worked out. What it amounted to was cutting up a number of old electrically heated felt shoes into sections large enough to fit around my regular G.I. shoes. With some help from the Parachute Department, where they had experts in sewing and the equipment, the sections were joined together. The heating wires were placed on the outside of the overshoes for easy access in case repairs should be needed. A pair of extra large flying boots was split and enlarged enough to fit around the overshoes to protect the heating wires from damage in use.

The overshoe design worked even better in high-altitude extreme cold than I expected. My feet felt exactly as if I were on the ground in mild weather. There was no sensation of either heat or cold. They were durable enough that no repairs were needed for the remainder of my missions. The design made so much sense that it was difficult to understand why the Air Force equipment experts stayed with those too-hastily designed electric felt shoes that were not what combat crews needed.

October 5

The training classes continued concerning bail out procedures and escapes from enemy-occupied territory. I can still hear the instructor droning: "Now when you see a wing fire, that means gasoline or oil is burning. Sometimes a wing fire will burn itself out but that is rare. When you see the flame streaming back from the wing, get ready to bail out. You will not have much time to ponder the situation. There is no need to panic. Snap on your chute and wait for the bail out order. Grasp the ripcord in one hand, fold your arms against your body and fall out. Count at least twenty and pull the ripcord. Never pull it too quick because it might blossom up an' hang on the tail of the airplane."

Then questions would interrupt the instructor. When the order was restored, the speaker would continue: "Don't worry about passing out in the thin air. You will revive when you get down to ten or twelve thousand feet. When you get close enough to see the ground clearly, look in all directions for dense woods or some other place to hide until dark. Determine if an army or civilian patrol is on the way to where you will land. If they are, do not resist or attempt to run away. If you do you will be shot on the spot."

Each instructor had different ideas about how to land safely. I liked the following because it was the same system I was taught at Brooks Field many years earlier. "At about a hundred feet from the ground reach out and grab as many parachute shroud lines as you can grasp in each hand. Just before you hit the ground, bend your knees slightly to avoid breaking a leg, and pull down hard on both groups of shroud lines in order to help break the impact of your fall. Immediately after hitting the ground, turn loose of the shroud lines with one hand and use both hands on the other lines. Pull hard enough to spill the air out of the chute and prevent the wind from dragging you. If you are not apprehended, stuff the chute under some bushes then take off fast for the nearest place to hide. Swallow one of these benzedrine tablets from your escape kit to prevent shock. Stay hidden until dark, then move out to put some distance between you and any patrol that may be looking for you."

If an escaped airman was picked up by the Underground Resistance people, as often happened, he would need an identification picture for forged papers. All civilians in Europe were required to carry identification papers with a picture attached. The Underground could easily forge a set of false papers, but no photographic paper or film was available to civilians in occupied Europe. So each crewman carried an escape picture of himself made under harsh light to make him look haggard. Since the combat groups were strictly military units they had a limited number of civilian jackets for those pictures. On the following page are seven pictures all showing exactly the same jacket. The Germans learned to identify captured fliers by the jacket in their escape picture.

I remember a lecture from an airman who had bailed out and made his way to Spain and eventually back to England. "Most Frenchmen will recognize who you are, but Germans in France may not. Never force a conversation with a Frenchman because you do not know if it is safe for him to speak to you or recognize you for what you are. A French family caught aiding an escaped American or English airman is executed. If you reach the point where you desperately need help, try to find a remote village. Watch it from a distance for signs of Germans or officials. If there are none, then just before dark saunter slowly through the town without speaking or nodding to anyone. Let the people see you. Keep right on walking down the road so they will know where you will be after dark. If it is safe, they will notify the Underground. Leave it entirely up to them."

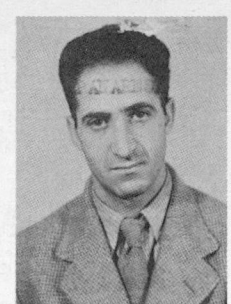

Examples
of
Escape
Pictures

Note that every man used the same jacket.

CHAPTER XII
Mission to Bremen

October 8

The nightly raids against England continued but were a civilian threat, not a military one. The Germans did not have the accuracy to pinpoint military sites at night. Hitler had given up the idea of attempting to invade England, and knew that his forces could not destroy her with the weapons presently available. The German air raids were as much in retaliation for the nightly R.A.F. destruction raining down on Germany as they were to wipe out war production.

If we thought Hitler was about to give up on the idea of subduing England, we were very much wrong. He could not accomplish it by means of conventional weapons, but his excellent scientists were working hard to develop new means of terror for the stubborn British. The Allied Commanders had no means to know how close to success they were, but alarming rumors were filtering into Allied intelligence centers. Some came from agents on the Continent. Other information of highly disturbing nature was picked up from the secret Turing Machine (code-named Ultra), a marvelous machine. It was developed by a brilliant Englishman named Alan Turing, and could decode the supposedly unbreakable German cipher as easily as the Germans could do so with their code books. The German high command never suspected that their cipher had been broken and the Allies read their secret messages throughout the War. Mr. Churchill thought that "Ultra" was one of the most decisive advantages that the Allies possessed. Thus the Allies knew the threat of new super weapons was not just an idle boast of the Germany propaganda machinery. In English language broadcasts we heard direct allusions to terrible instruments of death and destruction that would turn the tide of victory to Germany. We knew the Germans were capable of creating new machines of death if they had enough time. Even though we dismissed the threats as so much propaganda, we did not take the enemy lightly. I would not have been surprised at any time that some new weapon was thrown at us. We assumed that the Allies were working on super weapons, too, but there was the haunting fear that the German scientists were ahead of us because they could have started as far back as 1935 or 1936 and might be nearing success.

October 8 - Bremen   *Aircraft 755*

"OK! Wake up. Let's go! Listen to the roster: Comer, Counce, Balmore, Legg, and Harkness flyin' 755 with Gleichauf. . ."

"Wait! You mean 765," I said.

"No! 755 like I said."

"But 765 is our ship," I replied.

"Not today. Some other crew is flyin' it. Good luck."

Reese was gone before I could say anything else.

Jim exploded. "Damn those clerks at Operations! Giving our ship to some other crew an' makin' us fly one we've never seen before."

"It's an error in typing but too late to do anything about it. George, how about you standing by the Briefing Room door while Jim and I get to the aircraft early? I don't remember aircraft 755."

The aircraft was in excellent condition. An hour later I said to Jim, "Things are going too well this mornin' — not normal. We must be overlooking something."

George came out on the next truck. "Didn't sound too bad. I'd say medium tough."

"You think we need more ammunition?"

"Don't think so."

A Jeep pulled up and the Flight Surgeon stepped out. "Rub some of this salve on your face where the mask does not cover it. I hope it'll cut down on frostbite." Captain Ralston was a good one. He never succeeded in finding an ointment to prevent frostbite but he kept trying.

The crew chief drew me aside. "How long you fellows been here?"

"Since July."

The chief looked relieved. "Who is your pilot?"

"Gleichauf."

"Oh, good man."

Paul was well known to the veteran crew chiefs. They took pride in the condition of the aircraft assigned to them. When necessary the ground crews put in long hours. They became upset when an inexperienced crew abused an airplane. The chiefs, of course, expected battle damage, but they were incensed when planes returned with unnecessary wear on brakes and engines caused by pilots who did not have enough experience or did not care. Gleichauf had a reputation for respecting an aircraft and the men who kept them in good condition.

When the pilot arrived, I started sounding off about some other crew assigned to our airplane but Gleichauf cut it short. "Some clerk made an error. Forget the bitching and let's get ready to start engines." He waited for the rest of the men to gather around him. "We're goin' to Bremen today. The fighter opposition is not expected to be too rough. There are two hundred and fifty flak guns — very accurate. There are two hundred fighters in the area, so it could turn out rougher than expected. P-47's will go with us nearly to the I.P. The target is submarine installations."

As we approached the enemy coast I went into my regular ritual. "Oh, God, be with me today and keep me from danger . . ." Instantly my brain received a messge as clear as if it had come routinely over the intercom system, except it was not audible. "German pilots rising up to meet you are asking the same thing. How can you be so misguided, understand so little?" Where did the message come from? I put small credence in prayer in the sense of physical phenomena. It had always been for me more of a ritual or historical practice of Christianity than a direct communication with a higher power. I had never really expected a positive response. My mind reeled from the impact of a new dimension with which it was unprepared to cope.

"Navigator to crew, fighters nine o'clock. It's the escort right on time."

"Waist to Turret."

"Waist to Turret — come in."

I recovered when I realized that someone was calling my position. "This is the Turret — go ahead."

"Number four engine is vibrating too much — could be detonation."

"Turret to Copilot, what's the temperature of number four?"

"Two fifteen."

"That oughta be OK if the gauge is accurate. You can try two things: switch to automatic rich or open the flaps and drop it down to about two hundred."

I saw the cowl flaps open slightly and in a few minutes Jim called again, "Number four looks OK now." I made a mental note to tell the crew chief to check the cylinder head temperature gauge for number four engine.

We crossed over the edge of the Low Countries and entered the air above Germany. The P-47's dipped their wings and turned back toward England. What went through the minds of the men who flew the P-47's when they had to break off and leave us alone to face the fury of Goering's vicious fighters?

"Tail to crew! Fighters at six o'clock. More fighters low and coming up."

"Copilot to Tail, let us know what they're up to back there."

"Tail to crew — four fighters closing fast at six o'clock high."

"Radio to crew, I think they're gonna come on in."

"Turret to Copilot, watch forward an' call me if anything shows up — I'm goin' to help the Tail."

"OK, Turret."

When I spun around I could hardly believe what I saw. Four fighters were flying so close together they looked like one enormous four-engine aircraft. Surely they did not intend to attack us that way! The greenest German pilot should have known better, but they kept coming. At six hundred yards I saw the first flash of cannon fire which was the signal for the formation gunners to let go with a furious assault. Every fifth round was what we called a tracer. It was a projectile with a magnesium insert in the rear, which would ignite and glow brightly as it flew through the air. Immediately the sky was ablaze with tracers. Almost all top turrets, some balls and all tails poured a heavy barrage at those four unfortunate fighters. The enormous mass of fifty caliber slugs was so devastating that there were four puffs of black smoke and a sky filled with debris that erased four poorly-trained German pilots. They made two horrendous mistakes: one, flying so close together that they gave us a single target; and two, choosing the worst possible angle of attack where they would have to face the maximum fire power a B-17 formation could bring to bear.

"Tail to Turret, they were crazy. They didn't have a chance."

"A good way to commit suicide."

A curious thought ran through my mind. "Perhaps in their twisted teutonic thinking they were reaching for Valhalla — if so, I hoped they found it."

"Navigator to crew, fighters — nine o'clock level — eleven o'clock level."

They came at us from four directions. A Jerry defense commander must have stirred them up and they were breathing fire — mean and rough. It might have been what they saw us do to those four green pilots. For the next fifteen minutes it was a savage fight as intense as I can remember.

We were in the low location, called "purple heart corner." On the first heavy fire the turret clutch kicked out of position, stopping the action. I jumped out, removed the cumbersome gloves from one hand, reached high up into the maze of cables and reset the clutch. The turret was quickly back in operation. The next burst of prolonged firing kicked the clutch out again.

"Turret to Copilot, the damn clutch keeps jumping out! Must be a weak spring. I've got to try to wire it in position."

"Hurry it up. If the turret is out of action too long, the fighters will notice it."

As fast as possible, I re-engaged the clutch and wrapped copper wire around it to hold it in position — I hoped. As I climed back into the turret, a fighter zoomed by spraying us with machine gun fire. A slug knocked out my intercom phones. I did manage to repair the mike, but the ear phone system was dead.

As we approached the target the enormous field of flak ahead was unbelievable. And frightening! My thoughts were "Good God! Can anything fly through that?" I knew how accurate the flak was over Bremen. The German gunners had excellent radar control. Intense anti-aircraft fire was far less dangerous than fighter attacks, but more scary: there was no way to fight back at bursting shells.

WHAM! The heavy crashing noise came from below me. I dropped down to survey the damage. My first fear was that one or both pilots might be seriously injured, but as far as I could see with a quick look, both were OK.

"Turret to Copilot, over."

"Go ahead."

"Are either of you hurt? My earphones are dead, so give me some sign."

I leaned down enough to see him and he shook his head, which told me there was nothing too serious. Several fighters were circling high and to my left and I was watching them closely. I turned to the right for a quick look and was petrified! A huge rectangular mass the size of a large car was flying alongside, not far from me, glistening in the bright sunlight like a thousand diamonds. "What is that monstrous thing?" I said to myself. "Some fantastic new weapon the Germans are throwing at us? If that mass explodes it could blow us out of the sky." I hid on the opposite side of the computing sight to take the small amount of cover available, and peeked around it at the terrifying apparition. It began to lose speed and broke up into shimmering reflections that fanned out behind into a luminous cloud of particles. How could that huge mass have gotten twenty-five thousand feet up in the sky? What was it?

Fighters were streaking in straight ahead too low for me to get any shots. We caught a direct hit on number three engine and it began to vibrate heavily. I heard a loud smash underneath and suddenly my intercom was working. (Like a radio that you kick and it resumes playing.)

"Copilot to Ball."

"Go ahead."

"Can you see any oil leaking from number three engine?"

"It's throwin' oil real bad."

"Pilot to Copilot — feather number three."

The engine slowed down and eventually stopped.

"Copilot to Ball — is number three still leakin'?"

"It's about stopped."

I felt the bombs fall out and soon we were clear of that awful flak! I looked back and the sky was a solid mass of boiling black smoke. How in the hell did any of us get through it?

There was a loud bang from number two engine. It must have taken a hard smash from a cannon shell or a big piece of flak. I waited for smoke or heavy vibrations but when, after thirty seconds, it was still running smoothly, I relaxed. Had we lost another engine it would have been extremely hazardous for us alone among all of those snarling fighters. We could not have kept up with the formation on two engines.

Another attack came and I heard something strike the radio room with a sound of tearing metal.

"Copilot to Radio — Copilot to Radio — come in."

"Copilot to Waist, can you see Radio?"

"I can see him. Got some equipment damage, and he's rubbing his ass like he may have been zipped there, but don't think it is too serious."

"Go check out Radio an' call me back."

"He's OK now, Copilot, he's motioning that his intercom is knocked out."

"Waist to Copilot."

"Go ahead Wilson."

"765 has been hit — looks bad — don't think she can keep up with us."

I watched 765 fall back with mounting apprehension. Soon she was out of my range of vision.

"Ball to crew — 765 is gone! No chutes. Damn!"

After a few minutes the Ball continued, "Six fighters tore her apart. Looked to me like they had time to jump."

Our faithful old aerial warhorse was finished! As she rolled back within my sight far below, I felt stabs of anguish. It was like losing an old friend with whom I had shared both escapades and harrowing experiences.

A fighter zoomed up from below and cut loose at us with cannon fire.

"Tail to Copilot, a twenty millimeter shell damn near got me.

Knocked off one of my boots an' crashed on through without exploding.''

Aircraft Tinker Toy moved into the space that 765 had been holding.

''Tail to crew, look at Tinker Toy. She's riddled from the ball to the tail.''

''That's Tinker Toy doing her special thing,'' said the Bombardier.

''Copilot to crew, two fighters comin' in eleven o'clock high. Let 'em have it Turret! Hey, Navigator, blast the bastards.''

They were going for Tinker Toy and hit her dead center of the cockpit. I saw a small explosion.

Counce called, ''They got the pilot! Copilot is hit, too. The engineer is trying to move the pilot's body so he can get in his seat.''

''Turret to Copilot, I think I just saw the engineer put Tinker Toy on auto pilot until he can try to get control.''

Kels motioned for Gleichauf to switch over to intercom.

''What is it?''

''Keep your eye on Tinker Toy. Pilot is dead. Engineer put her on auto pilot. He's trying to move the pilot's body. The copilot is slumped in his seat — can't tell how bad he's wounded.''

''We'll watch her — don't want a collision with Tinker Toy.''

The fighters kept striking her. One wing was badly torn and an engine cowling knocked off. But she flew on. In my imagination I could hear her taunting the fighters: ''Yah! Yah! You kraut pimps! You can't knock me down. Go ahead! Try it! You square-headed bastards ain't good enough to get me. Yah! Yah! Yah! Go ahead and try to shoot me down! Yah! Yah!''

The wounded copilot raised up in his seat momentarily and helped the engineer with a control then collapsed again. How could the two men in the cockpit withstand that awful blast of super frigid wind blowing squarely in their faces without windshields?

Suddenly I realized my left hand was so cold it was becoming numb. That was normally a sign that the electric glove had burned out. I looked down at the hand. It was bare except for a thin silk glove. Where was the electric glove? Oh! I had removed it to wire the turret clutch in place. At thirty-five below, I was handling the metal gun controls with a hand covered only with the light silk glove normally worn under the electric outer glove. Impossible! My hand would have frozen solidly in a very few minutes. Yet, I was looking at the numb hand and the electric glove was resting where I took it off much earlier — before we reached the target. There was only one explanation: in the excitement of the action my blood pressure had gone sky high, pushing a large quantity of warm blood to the hands which replaced some of the lost heat.

When the fighter attacks finally faded out my relief was quickly punctured by the antics of number three engine. It suddenly unfeathered and began to revolve out of control. It required engine oil pressure to hold a propellor in a feathered position with the blades flat to the wind. If the oil pressure failed, the blades would shift to an angle, and the strong wind would rotate them. That was called windmilling, and with no means of control, the propellor revolutions would rev up to fantastic speeds. With no lubrication the engine would get hotter and hotter until it became red hot. The danger was that it might tear off of the aircraft with severe damage. The engine revved up and up beyond the twenty-five hundred R.P.M. red line limit. I watched with a sinking feeling as it shot up to three thousand. Then, to my immense relief, and for no reason that I could think of at the moment, it began to level off, then started slowing down. Eventually it stopped and resumed a feathered position again.

"Turret to Ball."

"Go ahead, Turret."

"Check number three again for an oil leak."

"No oil leak from number three engine."

"Pilot to Turret. What's wrong with number three prop?"

"Not sure. Could be a fracture in the oil pressure system in the prop hub that opens and closes. Ball says no oil leak down below so far. If it starts squirting out oil we'll have a runaway prop."

"Turret to Waist. Jim, how does this sound to you?"

"Don't see how it could be anything but a pressure leak."

Five minutes later the process repeated. All of the way back to Ridgewell that propellor would race up to three thousand revolutions and, having made its point, return to zero. Each time the speed zoomed upward my blood pressure went up with it.

We could have caught fighters again, but fortunately nothing else happened. Tinker Toy had serious landing problems but ended with nothing worse than slipping off the runway into sticky mud. A crowd gathered quickly to see what new horrors she had thrown at her crew. And again the question: was she really a jinx ship? For the men who flew combat raids in her it was more than a wartime superstition. It was a series of nightmares! That day her nose was blown off, both windshields were wiped out, one wing was battered, and she was heavily damaged from the radio to the tail. The cockpit was splattered with blood, bits of flesh and hair — a horrible sight to see.

When I climbed out of 755 the crew chief was waiting. "You had better put in a call for some sheet metal men, you will probably need two new engines, the radio is shattered, you will need two windshields, and one wing flap. The tail is also damaged. I think all of the main fuel tanks will have to be replaced because they are bound to be perforated. . .''

The 381st sent out twenty-one ships and lost seven. The 100th had another bad day and lost eight. The total loss for the raid was thirty-seven Forts. Of the returning aircraft, seventy-five percent were damaged.

As soon as we were on the ground, I asked Gleichauf and Purus about the huge mass of shining particles I saw near the Target. It turned out to be a new way to confuse the enemy radar by dumping out bales of thin aluminum foil fragments. The light pieces floating in the air confused the enemy radar by appearing to be aircraft. What I saw was a compressed bale of foil that had not yet begun to break up. Later on it was thrown in bulk from several aircraft regularly and was called ''chaff.''

After the mission I hit the sack, weary, exhausted and in a state of confusion. What did the message I received on the way to Bremen mean and where did it come from? I never expected to get an answer to a prayer, if indeed, that is what had happened. There was absolutely no doubt but that I did get a communication. The question was, ''Where did it come from?'' A simplistic answer would have been straight from God. I could have accepted that except it seemed too simple — too easy to draw such a conclusion as fact. I tried to think about it in rational channels, although I realized that at some point any religion steps beyond logic or reason into mystical or metaphysical phenomena. The danger faced each mission made me ready to turn to any spiritual assistance that was readily available, but I needed to separate the real from the dross that had accumulated in my mind.

Tinker Toy as the aircraft looked after the Oct. 11 mission.

CHAPTER XIII
Mission to Anklam

October 9 - Anklam, Germany   Aircraft 719 - Hellcat

It was difficult for me to get out of bed that morning. I felt tired and low on energy, which was unusual for me. When I got to Operations, Gleichauf was waiting. "They've given us a new airplane, John — one of those G Models that arrived two days ago — the number is 719."

"That's great! Now we will have twenty-seven hundred gallons of fuel. I wish we could have had one flight before we take her up for a combat mission. I hear there are a lot of changes."

"Oh, I don't think the changes will make much difference," Paul replied, "but get on out there as fast as you can and look it over. Find out what you can about those new electronic supercharger controls they told us about."

When Jim arrived I called to him, "We've got a new airplane — one of those new G models. Get your equipment quick and let's get out there and see what she looks like."

An ominous groan from the Briefing Room sent a shiver down my spine. Jim looked up, "Listen to that! We must have a real bitch today!"

"Wherever we're headed, it's gonna be mean. That much is for sure," I answered.

"I hope Chamberlain is on hand with plenty of extra ammunition, 'cause it sounds to me like we're goin' to need it."

In the personnel truck on the way to the ship Jim asked, "What do we know about the changes in the new models?"

"The main ones are the electronic supercharger controls and the new chin turret."

"Don't forget about those enclosed waist windows and the radio hatch cover. No more of that storm of cold wind gushing through the waist and radio room. The electronic controls are located near my position. I'll check them out with the crew chief and see what we can do in an emergency."

The early E and F models of the B-17 had open waist windows with guns mounted in those openings. The radio room upper hatch was removed and a gun was placed there. In most groups the rear radio room door was also removed, since it served no purpose in combat. The combined open spaces created an enormous suction causing a terrific frigid wind blast to roar through the radio room and the waist. This hazard was responsible for untold casualties of freezing and frostbite. The new G model replaced the open spaces using clear plexiglass windows with the gun mounts built into them.

"O.K. — we'll both check out the new turret for Purus. The guns have probably never been fired. I hope that remote control sight works out well."

"It will take Purus a while to get used to it — sounds awkward to me — but it ought to help up front where we need more fire power."

Chamberlain was there when we arrived and I asked him for four thousand extra rounds in case we needed them. How did he always manage the extra ammo? There wasn't supposed to be any surplus around the flight line.

I was waiting anxiously for Gleichauf to begin the briefing: "All ships will have twenty-seven hundred gallons of fuel today for the first time on a mission. Three Wings will cross Denmark at thirteen thousand feet and attack different targets. We will fly a little way over the Baltic Sea then turn right into Northeastern Germany to hit an airframe factory at Anklam. S-2 thinks the different routes, the unexpected lower altitude, and timing, will upset the opposition and divide the fighters. They estimate the opposition will be light. Jerry does not know we can strike a target this deep."

The crew was delighted at the lower altitude and mild temperature. My enthusiasm waned when I had time to reflect on the long route over Denmark so close to the German border. I found Purus examining his new turret. "You say S-2 doesn't expect much fighter opposition?"

"That is what they told us."

"Suppose S-2 is wrong? We'll be within close range of German fighter bases for six to seven hours. Every fighter they have can easily get to us at thirteen thousand feet."

"You're right. We could catch a long, rough fight in and out."

I turned to Gleichauf. "I don't buy S-2's estimate of the fighter opposition. There are too many fighter bases close to our flight path. We could catch half of the fighters in North Germany and we better put on all the ammunition we can carry."

"I don't like to carry more weight than we need," he answered.

He did not give me a flat no, so I put aboard more ammunition, raising the total load to thirteen thousand five hundred rounds. It was almost double the regulation seven thousand rounds.

When our turn came to takeoff, we roared down the runway and at ninety miles per hour Paul felt out the lift of the wings. Nothing. At a hundred miles per hour, still nothing. At a hundred and ten he tried again with no response! We should have been in the air at a hundred and five. At a hundred and fifteen the ship still would not begin a bounce. Kels glanced at Gleichauf with a questioning look. The end of the runway was rushing toward us. It was too late to abort the takeoff. Big beads of sweat broke out on Paul's face. At a hundred twenty-three miles per hour, there was a feeble bounce.

Paul screamed at Kels, "Raise landing gear!"

That desperation move lowered air resistance just enough to permit the aircraft to stagger drunkenly into the air. I have never been so frightened in my life! We barely skimmed over some trees and rose unsteadily to a little over sixty feet. Then the airplane started sinking, in spite of all Gleichauf could do and what should have been a safe airspeed. For the only time in my life I gave up all hope of survival. I knew that no one survived a crash on a takeoff with an overloaded airplane. We cleared some trees and reached a large open area of fields as the aircraft sank toward the ground. I expected at any second to spin off to the right or left and crash. That is what airplanes normally do when they can not maintain flying speed on takeoff.

Paul yelled to Kels, "Lower landing gear!"

John quickly flipped the gear switch and the main wheels came down before the plane struck the ground. The ship hit hard and bounced back into the air thirty or thirty-five feet.

"Raise landing gear."

Up came the wheels and we hung precariously in the air for a few seconds. Slowly the plane began to sink again. We got down to twenty-five feet and steadied. The engines had been wide open all that time and air speed was up to a hundred and thirty. Now the aircraft began to inch upward. I saw some trees ahead and we were able just to clear them. Ever so slowly the ship rose on up to a safe height.

Lucky! Lucky! Lucky! Nothing but pure, unbelievable and undeserved luck saved us from a complete wipe out! Ten men got a reprieve from what seemed certain death. Why? The aircraft was mushing on takeoff because of too much tail weight, upsetting its aerodynamics. Too much extra ammunition weight? I did not think so. The ships we had been flying could have handled it. Up to then I had not considered that a G Model, with the chin turret disrupting the air flow a little, might not have as good takeoff characteristics as the older ships. That may have had something to do with it, but was not the main reason for the near disaster.

I hurried to the radio room to check the weight distribution of the extra ammunition in the rear of the plane. I had placed as much as I could against the forward wall of the radio room next to the bomb bay and the center of gravity of the airplane and the rest as far forward as possible, along with some in the cockpit and nose. To my shock the boxes of reserve rounds were far back in the waist and some stacked right against the tail gunner's position. I was furious. "Are you guys crazy? You damned near killed us. You never move weight to the rear of an airplane!"

Jim knew better so why did he let them do it? Then I saw the Tail Gunner getting out of the tail. "You were in that tail on takeoff? No wonder we were so tail heavy." I was so incensed I could have choked Legg on the spot. "Get those boxes of ammo back against the radio room forward bulkhead an' leave them there until they are needed."

In the cockpit I explained to Gleichauf what happened. "The crew back there pulled most of the extra ammunition to the waist. And Legg was in the tail with all of his equipment on the takeoff. We were thirteen hundred pounds too heavy at the tail." That must have been the worst successful takeoff since Orville Wright made the first one.

The length of the mission cut out the usual feinting tactics. We formed up quickly and headed out over the North Sea toward Denmark.

"Bombardier to crew — Bombardier to crew — test fire your guns."

I listened to the guns chatter.

"Navigator to Copilot. How about this? No oxygen mask — and a decent temperature."

"I wish they were all like this," Kels answered.

"Pilot to crew, cut the unnecessary talk. Keep the intercom clear."

"Navigator to Pilot. Danish Coast in ten minutes."

"Bombardier to crew, we're close enough that fighters could hit us. Keep alert."

The Coast passed by underneath. We were flying parallel to the German border. Denmark looked green and peaceful below.

"Bombardier to crew, fighters at eleven o'clock level."

I counted thirty-two M.E. 109's. They made numerous attacks but were cautious and showed inexperience in opposing B-17 formation.

"Waist to crew — more fighters coming up — look like M.E. 210's."

"Bombardier to Navigator, my guns have jammed. Take a look at the ammunition chute."

The G Model eliminated the navigator side guns and placed two guns in the new nose turret. The Navigator had the responsibility of reloading the small ammunition cans by removing a section of the deck above the ammunition chutes. The long chutes were assisted by electric motors activated by the firing trigger.

The attackers were wary of the formation guns and we kept them at a distance with good protective fire coverage. Some large twin-engined craft came up and flew along with us on both sides of the formation just out of our gun range. Some gunners were firing at them.

"Bombardier to crew. Do not fire at those ships. They're out of range. I think they're trying to get us to use up our ammunition."

Over the Baltic Sea there was little opposition. We passed directly over a German naval base. I could see frantic action below as boats hurriedly attempted to clear the harbor before the bombs they expected started falling.

"Navigator to crew, watch those Krauts tryin' to get out of the harbor."

"Ball to Bombardier, lower the bomb bay doors and scare the hell out of 'em."

"Pilot to crew! I told you to keep the intercoms clear!"

The formation made a sweeping turn to the right into Northern Germany. Perhaps then the German Defense Command could narrow down the possible targets and alert the fighter air fields protecting those installations. The enemy could not be certain until we made the final turn toward the objective.

"Bombardier to Navigator, my guns are jammed again."

Later Shutting called Purus. "Your ammunition keeps jamming up in those long chutes. Must be somethin' wrong with the design."

"Copilot to crew, watch the F.W. 190's one o'clock high. They're comin' in but not on us."

We helped out another squadron with protective fire at long range.

"Bombardier to Pilot."

"Go ahead."

"We'll be on the bomb run in five minutes."

"Flak nine o'clock low — flak ten o'clock level."

When the doors came down the fighters stood away from us as they always did. I never figured out why. Were they afraid of our falling bombs? When the load released cleanly, I felt much better because the mission was half over. It would be a long ride back, but the Germans usually hit us harder before the target, so going back should not be too bad. That extra ammunition was not likely going to be needed. Gleichauf would probably give me hell about loading on too much ammunition: all of that extra weight for nothing.

Ten minutes later Purus called the Pilot. "Looks to me like we are goin' to be hit harder on the way back. By now every fighter in North Germany knows where we are and how long we'll be in their range."

Wilson came on the intercom. "Copilot, check ten o'clock level — is that a four-engine Dornier bomber with all of those guns sticking out?"

"I've never seen anything like that before — are they trying to use that big ship against us like a fighter?"

The formation continued the steady fire and it was effective. At that rate, if fighters kept showing up, we were going to have an ammunition problem before long. I changed my mind about the extra ammunition. We were going to be glad we had it aboard.

"Bombardier to Copilot, look at twelve o'clock! A small open-cock-pit training plane coming right at us — must be gunnery students."

I could scarcely believe what I was seeing! No doubt they were German students on a gunnery practice flight with a single small caliber gun. They were taking on a Flying Fortress formation bristling with heavy caliber guns . . . Teutonic Don Quixotes cheerfully facing impossible odds. (I thought that the little plane went on through the formation, but I rarely glanced at an aircraft once it passed by and was no longer a threat. Woodrow Pitts said he saw the aircraft shot down. I hope that the younsters in it managed to bail out — they had unusual courage.)

"Bombardier to Navigator, my guns are jammed again. This is the fourth time."

On the return over Denmark the fighters came up in relays. When one group ran short of fuel another group arrived to take over. One Fort after another was hit and lost.

"Copilot to crew — two fighters coming in twelve o'clock high."

The nose and turret poured heavy fire at them from a thousand yards out all the way in. Both the M.E. 210's were burning when they flashed by us very close.

"Pilot to Turret — did we get either one?"

"Both are badly damaged."

"Waist to Pilot, the pilot bailed out of one of them."

"Turret to crew — slow down on the ammunition. Some of the Forts are already out of ammo. Not many put on extra ammo like we did. At least one aircraft did, Ed Klein said his plane had 14,000 rounds aboard."

"Copilot to crew — Hendricks is hit. Don't know how bad. He's losing an engine, I think."

We were halfway across Denmark and I thought Hendricks had a good chance to make it to the coast where our escort was supposed to pick us up.

"Tail to Copilot, some M.E. 210's at fourteen hundred yards behind us, a little high. They're gettin' in some kind of a formation."

"Turret to Tail, what are they doing back there?"

"Nothin' yet, but they must be up to somethin' — I see what looks like big tubes under their wings."

Flak began to burst around the formation. It was larger in size than what we were used to seeing.

"Copilot to Navigator, where is that flak coming from? I don't see any cities or plants down below."

"There is not supposed to be any flak in this area."

The bursts got more consistent.

"Tail to Copilot, those 210's are firing something at us. The flashes are bigger than cannon fire."

I turned around to watch. Flashes of flame were coming out of those funny looking tubes. I looked closer — there was a faint vapor trail coming from a fighter and I followed it into the formation where it burst like a flak shell. Rockets! Jerry's much heralded rocket defensive weapon.

"Turret to crew. Those ships are throwing rockets at us. It's not flak. Its rockets."

"Tail to Pilot! Quick! Pull left — fast! A rocket is heading straight for us."

Gleichauf responded and the rocket passed a few inches from the horizontal stabilizer, then slowed down to our speed.

"Turret to crew, look at that damn rocket! It's spinning like a huge disc."

It was not more than twenty-five feet from my turret. Another ten feet and it would have struck the right wing. I took cover, expecting it to explode any second. The rocket slowed some more and spun away from us before it exploded. It was the first time I actually saw a lethal projectile clearly aimed at me.

We had experienced a few rockets before. We knew the Germans were working feverishly to get them in shape to try to stop the Forts on daylight raids.

"Turret to Bombardier, that last rocket was much too big to fit in those tubes under the wings of the 210's."

"You saw a malfunction, Turret. It was spinning end over end. That's why it moved so slow and looked like a big disc."

"Pilot to Tail, any way we could reach them with our guns?"

"Turret to Tail, let's aim high and try to lob some rounds into them."

We tried numerous elevations, but it was too far — we had a

thousand yard trajectory with our guns. Beyond that the projectiles lost velocity rapidly. Jerry had the distance figured exactly right.

The 533rd Squadron began slowly falling behind and as a result we were drawing more of the rocket fire. Purus kept warning us not to waste ammunition, because we did not know how much longer the fight would continue. It seemed to me that seventy to eighty percent of the gun positions were out of ammunition already.

Major Hendricks was in the lead ship and we were on his left wing. I saw him leave the cockpit and go toward the bomb bay. A few minutes later he returned to his seat. Immediately he dropped down out of the formation. Perhaps he hoped to get close to the ground, below the radar, and try to slip through. I doubted he could make it. There were too many fighters circling about us. A lump came into my throat and I said to myself, "Take a good look at Hendricks — I doubt if we will ever see him again."

"Ball to Pilot, is Hendricks trying to surrender? His landing gear is down."

"No, that's his signal for the deputy lead to take over."

Gleichauf moved up to take over Squadron lead and I lost sight of Hendricks.

I could sense the pain in Gleichauf's voice. He and Hendricks were good friends and it was hard to lose a friend in plain sight with no chance to help him.

Kels called the Pilot. "Hendricks saw he was slowing down the Squadron and did what he thought was the right thing for the Squadron."

"He didn't have to do it — we could have made the coast. The escort will meet us there."

"Legg to crew, four 210's trailing us — may come in ."

"Turret to Tail — if they start in, fire two quick bursts an' I'll turn around and help you."

When I heard Legg open up I whirled around. Two 210's were closing fast at six o'clock slightly high. Both of us threw burst after burst at them and they broke off the attack. The other two 210's must have absorbed some hits, too, because they also turned suddenly away and vanished from sight.

"Ball to crew, 210 trying to come up at us."

Harkness tore that ship apart. The Ball had a large advantage when a fighter tried to sneak in from below. A J.U. 88, used that day as an interceptor, tried the same thing and Harkness drove if off, but the 88 took all he could throw at it with no outward signs of damage. It was a rugged ship.

"Tail to Waist, any ammunition left?"

"A full box. I'll shove it back to where you can reach it."

"Navigator to Bombardier, most of our planes are out of ammunition."

"Copilot to crew, don't talk about ammo — it might leak through to Jerry."

The fight was showing no signs of abating. Ammunition became deadly serious. By that time we were one of the few aircraft with ammunition. I realized that if Jerry discovered we were defenseless, few of us would make it through the day because to ditch, or bail out, in that ice cold water would amount to a slow death.

A few minutes later, when I saw the fighters fade away to the south, I thought we almost had it made because the rendezvous time for our escort was a few minutes ahead. Five minutes later the Bombardier called, "Bombardier to crew, the escort at nine o'clock high."

They were a welcome sight. It had been a long day and now we could relax and let them worry about the fighters, if any more showed up. All of a sudden I saw something odd. What in the hell were those 47's doing? They knew better than to dive on a B-17 formation! Oh, my God! They were F.W. 190's! If they knew about our ammunition, we were done for (F.W. 190 fighters did look like P-47's at a distance and they had appeared at the same time and same direction that we expected P-47s.)

"Turret to Waist — Wilson."

"Go ahead."

"They're comin' in on Cahow. Let's give him some help."

I fired so close over Cahow's head that he might have preferred the fighters if he had a choice. There could not have been much, if any, ammunition left in the 381st Group — certainly not enough to hold off another attack. Until the P-47's arrived we were helpless. The German fighters made one run through the formation, then pulled away and began circling us. All they had to do was drop flaps to slow down to our speed and blast us out of the sky. Never before had Jerry had a formation of B-17's of this size on the ropes. Any minute the slaughter would begin. Wait! What was happening? Were they really turning away to leave? It was hard to believe. Didn't they know they had us whipped? I watched with a combination of amazement and jubilation as those fighters vanished into the haze. I will never know what saved us. It is possible that the fighters intercepted us at the outer limit of their fuel range.

"Waist to Copilot, you think they're gone for good?"

"You better hope so."

Five minutes later I called Jim. "We are not out of the woods yet, but it's looking better every minute.''

The formation droned on toward England and I watched the Danish Coast fade away to the east. Was it over? Where was the escort? What had happened to Hendricks? I would have prayed for him and his men if I had known how, or what to say. For the next fifteen minutes I anxiously scanned the skies to the south and east until I finally felt that the long air battle was over.

When I heard about Carqueville at interrogation I went numb. The information was meager: ''He was last seen with engines smoking heavily headed downward but still under control.'' Herb was with another squadron and I did not know he was on the mission until after interrogation. We went by Operations to ask if there was any word about Carqueville or Hendricks. Nothing!

In the hours before dawn, after a sleepless night, my thoughts turned back to Carqueville. Did he make it to Sweden? Did he go down in the ice-cold Baltic Sea? Maybe he bailed out over land. I wanted desperately to believe he was all right, but somehow I had the feeling he did not make it. There was that sickening sensation deep within me that told me Herb was gone.[1] How did such a communication reach my brain? I frankly do not know. But during the days in England, I developed a psychic ability to perceive things about some people in combat unrelated to facts from the sensitory world. Although he was not a great pilot, Herb Carqueville was my friend. How often we use the word 'friend' when we really mean an associate or a neighbor. Often it is because of eccentricities or shortcomings that the attraction develops. The pain of losing a friend never subsides. Could it have been only last April when our crew first came together? It seemed much longer.

October 10

Bomber command sent another large force against Munster and caught heavy opposition and lost thirty Fortresses. The 381st was bypassed no doubt to permit more time to repair damaged aircraft. The unlucky 100th Group had another disaster. They lost all twelve of their ships. A sizeable consignment of new planes and crews arrived at our base

---

[1]No trace of Carqueville or Hendricks was ever found. In 1982, while attending a memorial service at the beautiful American Cemetery near Cambridge, I found their names carved on the long white stone wall dedicated to all of the service people who were missing in action in that part of the war. I looked at those two names a long time, and memories, long buried by the passage of years, came flooding back.

during the day and they were indeed welcome. Our strength was below par, which put a strain on the crews and repair personnel. I watched the newcomers at the mess hall that evening and could not help wondering how long they would last. Which ones would be shot down before we had a chance to learn their names?

Johnny Purus and I were greatly disturbed by the jamming malfunctions of the chin turret guns on their first test under combat conditions. We got by with it the day before only because the attacks, while strung out over five or six hours, were at no time an intense action of fighters coming in right behind each other; we had time to get the jammed ammunition straightened out between attacks. We could not afford to have the nose turret out of action in an all-out fight. We carefully re-examined the new weapon and concluded that the problem was caused by the assist motor in the ammunition chute. The electric motor was put there to help slide the ammuntion along an extra long chute. The idea was fine, but as we saw it, the motor continued to revolve for a few seconds after the firing ceased, causing the ammunition to jam tightly in the chute creating a stoppage. We decided that if an adjustable restrictor could be fitted into the chute behind the motor it could be adjusted to exert just enough back pressure to relieve the problem. I borrowed a ruler and we took careful measurements. That night at the barracks I prepared a drawing to proper scale of the modification we thought would work. The officers at the Turret Shop and Armament studied it and agreed it might solve the problem. They sent it to the machine shop with a rush order for four of the devices to install on the two G Models on our base.

My other concern stemming from the Anklam Raid was the rocket fighter menace. Most of the men on the mission were not that worked up about it, because the enemy did not have spectacular success with the rockets. Jim told Lt. Adkins, the Gunnery Officer, that the pattern of the rocket weapon was very good. I agreed. It was, he contended, merely a matter of time until Jerry would apply it against us with ten times that many rocket carriers. I felt that it worked much too well for a new weapon and we could expect accuracy to get better. They already had the distance worked out perfectly.

Adkins said, ''We've got people smart enough to develop a new weapon with a two or three thousand yard range, but it would take a year to get it to us. We need it now.''

Jim replied, ''Then you think the only fast answer is long range fighters?''

''Yes! I do not see anything right now that will work except fighters who can stay with you fellows to the target.''

That was discouraging news because, if Adkins was right and our only practical defense was long range fighters, where were they coming from? Did we have such fighters?

One other worry had been solved the day before. When Nick was wounded, it meant a new man in his position. Harold Harkness showed me over Denmark that he was a top notch ball gunner. We were lucky to draw a man so solid and steady from the unassigned gunners on the base. When lethal flak shells were exploding around the ball, it took some kind of man to hang in there calm enough to do his job. The shells were fused to burst under the aircraft, so the ball always caught more of it than the rest of us. There was no place for Harkness to take cover. Of course, there was little cover anywhere in an airplane, but for most positions there were barriers that flak shrapnel had to penetrate from at least some directions. The rest of us donned heavy metal-lined flak vests when we approached the flak areas, but it was impossible in the ball, due to the restricted space. Harold had traded a farm tractor for a weird glass and aluminum ball hanging under the belly of the B-17 like a single giant testicle. Did he wonder at times if the ball was securely fastened to the aircraft? I would have. Suppose the plane took a heavy hit! Could he get out of that awkward prison in time to jump? Nick was impetuous and unpredictable. Harkness was the opposite: steady and methodical. I often speculated about the problem of an overflowing bladder in the ball. What did the gunner do? I suspected that I knew the answer, but never discussed it with Harold.

That night Jim said, "How in the hell did we get by with that takeoff? When it sunk to the ground I thought we were all gone!"

"So did I! No way we could have cut it thinner!"

"That's the second time we almost got it on takeoff. Remember that night at Boise when Capt. Glenn almost got us killed?"

"I'll never forget it," I answered.

Pitts spoke up. "You say some Captain almost crashed the plane?"

"No, we were scheduled for a night instrument takeoff check for the pilot. I got to the ship ahead of the others and Captain Glenn, the instructor pilot, was already there and impatient to get the flight over with. He told me he had already done the preflight inspection, so let's get the engines started. I climbed into the copilot seat and reached for the checklist.

" 'I've already been through the checklist — don't need it again.' " he said.

"But I thought we had to do . . ."

" 'Sergeant, I told you I have already been through it! Now start those engines!' ''

'' 'Yes, Sir!' ''

When Carqueville got there the Captain told him, 'We've already done the checklist. We'll get the hood in place and takeoff.' (With the hood in place, the pilot could see only the instruments). The flight was an instrument check. A few minutes later we roared down the runway and at ninety-five I saw Herb pull back on the elevator controls. Great Gods! The elevator was locked! I was standing alongside the copilot (Capt. Glenn had his seat) directly over the elevator locking device! Both of us instantly dived to the deck to try to unlock it in time for the aircraft to get airborne before we ran out of runway! All we managed to do was knock each other out looking very much like a Stan Laurel and Oliver Hardy comedy. Herb jammed brakes, released them and jammed them again and again. Near the end of the runway he revved up an outboard engine and skidded the aircraft around. We slid sideways up to the end of the runway. We ruined the brake system and both tires and were lucky to get by with nothing worse.''

Balmore said, ''I think that day we almost crashed into the mountain in Oregon was the closest thing we've had. It was worse than the takeoff this morning.''

Counce added, ''You're right! We were seconds from a head-on crash and it looked like there was no way to avoid it.''

Jim was talking about a hazardous incident that took place on a training flight over the Pacific Ocean. I was not on the flight and Jim was serving as engineer. It was a check out of the Navigator and Radio Operator on over-water procedure. In a short time we would be heading out over some ocean for an overseas assignment. The flight started at Marysville, California. Soon after takeoff, fog closed in solidly up to twenty thousand feet. The Operations Tower directed them to continue the flight as planned because there would be no break in the fog for several hours. That put Lt. Shutting on a pure dead-reckoning course with no means of checking his position for wind drift until the fog dispersed. Carl did fine for the first five hundred miles over the water. Radio contact indicated that they passed over a check point on time. But the Navigator listened to considerable radio talk from ships and decided that the wind had shifted direction from the early morning briefing. After an hour or two on his changed heading (he had shifted the heading some to allow for the supposed change in the wind direction), he realized that the change was probably in error and he could not pinpoint where they were. The Navigator had downed too many cups of coffee and had to take time to go to the bomb bay to urinate. But he found the perchant tube hard frozen.

He located Jim in the cockpit.

"What am I going to do? Let it go in the bomb bay?"

"Here, take one of these paper bags the lunches came in. Urinate in this and throw it out of the waist window." Jim solved his problem. It worked fine until Shutting tossed the sack out of the window; the swirling wind caught the sack and flung it back into the Navigator's face. There was not much Jim could do for him except offer a handkerchief.

In the radio room Balmore was trying to make contact with any station that might help. At that time of crew training, the radio operators had not yet been instructed in how to get a "fix" or a "Q.D.M.," but fuel was running low and they had to know exactly where they were. George raised a Coast Guard station and the operator suggested a fix. An officer was called in and explained the procedure to Balmore by Morse code. A few minutes later he was able to give Shutting his exact position at a given time. With that definite information, the Navigator brought them over the Air Base at Eugene, Oregon. The fog was still solid over the western part of the U.S. Visibility was near zero and fuel too low to proceed east far enough to clear the fog. Below were rugged mountains. An instrument let down in unfamiliar mountain surroundings was beyond the experience of the pilot.

Carqueville turned to Jim. "How much fuel do we have left?"

"Less than an hour."

"We're goin' to have to do somethin' before long, even if it means takin' some risks."

The control tower at Eugene understood the gravity of the situation and called Carqueville. "We can hear your engines so we're going to try to talk you down by sound. Keep circling and start lettin' down an' we'll call your turns and headings. Let down at two hundred feet per minute."

"OK — we're ready."

"Pilot to crew. The tower is goin' to talk us down. We will be lettin' down in mountains, so everyone get in position an' keep a sharp lookout. If you see anything up ahead call me quick."

"Navigator to crew. We'll be lettin' down in a valley with mountains on each side. You know what that means."

Cautiously they began easing down, following the instructions from the tower. The tension was intense. Every eye strained into murk, hoping to spot an obstacle in time. Surely there is no experience in flying more nerve wracking than to know you may, at any second, hit a mountain head on.

Down! Down! Down! Down!

"Pilot to Navigator, we're below the height of the mountains on either side of us now.''

''MOUTAIN — STRAIGHT AHEAD,'' screamed the copilot.

''Oh, my God!''

Out of the gloom was the sight that all pilots hope never to see coming at them from close range! Carqueville jerked the nose of the aircraft sharply upward so that they were flying parallel to the sloping side of the mountain, almost brushing the tree tops. They could not maintain that steep angle of climb more than a few more seconds before the ship stalled out. Then number three engine could not take the strain of prolonged high power and conked out. That appeared to seal their doom, if it was not already certain! Seconds before stalling out, the ship cleared the top of the mountain and Herb quickly leveled off. There is no way it could have been nearer to a disaster!

Suddenly Wilson roused himself.

''Hey John, remember the day we left Boise? We were about ready to clear the field, and a horrible accident took place right in front of our eyes?''

''I certainly do remember — I'll never forget it!''

When First Phase Training was over, our crew, along with another crew, were ordered to proceed to Casper, Wyoming by train. There was a delay on the morning of our departure, however, because the pilot of the other crew had to be pressed into duty as an instructor for a two hour flight. Men of both crews were waiting together, in front of the orderly room. Fifteen minutes later we heard the roar of a B-17 taking off. Then suddenly, there was the earth shattering sound of a horrendous crash, followed by intermittent explosions.

''Look at that parachute!'' shouted Jim.

How weird! I saw a parachute billow into the sky with no one in it! The next second the air was filled with debris, flames and smoke. We were stunned! The pilot we were waiting for was in the aircraft that just crashed! The plane ran wild on takeoff, veered from the runway and streaked across the parking ramp crashing into several B-17's. It ended up in a pile of burning wreckage against one of the school buildings where our training classes had been held. Two men were pulled from the flaming wreckage and seven others died.

It was so pathetic. The lives of seven young men wiped out instantly, either due to a pilot error or some mechanical failure of the plane. I could visualize the arrival of telegrams, and the tears of grief and anguish! I could see the flag-draped coffins and the solemn services. I could hear the lovely haunting echoes of ''Taps,'' bidding the young men a final good-bye. I knew that after a short time the memory of those men would begin to fade. In a little while only their families and a few close friends would remember. The rest of the community would soon forget them. After a year or two, most of the people who once knew them well, would have a hard time recalling exactly what they looked like.

THE AVAILABLE PICTURES OF THE GLEICHAUF CREW

Lt. Paul Gleichauf
Pilot

Lt. John Purus
Bombardier

Sgt. John Comer
Flight Engineer, Gunner

Sgt. James Counce
Waist Gunner

Sgt. Harold Harkness
Ball Turret Gunner

Sgt. Raymond Legg
Tail Gunner

Lt. Carl Shutting
Navigator

Sgt. Carrol Wilson
Waist Gunner

Lt. Herbert Carqueville
Co-Pilot

THE AVAILABLE PICTURES OF THE CAHOW CREW

Lt. William Cahow
Pilot

Lt. Stanley Parsons
Co-Pilot

Sgt. Hubert Green
Waist Gunner

Sgt. Woodrow Pitts
Flight Engineer, Gunner

Sgt. Ugo Lancia
Radio Operator

Ugo Lancia and Moe Tedesco
Waist Gunner

Ray Bechtel — Tail Gunner and Hubert Green
In the background is our metal hut.

Sgt. William Kettner
Ball Turret Gunner

Col. Joseph Nazzaro
381st Commanding Officer

Major Landon Hendricks
533rd Squadron Commanding Officer

The triangle ''L'' insignia that identified the 381st bomb group.

''The Joker'' — a well known aircraft of the 381st group.

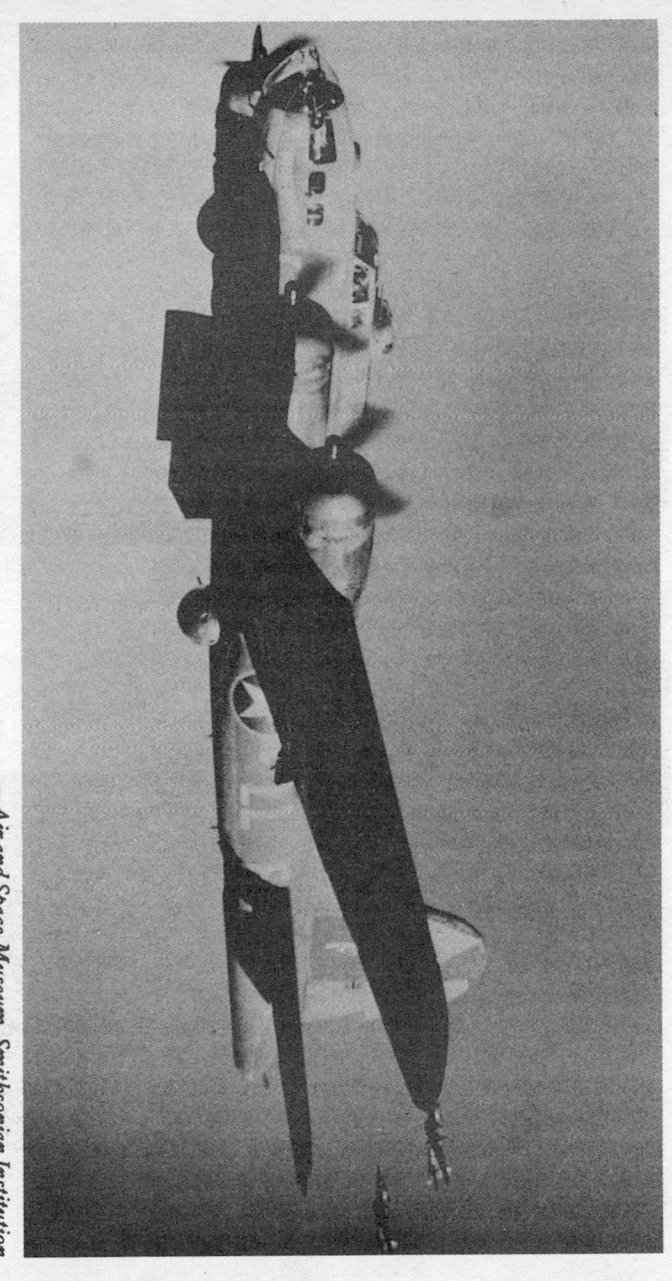

Boeing flying fortress B-17 G that was modified to add more fire power up front. Note the extra large side windows in the nose and guns in those windows. It must have had some special use.

—Air and Space Museum, Smithsonian Institution

—*Air and Space Museum, Smithsonian Institution*

Lockheed Lightning Fighter P-38. It was the first escort fighter that could go deep with the Flying Fortresses into the heart of Germany.

— Air and Space Museum, Smithsonian Institution

Republic Thunderbolt P-47 Fighters — the escort that was most often used to help the Fortress formations in the high thin air over the European continent.

The Mustang P-51 Fighter — most experts agreed that it was the finest fighter of the war. The aircraft could hold it's own in combat performance against anything in the air and with disposable fuel tanks could go with the bombers on their deepest missions.

—*Air and Space Museum, Smithsonian Institution*

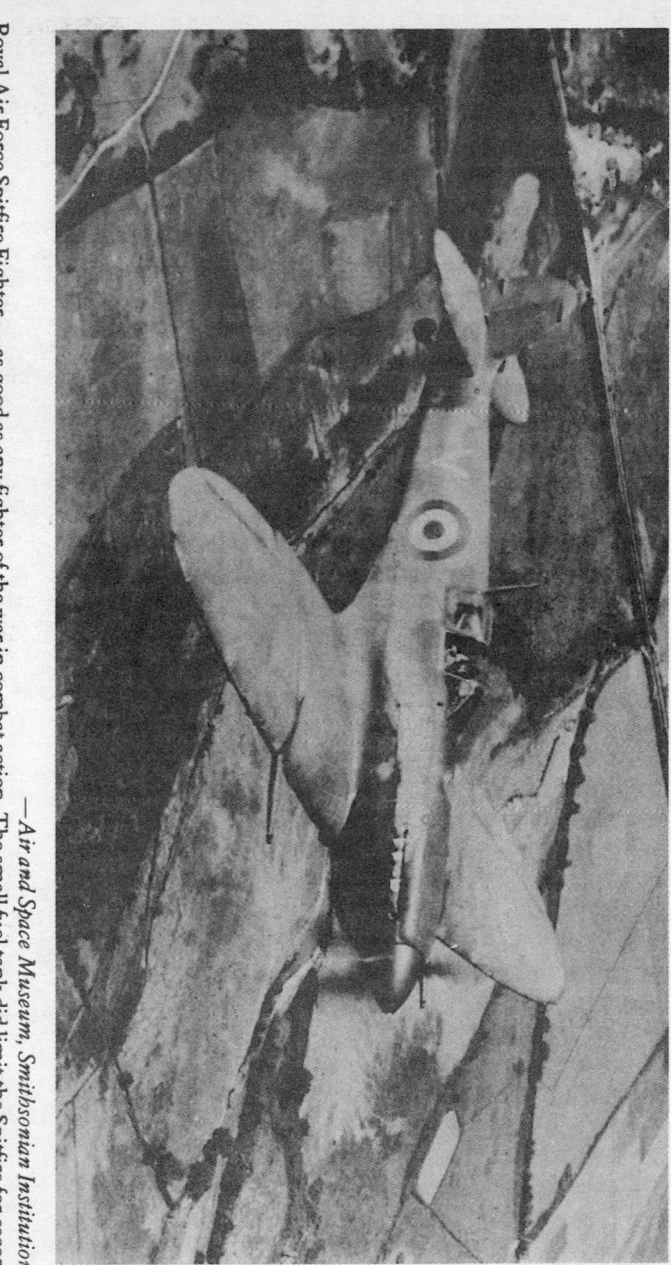

Royal Air Force Spitfire Fighter — as good as any fighter of the war in combat action. The small fuel tank did limit the Spitfire for escort service.

—*Air and Space Museum, Smithsonian Institution*

German Focke-Wolfe 190 Fighter — probably the best fighter the Germans had for the early stages of the war. There was a bulge of the nose that does not show up in this picture that made it easier to identify.

—Air and Space Museum, Smithsonian Institution

German Messerschmitt 109 Fighter — when the 109G model was activated in late 1943 it probably became the best propellor driven fighter that Germany developed.

—*Air and Space Museum, Smithsonian Institution*

—Air and Space Museum, Smithsonian Institution
German Messerschmitt Fighter — often used to carry rockets.

CHAPTER XIV
Second Mission to Schweinfurt
(BLACK THURSDAY)[1]

Johnny Purus was an unusually good man to have on a crew. He was as steady in the nose as Jim Counce was in the rear of the aircraft. The rest of us would screw up at times, but Johnny never did, except on that first fighter attack when three of us failed so miserably. He entered the service as an enlisted man and had some aircraft mechanical experience. Purus could handle the controls of a B-17 well enough to get back to the base if something happened to the pilot and copilot. Counce showed natural flying ability, and I had flying experience also. That was good insurance for the crew.

Coming out of the mess hall at noon, Purus was waiting for me. "Paul's got a flu bug an' a bad case of the G.I.'s, so Capt. Ralston has grounded him for the rest of the week an' sent word to Operations that none of the rest of the crew has to fly any missions 'til Gleichauf recovers.''

Jim spoke up, "Well, maybe we can get a four day pass to London."

"Go ahead an' try, but John can't go 'cause he's goin' to be busy with me putting in those two restrictors in the chin turret."

"You mean they're ready?" I asked.

"They'll be finished today. I was at Armament this mornin' checking on them."

By mid-morning the next day Purus and I were working with an armament mechanic on the tricky job of installing those hastily made assemblies at the best positions. We did not know how much back pressure would be needed to correct the malfunctioning of the ammunition, or at what point too much restriction would interfere with the movement of the ammunition to the receiver of the gun. Late in the afternoon the Major who commanded Armament, which included turret maintenance,

---

[1]The name of a book written about this mission by Martin Caiden.

came out to 719. After examining the installation he remarked, "Looks to me like you're about finished."

"Another thirty minutes will do it," Purus answered.

"How do you know how to adjust it?" asked the Major.

"We don't," Purus said, "that will have to be done under fire."

"That's what I thought. If 719 goes out in the morning, who is goin' to do the adjusting?"

There was complete silence while the Major waited. Then he looked at me. "Wasn't this your drawing? Isn't this your ship?"

"Yes, sir."

"Well, I think I can get you on it as Navigator — OK?"

"Wait! Wait! I'm not on combat status for the rest of the week," I answered.

"What's wrong with you?"

"Nothing. Our pilot is sick an' Capt. Ralston gave the rest of the crew time off 'til he recovers."

"But you could go?"

"I suppose I could."

"I think you should — it's your ship an' you're the engineer. We don't want some damn navigator foulin' up this test and that is what we're going to get unless one of you does it. I never saw a navigator who knew anything about guns except which end the bullets come out." (That wasn't quite fair to navigators. Even though they did not have as much opportunity to fire the guns, some navigators did take their gunnery seriously.)

"You got a good point there, Major."

"Well, how about it?" he answered.

"I'd like to, but hell, I — uh — you know what happens when you volunteer. You get the shaft ever' time."

He laughed. "Oh, that's just barracks talk — let's go to Operations and see what they say."

At Operations Franek said, "You can go if you want to, but you got a medical excuse for the rest of the week. It's your choice."

The Major asked, "Can't you give him some hint about where we might go in the morning?"

"We don't have the target yet an' couldn't tell him or anyone else if we did know where it was. But you have the bomb load. You could tell him what your men are goin' to load tonight."

He turned to me. "I'm not supposed to talk about the kind of bombs, but I guess it won't hurt to tell you. We're loading block busters."

Block busters? Where did we use those two thousand pound big ones? Wheels turned in my brain. Lights flashed on and off. Submarine pens! That's the only place we had ever used them. Where were submarine pens? On the coast! It was going to be an easy target somewhere on the coast. I was not about to let a milk run get by me. The easy ones counted the same as the mean ones.

"OK, Major, I'll do it."

Turning to Lt. Franek I asked, "Can you put me on 719 as Navigator if we go out in the morning?"

"I guess I could this one time. I hope to hell 719 don't get lost with you doin' the navigating." He paused for a moment. "I'll put Cahow on 719 'cause his navigator is sick."

"That's fine with me."

Franek called as I started out the door, "Not a word to any of Cahow's men until wake up call if we go in the morning. Got that straight?"

"OK, not a word."

October 14 - Schweinfurt Ball Bearing Plants   Aircraft 719 - Hellcat

At three-thirty, George Reese turned on the lights. "Pitts, Lancia, Tedesco, Green, Bechtel, Kettner, and Comer flying 719 with Cahow — briefing at 0530 hours — good luck."

"Hey, wait," said Lancia. "Comer is not on our crew."

"He is today," Reese replied. "He's your Navigator."

"Navigator! That bastard, a navigator?"

"I've been taking a correspondence course in navigation for the last week." I answered.

"Come off the bullshit! What are you doin' with us?"

"Seriously, the chin turret guns jam up real bad on these new G Models. Yesterday, we put some special made restrictors in the ammunition chutes. I'm going to adjust them in action an' see if they work."

"You think they'll work?" Tedesco asked.

"You better hope so, 'cause Franek told me he is goin' to assign the other G Model we have on the field to your crew."

Pitts moaned, "God! I hope we don't get lost today with you up there in the nose."

They had decided that this mission was going to be an easy one, probably because Operations assigned me as navigator. As they saw it, I would not be up in the nose if it was going to be a long, tough raid. So no one on the crew stood by the Briefing Room that morning to catch the reaction when the curtain was pulled back revealing the target. We had the usual early morning murk, but there was a good chance it would break by takeoff time.

In the briefing room when the curtain was pulled and they saw that long string pointing straight to Schweinfurt, the pilots let out one loud obscenity in unison — the last place on earth any of them wanted to go.

Dawn found the gunners in a breezy mood. The copilot, Lt. Stanley Parsons, got out of the personnel truck looking glum.

"Where are we goin' this morning?" asked Pitts.

"Schweinfurt," Parsons replied.

"Very funny," said Lancia, "where are we really going?"

"Now listen, you've had your fun! Get this straight! We're goin' over the middle of Germany to Schweinfurt an' back." He hesitated a moment, then added, "If we get back."

My mind recoiled in disbelief. "No! No! No! Not Schweinfurt! Was this some kind of joke? If so, it was on me. But I thought we were going on a milk run! Thought? If I had done any thinking, I would have been back at the hut," I said to myself, "Anyone stupid enough to volunteer for a combat mission deserves exactly what you are going to get today." I looked around at the other men. The silly grins had faded out. Tedesco tried some comic remark. No one laughed. Only the sound of the electric generator broke the silence. Gunners started drifting back to the aircraft. A little more head space for heavy firing. More ammunition. The oil buffer could be adjusted to allow more rapid firing. I came out of my shock and decided to recheck the two nose guns I had already set up for the bombardier, Lt. Jim Leverette. They had to be right for what I knew was coming.

When Cahow arrived I wondered if he was as calm as he looked. "I see that you already know what the target is. No need to tell you about the fighters. You know what to expect, so be careful with ammunition. Don't waste one round 'cause we're going five hundred miles into Germany. Three divisions will participate on this mission. The First Division will lead the attack and the 381st will be the low group. . ."

That drew heavy moans and sarcastic remarks. "Here we go again! Is the 381st on the Wing shit list?"

"Knock off the bitching and listen to what I am telling you. We'll have an escort going in — P-47's — as far as their fuel will permit. . ."

The whole thing sounded ominous. A low position against the heavy opposition we knew would be waiting meant a brutal fight for survival for hours over Germany. The thought went through my mind that many of our 381st men would not survive the day.

At engine starting time the fog was expected to be no higher than four thousand feet, but we had to grind up slowly through ten thousand feet of murk before breaking clear of it. I recall how bitterly I cursed that miserable English weather and the ever present chance of a sudden collison in the soup. By the time we pulled out on top of the fog the Group had to circle and circle until our widely scattered planes could be gathered into a formation. They were always in confusion when climbing that high through fog. Meanwhile, other groups in the Wing broke into good weather at four thousand feet and were on schedule, but we lost too much time collecting our scattered aircraft and were late. Major George Shackley, leading the Group, set out to try to intercept the Wing over the Channel. But we were not the only group that missed their rendezvous. The 305th was behind time and their Wing was out of sight. When the 305th commander sighted the 1st Division with the low position open he pulled into it. A little later, when Shackley caught up with the Wing, he was astounded that our assigned position was occupied. At that time I did not know what group had usurped our position or why.[2] The 91st was leading and I noticed that they appeared to be under strength. I watched with delight while the 381st pulled up to a position adjacent to the high group. It was a peculiar combat formation but certainly a fortunate one for us. (Recently George Shackely told me he made that decision.) The escort arrived much too early, in another failure of timing, and therefore was of little help, because they had to turn back before we passed Aachen. As we started angling in toward the Rhine River, various gun positions began to call out warnings of approaching fighters.

When it was time for the escort to leave us I watched with growing apprehension as enemy fighters gathered in unusual strength for the opening attacks. I had other things to do when the fighting began so I could not estimate how many fighters hit the Division. One report said that the Germans threw two hundred interceptors against us early in the fight. The action was a lot like the Aug. 17th mission. They came in from all angles but what I remember most is that they seemed to line up in groups of three to six and come head on thus dividing the defensive fire of the formation. Once while looking down at the heaviest action the thought struck me that it ws an aerial version of cavalry tactics. I saw single engine fighters carrying rockets that were fired from close range. Fortunately for me most of the worst action was below the high position of the 381st. I could not see the 305th very well but the reports of the Ball and Tail indicated that it was being struck hard. I could not keep from remembering that our group was supposed to have been down there. One

[2]Until I read *Decision Over Schweinfurt* by Thomas Coffey.

Fortress after another was reported as hit. Some I could see, but most were out of my viewing range. Some blew up. Others were set on fire. Possibly a third of the men were able to bail out in time. The battle was as furious as any I saw over Europe.

During the early firing action I was lying face down on the deck watching the ammunition slide in the chute and tinkering with the restrictor adjustment. The device worked perfectly and the ammunition jamming problem was solved. From that point on, my main responsibility was to reload the chin turret cans when the ammunition ran low.

The pilot described the action as he saw it from the cockpit: ''When I saw the fighters go through the formations ahead and come at us without breaking off, and seeing Fortresses going down everywhere I looked, I knew our chances for survival were not too good. But the luck of the Irish, and a few side-slips as they came at us helped. I had a theory that if I slipped a Fortress up or down, and into the fighter's attack curve just as he started firing, it might throw him off just enough to miss us in the few seconds of his pass. But if the fighter was not aiming at our plane I flew a level path and gave the gunners a better crack at him.''

At first I did not pay much attention to the Ball and Tail reports about two engine fighters standing back out of the Fortress gun range and steadily throwing rockets into the formations.

''Ball to Pilot.''

''Go ahead.''

''That low group is takin' a helluva beating — they're getting rockets and fighter passes at the same time.''

''Waist to Bombardier.''

''Go ahead, Waist.''

''When the rockets explode it looks like they throw out something like hand grenades that also explode.''

''Bombardier to crew — watch those rocket explosions. Tell me if they are throwing out other explosives.''

''This is Radio! M.E. 109 is right above us — something is hangin' below it — on a long cable. The sonnuvabitch is tryin' to drop a bomb on us.''

Fortunately, the bomb fell through the formation and exploded too far below to do any damage. The rocket-carrying twin engine fighters increased in number as we battled deeper into Germany. The rockets were hurled steadily into the formation with devastating results. A few made direct hits, but mostly Forts were damaged too much to be able to stay up with the formation. When they fell behind, away from the protection of the concentrated defensive fire, the single engine fighters ganged up on them, and their chances for survival were slight.

We turned toward the target at Wurzburg. Cahow called the Tail Gunner: "How many Forts has the low group lost?"

"Eleven I think — don't know if any of 'em are gonna make it."

With that final left turn, the Germans knew for sure where we were heading. They must have suspected that the ball bearing plants were the objective thirty or forty minutes earlier. The modest city of Schweinfurt now lay straight ahead. The fighter fury intensified; their attacks became more savage. In the distance, sunlight reflected from a maze of red tiled roofs. There was a slight haze and some smoke, but visibility was excellent. At that point I could not pick out the bearing plants for certain, but I did see sizeable buildings along the Main River that wound through Schweinfurt, and I suspected they were the targets.

Flak began to burst all around the formation and I could hear heavy shrapnel striking the ship. To my surprise the fighters kept on coming after us in the middle of that inferno of fire and smoke. The enemy showed great tenacity in defending those plants that were so vital to their military production. I knew there were three hundred 88 and 105mm anti-aircraft artillery pieces in the Schweinfurt defense perimeter. With no guns to fire, I felt stripped of protection. The act of doing familiar things provides some sense of security in combat. In a strange position with little to do, I was shaking as if I had a chill. There was too much time to look and think about the paper thin aluminum sheet metal and transparent plastic separating me from the hideous white-hot shrapnel. I wished I had Shutting's special armor devices.

Below, and to my right, I noticed several Forts trailing us on a strange bearing that would cause them to miss the target if maintained. There was no heavy damage that would explain why the Fortresses were out of formation. They must have been remnants of some badly mauled outfit. It was soon evident that they knew the turn we would take after the drop, and were cutting the target short in order to pull into one of the groups low on aircraft. (It was the only time in seventy-five missions over the Continent that I saw, or heard of, undamaged Flying Fortresses deliberately by-passing the target.) None of the documentary accounts I have read mention that incident. It was one of the few times I was in position to see the bombs strike the target. The drop pattern blanketed what I thought must have been the bearings plants. The strike looked real good, but I wondered if it was really worth the high price we were paying. There had been strikes before that we thought to be excellent, but the plants were back in production in a few weeks.

The 381st fared better than I expected, only because we were high up in the formation escaping the worst of the rockets and fighters. The lowest group was always easier to attack because the enemy fighters performed better lower down, and the defensive fire was reduced. Halfway back to the coast the two remaing aircraft of the ill-fated 305th Group pulled into empty positions in the 91st. Thirty minutes from the coast the interceptors faded out. Were they really gone? I searched the sky for a while then slowly unwound from the high tension that had gripped me for the last seven or eight hours. It was the first time I relaxed since I heard the dreaded word "Schweinfurt" early that morning.

Counce, Balmore and Wilson were waiting at the hard stand when we climbed out. They had heard what the target was and knew only too well what we were catching. They told me that Purus was on the mission with Hutchins and his crew and their plane was reported missing. My elation at getting back was short lived. The interrogation was long and tedious, but I barely listened, wondering what happened to Johnny. I felt numb, almost devoid of energy, my vitality drained down to empty.

The way I saw it, on October 14 the Germans achieved a victory over the Fortresses. The enemy losses in planes shot down were small in view of the intense action. The rockets were devastating. Standing back just out of the gun range of the Forts, the Jerry pilots had tremendous success throwing rockets into the Fortress formation. At Luftwaffe headquarters they must have been elated that at last they had a weapon that would either stop the American attacks, or wipe out the attackers if they persisted on deep missions into Germany. Albert Speer described Goering's trimphant report to Hitler about the success of the rocket defense against the Fortresses earlier in the day — sixty bombers smashed out of the sky.[3] Goering was positive that long-range fighters could not be designed or built with the technology of that period, as were many other aviation experts. Without deep fighter escort, the German Defense Command thought that they now had the much needed weapon to stop deep raids into Germany in daylight. And in the weeks following, it looked that way to the American flight crews also.

Back at the hut a long time later, I hit the bed quickly and closed my eyes. The station loud speaker came on: "Now hear this — now hear this — Lt. Hutchins landed at an English airdrome on the coast with all crew members safe." It was a good day for me after all. But I vowed that I would never again volunteer for anything as long as I was in the service.

---

[3]*Inside The Third Reich,* by Albert Speer.

The Official losses were:

Sixty two Forts shot down.

   Seventeen Forts damaged too much to be repaired.

   Ninety-nine enemy planes shot down.

   Thirty enemy planes probably shot down.

   Thirty-six Forts damaged but could be repaired.

A day later the damaged figure was raised to one hundred forty-two. Which figure was correct, if either was, I did not find out. Perhaps it depended on how to define "damaged."

Unpredictable factors, impossible to foresee, sometimes decide the fate of men, or shift the course of history. For me — and the 381st Group — that high bank of fog hovering over our air assembly space that morning was an incredible stroke of good fortune. Although we bitterly cursed the fate that put us in that ten thousand foot layer of murk, it turned out to be the difference between acceptable losses and disaster! Had we been in our assigned low position, the odds against getting back would have been twelve to one (based on the losses of the 305th Group.)

In the days that followed the second Schweinfurt Raid, it received widespread publicity, ranking alongside Doolittle's Raid on Tokyo, and the sensational Raid on the oil fields at Ploesti. Mr. Roosevelt had to make a public statement about the raid to soothe over the disastrous losses. It represented to me the zenith of German aerial resistance to the American Air Forces. Never again was Goering able to achieve an out and out victory over the Fortresses. There would be days when the B-17's would suffer losses of comparable numbers in the future, but against much larger fleets with a far lower loss percentage.

Some persons can point to a spot in their lives — a name perhaps — that represents to them an intangible emotional height beside which all other days pale. The name of the obscure Bavarian town "Schweinfurt" means nothing to most Americans but a name on a map of Germany. But the men who endured the fury of either of those historic battles will never forget what air combat, at its epitome, was like. Some historians contend that the collision of those two large forces over Germany marks the highest point that aerial combat has ever reached — the greatest air battles of all time. That is, of course, merely an opinion. There is no way to compare the great naval engagements of the Pacific involving carriers and their planes with the savage conflicts over the Continent. In the Pacific, the great air battles covered vast distances and sometimes lasted several days. The two Schweinfurt raids were a powerful, determined offensive air fleet clashing with an equally potent defensive force in a restricted air passageway in a time span of four or five hours. There had never been anything like them before. Never again will two air forces of such magnitude collide head on in a single afternoon.[4] By some criteria the Oct. 14th mission was the most savage in the history of the Air Force. It depends on how a historian looks at it: there was a devastating 19% loss of the aircraft participating.

October 15

No matter what the conversation started out to be, sooner or later it would inevitably shift back to the thing most on our minds. The raids were flown over and over. Bits and pieces that were missing fell into place because other men in different aircraft saw things I could not see. I could reconstruct the whole action only by gathering the observations of others who were in different positions, and fitting them in with my fragmented memories of what happened. In the process of doing this, there was a tendency to combine the ideas and impressions of others with my own in such a manner, that a month later, what I actually saw could not be separated from what I heard from them. I am sure that I have some vivid memories of incidents that I did not see so indelibly imprinted in my mind that now I think that I personally witnessed them.

There was a divergence of opinion about how the odds for survival worked out. Rogers led one school of thought on the subject and I was the foremost proponent of a different way of looking at it.

"Now, Buck, you say that ever' time I fly another mission my luck and chances for survival stretch thinner?"

"That's right. The more raids you get, the more the odds catch up with you."

"You mean to say that the odds on my twentieth mission will be twenty times more against me than on my first mission?"

[4]Long after the War I visited Schweinfurt. It was a beautiful Sunday morning. The burghers were on their way to Church. The city was so quiet and tranquil that it was hard to imagine the carnage that once rained down on it. The streets and buildings looked as if nothing had disturbed them in the last hundred years. The bearings factories were still there, now turning out assemblies for Mercedes Benz and B.M.W. vehicles, instead of Hitler's fierce war machines. I rode slowly through the city and let my mind drift back in time to August 17 and October 14, 1943. The faces of fine men lost those two days flashed through my mind; some I could recall distinctly and others would not quite come into focus, like a television picture out of adjustment. So many men lost and so many families bereaved! Did those two gigantic efforts of men and machines really shorten the war and save far more lives than they cost? There was no answer.

172

"You're damn right, if you make it to twenty missions. Those odds stretch and stretch. That's why so many men go down on their last two or three missions."

"The way I see it the odds start all over every day or every mission," I answered.

"I can't buy that. The more you fly, the closer you get to the breakin' point. Then bang! They catch up with you," Rogers said.

"The laws of chance don't change just because we're talkin' about missions," I insisted.

"Sure they do," said someone, "they're bound to catch up with you."

"Look, you take a pair of dice — you roll them and the mathematical chance to get a seven or eleven will repeat every time you throw those dice. It's the same for a mission. What's already happened doesn't count. It's a new ball game ever' mission morning."

Jim cut in, "You are right. But each raid you learn something new, so you can change the odds a little in your favor with experience."

But Balmore disagreed. "Buck's right, your odds keep stretching like a rubber band — unless you are lucky, one day the rubber won't stretch any more an' it snaps."

"I can't figure your thinking. You're trying to tell me that if I roll dice ten times the odds for me to make a seven get less each time I pick up the dice. The professional gamblers sure wouldn't agree with you. And the laws of chance are a matter of mathematics. It makes no difference if it is cards, dice or missions."

Neither side would budge from their positions and the arguments went on month after month.

October 16

It was a cold night, too rainy to get far from the hut. The small depressing building was quiet for a change. Only four of us were there. Woodrow Pitts walked over to my bunk.

"Comer, how did you like your ride with us to Schweinfurt?"

"I felt strange. I was out of place. It was like a bad dream when I suddenly find myself in some public place with no clothes on."

"Because you didn't have any guns?" he asked.

"Partly that — an' I couldn't see the action behind us. I heard all those comments about the rockets on the intercom and could not see them from the nose."

"You had a lotta time to look around. Could you see the strike?"

"Yes," I answered, "I could see the strike OK — one of the few times I ever saw them hit — an' I saw too many Forts on fire or out of control.''

"I saw too many of those myself.''

"Woodrow, I used to feel nauseated an' sick when I saw a Fort go down an' no one get out. But that day I watched them fall with a cold, impersonal feeling — like there were no men in them.''

"You're just getting used to it. When you see so many lost, you quit thinking about it.''

"Are we becomin' so callous we don't care when we see our own men trapped in a falling airplane?'' I asked.

Jim Counce spoke up. "Don't you think it's nature's way of conditioning a man for what he has to do? People can get used to worse than what we've seen.''

"In combat you have to become accustomed to death all around you or you'll blow up inside,'' Pitts added.

"Think how much worse it would be if we were fighting hand to hand with bayonets. But we could get used to that, too, if we were in it long enough,'' Jim said.

Of course they were both right and it was a good thing. One could not dwell on what happened to other men — even those he knew well — and maintain his sanity.

October 18

After lights were out that night and I thought the others were asleep, Lancia muttered into the darkness: "We've gotta have long-range fighters.''

He was voicing the thought uppermost in the minds of all personnel in Bomber Command, from the Commanding Officer down to the newest gunner. Without some way to stop those rockets we were all but finished as an effective deep offensive force.

"Where ya goin' to get 'em?'' came from a voice at the other end of the hut.

"They could send us some P-38's.'' I recognized Pitt's voice.

"But are they good enough to go against the 190's and that new 109G?'' I asked.

"That leaves us nothing but the P-51's — the new models we've heard about. But no one has seen them in combat yet, so we don't know what they can do,'' Pitts added.

"Well, the P-38's would be a lot better than nothing,'' said Jim. "They could tear up those rocket-carrying fighters — that's for sure.''

October 22

On days that missions were not scheduled, Operations often called crews for wearisome practice flights, or to slow-time aircraft with new engines. There were also flights to test repairs that could only be checked out at high altitude. With a shortage of crews, we caught a lot of those assignments if Operations could find us. We developed a sensitive ear for the sound of the Operations Jeep, and if we heard it in time escaped quickly to other locations. If they could not find us, they picked up others less fortunate, especially flight engineers, radio operators and pilots.

Ridgewell Airdrome was located at about fifty-two degrees latitude, which corresponds with the lower end of Hudson Bay and Labrador. Only the warm waters of the Gulf Stream make the British Isles a decent place for people to live. But the Northern latitude meant that long winter nights were rapidly approaching. Our crude metal hut was ill equipped to withstand the ordeal soon to descend. So Jim and I went into Cambridge and managed to procure wire, receptacles, lamps and insulators to install individual lights for each bunk. We also got caulking compound and sealers to plug up the cracks that let the north wind blow in unhindered. The English electrical system was two hundred twenty volts requiring more care in installation than our one hundred ten system. We made some crude chairs from wood we could scrounge, and a table for the poker games and for writing. A few pin ups of nude women provided the remaining touches, and we were more ready for the cold days and long nights of mid-winter.

Balmore was on pass in Cambridge doing some shopping the day we nailed shut the back door and sealed it securely. Early the next morning George heard the Jeep coming. He hastily grabbed his jacket and coveralls and made a run for the back door. While he was frantically trying to open it, Lt. Franek, the operations officer, came in the front door.

"Well! Well! Where you heading so eagerly? Do you always run around in your long handle drawers? Maybe we can find something for you to do. Be at Operations at nine hundred hours for a slow-time."

He turned to go, then came back to George's bunk. "I'm glad to know we have such eager men who leap out of bed so early in the mornings. We will try to find some more interesting flights for you, Balmore."

After Franek left George glowered at the rest of us who were shaking the hut with loud laughter. Lancia said, "How about that? You are getting to be Franek's favorite boy." And he rolled out of the way of the vicious kick he knew was coming. Balmore could be pushed just so far and that temper would explode!

"What the hell is the matter with that back door? I couldn't budge it."

"No wonder," Counce replied. "Me an' John nailed it up yesterday."

"You could have told me about it, instead of lettin' Franek catch me with my pants down. Now he will have me on one of those miserable slow-times for two or three days a week."

October 23

In Washington doubts were developing about the ability of the Fortresses on daylight strategic combat missions into Germany, where it really counted. The R.A.F. Command was still unconvinced about the accuracy of the bombing or the ability to resist the certain fierce attacks on deep daylight missions. General Eaker was unshaken in his feeling that the American concept could hit the enemy harder with fewer men and materials. What had the October raid on Schweinfurt proved? One, that the Fortresses could severely damage any target in Germany regardless of enemy opposition. Two, the losses of men and machines were too severe for continuous attacks into Central Germany without long-range fighter escort.

It is unfortunate that the Lancasters and the Fortresses did not concentrate their bombing offenses jointly on a few key German industries, using daylight and night raids to obliterate them. Eaker could never get the R.A.F. to help destroy the bearings production, regardless of the fact that the enemy only had five or six locations that could have been eliminated with better cooperation and understanding of what such a blow could have done to German military production. Then there were the oil and transportation industries, and they were almost as vulnerable. An oil refinery or large storage tank site was difficult to conceal. In late 1943 it seems to me that the Allies had the combined air strength to wipe out at least one or two of those industries. No modern army could fight long if deprived of any of them. Instead of concentrating on a few vital targets, we scattered our air strength over so many kinds of targets that in truth we succeeded in destroying none of them. German war production continued until the Allied armies broke into the interior of the Fatherland.

October 25

There was some free time that morning. At the hut I asked, "Anyone want to join me? I'm headin' for the bath house."

"You better hurry and get in line," Green said.

Jim chipped in, "I do like the big windows in the bath house — such a good view. We don't really need any glass in the windows — better ventilation an' no mildew.''

"Well, is anyone else comin'?"

"Hell no! Not me. I'm not gonna freeze my ass in that ice box," Buck answered.

"You know somethin'? You guys from the North are always the first to bitch about being cold. In all barracks you will see men from Maine and Michigan near the stove an' the men from Texas an' Florida at the end of the room.''

The bath house was located in the middle of the personnel huts but in winter it was shunned as if the plague lurked in its murky interior. An icy North Wind blew unhindered through the open window spaces. This is what went through my mind: "Why don't I put it off? Hell, I had a bath last week. No! You got to get on with it. Won't be any warmer tomorrow. Well, here we go! Get undressed — that's it. Hang your clothes on those nails. Forget about that freezing wind. Now off with those shoes. All right, go ahead and yell! That cold mud is hell. Come on, let's get it over with before pneumonia sets in. Over to the shower — now turn on the water. That's it, leap back when the water starts squirtin' out. Now hold the wash rag in the water and get it lathered up real heavy. OK, now soap down all over. Quit shaking; the blue skin will recover in ten or fifteen minutes. You are committed now! You've got to get under that shower to get the soap off. All right! Step under the shower. No! There's no hurry. Yes there is. Now get under that water! Owwwww! ! ! Yell louder! You're not going to disturb anyone. Do those yells actually make me a little warmer or is it my imagination? That's enough. Get out of here, you're wasting water. Turn it off and make a run for the towel. Where in the hell did I hang the clean underwear? Oh damn! It fell off into the mud on the floor. Well, put on the dirty underwear. Now on with the shirt and pants. You are feeling much better now. Right? Sure you are. Now rinse off the mud from your feet. You feel great! Just great! It was worth the ordeal, wasn't it? Tell that to the boys back at the hut!''

October 29

George, Hubie Green and I were lingering over a last cup of coffee at the mess hall. The building was almost empty as most of the men had departed.

"Hey, look comin' in — some brand new officers," I said.

"Yeah," said Green, "you can see that look on their faces. They must have arrived today.''

Five minutes later they had their trays and were seated at a table next to us. The temptation was too much to resist: it was time to start their initiation. Immediately we launched into a morbid discussion of combat raids in drastic detail, explosions, aircraft fires, dead crewmen, amputations, planes falling in spins out of control. We made it a point to act as if we did not realize they were listening. When the conversation was particularly gory, there was no sound of knife or fork from the next table. I noted with satisfaction when we left that the newly arrived officers were no longer hungry. It was our warm and friendly welcome to the 381st Combat Group and Ridgewell Airdrome.

November 1

There were nights when we could hear the faint sound of air raid sirens from the east toward the coast. We would lie there quietly listening to the spine-tingling wails, hoping they would fade away to the north or south. But some nights sirens closer to us would open up, then the nearby towns would come alive, and we knew the German bombers were coming in our direction. There were no air raid shelters at the base. There were some slit trenches near each hut, but they were always half full of water and mud. Most of us had rather chance the bombs than the freezing water and mud. If the weather was clear, men swarmed outside to find a vantage point and try to catch a glimpse of the action. Sometimes a dark shape of a bomber could be seen in the sky, silhouetted against a searchlight beam or the moon. On those rare occasions when a Jerry plane was caught by a blinding searchlight beam, it would shine brightly in the night sky, a perfect target for the R.A.F. night fighters. One night in October, eight parachute flares burst into brilliance over the base but floated over an adjacent village and burned luminously. It was clear that the bombers were after the 381st that night.

CHAPTER XV
Mission to Wilhemshaven
and Gilsenkirchen

November 3 —
Wilhelmshaven, Germany   *Aircraft 719 — Hellcat*

The weather looked questionable when I left the hut. The first man I saw at Operations was Chaplain Brown watching each man as he arrived. What did he look for? And if he pinpointed a man who appeared shaky, what did he say to him? Did he say, "God will watch over you and protect you," knowing that the man was on his way to kill and destroy.

When Gleichauf arrived at the aircraft, I had no idea what kind of mission we would face for the day. "We're hittin' Wilhelmshaven in Germany. Fighter opposition will be about the same as we get over Bremen, which can be rough. Flak is estimated from medium to heavy concentration. We'll pick up fifty P-47's at the coast on the way in. But the big news is we will have P-38's with us over the target."

There were whoops of joy! We were completely unaware that P-38's had arrived in England until that day. The Lockheed Lightning was powered by two liquid cooled engines and had a double tail boom. Its main feature was long range and strong construction. Fighting characteristics were good, but not great. It had performed well in the North African campaign against German aircraft, but how it would stack up in the rarified air of twenty-five to thirty thousand feet, against the best pilots the enemy could muster, was yet to be determined. But even a fair performance on those long penetrations, with the rocket menace hovering in the background, would be a tremendous help. There was no doubt that they could easily handle the rocket-carrying fighters with those awkward chutes hanging under each wing.

A few minutes after the P-47's turned back toward England, the Tail gunner came on intercom: "Tail to crew — here come the Bogies — five o'clock low."

The fighters climbed rapidly to our altitude and began circling to look us over as they usually did.

"Turret to crew — turret to crew — those Germans got a big surprise coming. P-38's at four o'clock high."

I watched a P-38 lead plane pick out a target and go into a steep dive. To my surprise the P-38 caught a blast of fire from somewhere and broke into two pieces and fell away in flames. The other P-38's pulled back up and decided to look things over a bit more carefully.

"Navigator to Copilot."

"Go ahead."

"Did you see what happened to that P-38?"

"He got caught by a 109 he never saw — it'll take a while, but they'll learn to use the P-47 tactics — get careless with those 109's an' they'll blow your ass off."

German and American fighters were evenly matched in numerical strength. I noticed that 38's seemed to fight in elements of two, while the P-47's used elements of four. But the 38's did better than I expected on their first encounter with the more experienced foes.

"Ball to crew — fighters comin' up at us from below."

I heard his guns chatter again and again. No one could help him down there. Attacks I could not see always worried me.

"Bombardier to Pilot — Bombardier to Pilot. Over."

"This is the Pilot . . ."

"We're on the bomb run."

"Tail to crew — flak at eight o'clock level."

It was spotty, but what they threw up was devastatingly accurate. Numerous Forts took hits, but none that I saw had to pull out of the formation in our Group. The Wing following us was not so lucky.

On the return P-38's chased away the few Jerry fighters who came up to our level. No rocket-carrying craft showed up. Actually, I would have liked for Jerry to have attacked us with rockets to see what the P-38's would do to them. On the way back I began to calculate the way long-range escort was going to shift the odds of survival for me. Until that day I tried many times to compute what the odds really were, using the total number of men who participated on raids since I arrived against the total casualties. This figure I projected over twenty-five missions. But the statistics I played with were too unreliable to have real meaning. My guess was that from July through October the odds must have been at least four to one that we would not make it. With the P-38's those odds were going to improve. That was the great news of the day. How much they would improve would depend on how many P-38's were in England then and how fast the force would be built up. At that time no airman at the 381st had succeeded in completing twenty-five raids. It was past the time that some of the earliest arrivals should have been through. For the first time I began to feel a cautious optimism that before long the 381st was going to turn out some graduates.

November 4

The Flying Fortresses were originally designed to fly as individual aircraft at high altitudes up to thirty-eight thousand feet using the accuracy of the Norden Bomb Sight. In practice this concept turned out to be impractical for two reasons. First, thirty thousand feet was found to be the highest altitude that crews could stand with consistency, due to the crude oxygen equipment and the intense cold in some areas of the airplane. Two, the opposition was so fierce from enemy fighters that the bombers had to attack in tightly flown formations to concentrate defensive fire.

In late October some officials of Bomber Command raised the question as to whether the Fortresses needed a highly trained navigator and bombardier in the nose. Could one officer be quickly trained to perform enough of the duties of both so that a well qualified gunner could be used up front where the main attacks were? Some bombardiers proved to be top notch gunners, like our Johnny Purus, but others could not get over the notion that their main job was to drop the bomb. That was important of course, but I can tell you for certain that the primary thing nearly all of us had in mind was to get back to England one way or another. Some training toward combining the two positions had already been started. After all, a navigator was needed only when an aircraft was separated from the formation or lost in murky weather on the way home. The navigator in the lead plane did the rest of the navigating for the Group. And the bombardier in the lead aircraft did the work with the Norden Bomb Sight. All of the other bombardiers watched for the first bomb to fall from the leader, then instantly released their load. But if the aircraft became separated deep in enemy territory, a bombardier would be needed to find some target of opportunity to keep the mission from being a total failure for that aircraft.

Shutting and Purus took this idea as a big joke. "Why we need you, Johnny?" Shutting asked. "I can toggle out those bombs when the stud bombardier lets go, and we can get us a good gunner on those nose guns."

But Purus retaliated, "No! It's you we don't need any more. If we get lost comin' back home, all I gotta do is call Balmore an' ask for a fix or a Q.D.M. — why we need you?"

(The concept of a single Bombardier-Navigator never caught on. A great deal of time had been spent in the training of both positions, and resistance to combining the two positions was too strong to overcome. After a few weeks we did not hear any more about it.)

November 5, 1943 — Gelsenkirchen   Hellcat #719

On the way to the mess hall that morning I could hear the last of the Lancasters up above, returning from a night raid against the Germans. I wondered where they had been and what it was like up there alone at night. They had to have a hell of a navigator to find the target, and the way back to their base in the dark.

The briefing sent a shudder up my spine: "We're heading for Gelsenkirchen in the Ruhr Valley. We'll have a P-47 escort at the coast — the navigator will give you the rendezvous time. Spitfires are due on the way out. Be careful not to mistake the Spits for 109's. There are seven hundred gun emplacements in the Ruhr so the flak will be intense, rougher than any we've seen so far."

There was an audible groan.

"Ball, keep a watch underneath for flak damage. There can be up to two hundred fighters, but they may not be too eager to come after us in all that flak."

After the briefing Kels said, "We got us two Navigators now, so which one of you jokers is gonna give us the headings today?"

Balmore stepped up. "I've got the solution to that problem." He presented small bail-out compasses[1] to Carl and Johnny. With a serious expression on his face he said, "I'm giving compasses to both of you, so when the pilot calls for a new heading, the one who comes up with it first gets to call it in."

Shutting and Purus solemnly shook hands with Balmore and accepted their tiny compasses.

"Balmore, your thoughtfulness is greatly appreciated. Now each of us has his very own compass!" responded Shutting.

At the coast the Tail came on intercom: "Fighters at six o'clock high."

"Radio to crew — they're 47's."

"And right on time," added the navigator.

The P-47's were using some larger disposable belly tanks made from pressed paper by the British that extended their range considerably. A few fighters broke through the escort cover but were ineffective. Losses to the

---

[1] Fingernail sized compass included in bail-out kits.

Bombers were slight, but the flak was awesome. There seemed no end to it and the accuracy was unbelievable. Numbers of times we were bounced about by the concussion of close ones. I heard frequent shell fragments crash into the aircraft, and could see some damage from my position. Lt. Butler's ship was hit, and he began to fall back. One of his engines was smoking. Then Colonel Nazzaro's ship was hit and the engine trailed black smoke for two hours.

Wham! A big piece of shrapnel slammed through the accessory section of number four engine.

"Turret to Copilot."

"Go ahead."

"How do the instruments look on number four?"

"Instruments are normal."

"All we can do is hope there is no fire."

The wings were perforated with holes to the right and to the left. My greatest concern was an oil or fuel system rupture that would ignite from the red-hot exhaust collector-rings of the engines.

"Turret to Ball — can you see any serious damage under the right wing? Look for fuel leaks."

"I see a lot of holes, but no leaks yet. Maybe they self-sealed."

A large chunk crashed under me and was deflected by an oxygen tank. Another slashed through the narrow space between the turret and copilot, and on out of the aircraft.

"Bombardier to Pilot — Bombardier to Pilot! We're on the bomb run!"

"Drop 'em quickly so we can get out of this damn flak!"

A few minutes away from the target coming out I heard an extra loud clang down below. A close one had showered the ball turret.

"Ball to Copilot — Ball to Copilot!"

"Go ahead."

"The Ball was hit an' both my eyes are full of glass. I can't open 'em to see."

"Are you hit anywhere else, Ball?"

"No, just my eyes full of glass slivers."

"You want us to get you out now, or wait 'til we're over water?"

"You can wait. I'm as well off here as I would be in the radio room."

Number two engine took a heavy hit squarely on the propeller hub, but continued to operate normally. A hunk of flak, a lot bigger than most of the fragments, tore through the empty bomb bay with a fearsome noise.

"Bombardier to crew — fighters at one o'clock level — 109's, I think. They don't seem too eager . . ."

"If you were a Jerry would you want in this damned flak?"

"Hell no!"

The Spitfires scheduled for the return escort did not show, although they could have been flying low cover below us. When the coast hove into view, a small flak field opened up. The Colonel expertly moved the formation around it. Lt. Butler was having double trouble. He was in doubt that he could make it over the North Sea. Later he insisted that the copilot gave orders for the crew to bail out while over land without his knowledge or consent. The navigator, four enlisted men, and the copilot jumped, including a special friend of ours named MacGinty. "Mac" was often a visitor to our hut. We would miss him. He had thirty-three raids with the R.A.F. and this raid would have made a total of fourty-two. Lt. Butler, with only three of his crew left, made it back to Ridgewell.

As soon as we got to lower altitude, and the threat of fighters had eased, I got out of the turret and looked for any damage I could see. After checking the hydraulic system I stood where Gleichauf and Kels could hear me.

"We got trouble with the hydraulic system. No pressure! We won't have any brakes on landing."

Paul asked, "Are you sure we can't raise any pressure temporarily?"

"Yes, the fluid is gone."

"Pilot to crew. We will have to land without brakes. I'll try to touch down at the end of the runway, then rev up number one and two engines. If we can ease off into the sticky mud to the right of the runway, that ought to stop us."

On the final approach Paul brought #719 in as slow as he dared — aiming at the end of the runway. What he saw ahead was unbelievable! Kels screamed out, "Paul, look at those damn people, lining both sides of the runway!"

"What are they doin' out here in our way!" Paul was frantic with helpless rage. "We can't turn off the runway and kill a dozen people!"

When the wheels touched down, Kels opened his side window and leaned far outside, trying to attract the attention of the people lining the runway. He frantically motioned the crowd to get out of our way. They smiled brightly and waved back at Kels. Gleichauf was infuriated! "Those stupid people are gonna make me wreck this airplane! We can't stop!! Who the hell let them out here?" The pilot was turning red with rage. Kels was still trying to signal the crowd to get out of our way. Total failure! The high speed of the aircraft meant nothing to them! Then it was too late! The end of the landing strip was coming up fast and we were still rolling at considerable speed with no possible chance to make the turn onto the taxi strip.

Number 719 sped toward rough ground, roads and ditches, but little soft mud needed to slow us down. This was long before a pilot could reverse the propellor pitch to slow down an aircraft. (There was a large field of sticky mud to the right side of the runway, if only we could have turned into it.) I asked many questions about why that unwanted crowd of people was lining the runway, not only in the way but in danger from the damaged aircraft coming in to land, some of which were without the usual landing controls. No one would tell me why the men were there, or who was responsible for an absurd situation that defied common sense. I suspect some officer ordered the men out to welcome "the boys back home." It might have sounded like a great idea to someone in an alcoholic daze.)

The aircraft was coasting toward a country lane when I saw an English soldier blithely pedalling along on a certain collision course apparently unaware of impending doom. I watched in horror! At the last moment the man looked to his left and saw those huge whirling propellors coming right at him. Then he passed out of sight under the wing and I felt a slight impact as we struct something.

I said to Paul, "I'm afraid we got him!"

"Oh, God! I hope not!" Gleichauf replied.

"Last I saw he was about ten feet away with number four prop headin' right into him."

We bounced crazily this way and that, over more ditches and obstructions, slowing down. I saw with dismay that we were heading straight for a barnyard and two elderly ladies were sitting on a wooden fence directly in our path. There was a sizable ditch and the wheels dropped into it, throwing one wing into the ditch, and the other up at a grotesque angle. The aircraft came to a lurching halt, with the nose of the plane resting about where I saw the two women sitting a few seconds earlier. Among the crew our only serious injury was to Harkness.

Paul leaned out of the window and called to some men nearby. "Did we hit those ladies sittin' on the fence?"

"No, it was a bit of a scramble, but they made it, you know."

That was a relief. The soldier on the bike was the only casualty. There was nothing we could have done to have prevented killing him. Number 719 was a sorry mess and it was all so stupid and unnecessary. A man killed and a new airplane wiped out for no sane reason! We should have gotten by with nothing more serious than a lot of sticky mud and perhaps a twisted landing gear.

The medical team arrived quickly to take Harkness to the hospital and get that glass out of his eyes. Those Medics were always efficient and fast when we had wounded men aboard. A crowd gathered around the plane, but I was concerned about the extent of damage to #719. One wing tip would have to be replaced and the landing gear was destroyed. The bomb bay was in sad shape and the bomb bay doors would definitely have to be replaced. One engine was shot, and possibly a second from the collision with the ditch. While I was climbing around estimating the repairs that would be needed, a muddy English soldier walked up and tapped me on the shoulder. His clothes were badly torn and he looked like he had been in a fight.

"Your bloody machine nearly got me, Yank," the soldier said.

"What's that?" I turned to stare at him.

"The propellor damned near cut me haid off — and I fell between the wheels — smashed me bike to bits. Bloody ruined!"

"I thought we killed you, soldier. Don't know how you escaped."

"I was on my way to the pub, I look up, and was never so scared in me whole life. I see that bloody propellor comin' right at me!"

Shutting climbed wearily out of the airplane with his briefcase of maps and his bag of flying equipment. He looked around until he located the radio operator. "Balmore, you saved us today!"

"What do you mean by that?" George responded.

"If it hadn't been for this little Boy Scout compass you gave me early this morning we couldn't have made it back. All my instruments were shot out!" His voice was almost breaking with emotion as he continued. "No compass! No drift meter! No nothing except this little doo-dad. So I says, 'Carl, this is it! The whole Wing is depending on you to navigate us home,' so I brought 'em back with this little Boy Scout compass. I want to thank you for giving it to me, Balmore."

George and Shutting shook hands solemnly. Those of us who were close enough offered our solemn congratulations. Of course, all of this was pure nonsense! Shutting had no more use for a compass that day than I did. Our plane merely followed on the Colonel's left wing all day, while the lead navigator did the navigating. But unknown to us, an Associated Press reporter was in the crowd writing down this insane foolishness word for word. The next morning the A.P. all across the U.S. carried a front page story of the incident. The account hinged on Shutting's supposed heroic leadership in navigating a wing of Fortresses home by means of a Boy Scout compass. It made big headlines in all the home town papers of the crew. Within two weeks some of us began getting letters from home asking about the crash. Was anyone injured or wounded? At first it sounded like they had us confused with some aircraft that crash-landed in England. Then Shutting received a letter containing a clipping from a Chattanooga newspaper. It read: "CARL SHUTTING LEADS FORTS HOME WITH SCOUT COMPASS" in big, black, front page headlines. Before Carl could recover from his shock, someone spirited the clipping out of his hut, and the next day it was pinned on the 381st bulletin board. That embarrassed our bashful navigator no end! It looked like Carl had been sending home some fanciful stories of his heroism.

Carl Shutting Leads Forts Home With Scout Compass

Chattanoogan in 700-Bomber Raid Falls Back on Small Guide After Instruments Ruined

LT. CARL SHUTTING

A U. S. BOMBER BASE IN BRITAIN, Nov. 5 (AP)—Lt. Carl R. Shutting, 107 North Seminole Drive, Chattanooga, Tenn., used a Boy Scout compass to lead his division of Flying Fortresses home safely from the 700-heavy bomber raid over western Germany today.

Navigator of the "Hell Cat," Lt. Shutting used the small compass to keep on the beam after the regular navigating instruments had been rendered hors de combat by enemy fire. As it was, the "Hell Cat" was forced to make a landing which sent it bounding over two ditches and through three fences because the hydraulic brake system had been shot up.

(Lt. Carl R. Shutting is the son of Mr. and Mrs. Rudolph Shutting. His father is a well-known commercial artist and map maker in Chattanooga.)

The Fortress with the lofty name, "Spirit of Franklin County, Mo.," which citizens of that county bought with their war bond purchases, led another division and stoutly maintained the lead position all the way back to the English coast although badly shot up.

With one engine out, gas flowing from the left wing, the windshield cracked and the fuselage perforated from antiaircraft fire, the "Spirit" reluctantly turned over leadership to another plane and

See Page Two, Column Seven

November 6

One man that I remember so well was always welcome at our hut. We saw him nearly every day. His name was Pete Ludwigson. It was a relief to see such a clean and wholesome young man untouched by the sordid aspects of war. We had traveled the same path since the days of the Engineering School at Boeing Aircraft, Seattle. His crew and ours went through training procedures at the same time, and we ended up at the 381st on the same day. Pete did not let anything bother him. He was always the same. When the rest of us would get worked up over some fancied abuse, Pete would say, ''Quit bitching. It's all part of the game. A week from now you won't remember what you're so hot about now.'' And he was right: gripes, shortages, inconvenience, dirt, mud, cold, military orders that made no sense, fear, and above all, sheer boredom, were the things that made up the military life. I wished that I could be more like Pete and take things of no real importance less seriously. On the mission yesterday our good friend, Ludwigson, was lost somewhere over the Ruhr Valley. That was all we knew because there were no witnesses to what happened after the aircraft had to drop out of the formation and fell far behind us, struggling along on two engines and a third operating at half speed. I had a hard time going to sleep last night wondering what Pete endured and if he made it out of the plane when it finally gave up. We knew that the Fort did not get back to England. It was a blow to lose a man like Pete. We hoped that he was able to bail out in time. Often I could achieve a psychic feeling about a crew that was lost, but in this case I had no impression about their fate.

In early November we began to hear more rumors about super weapons being hastily developed by the Germans. Hitler made numerous veiled references to frightening new instruments of destruction that he said would turn the war in Germany's favor. Goebbel's propaganda machine turned these dire predictions to advantage in raising the spirits of the German workers. Allied Intelligence slowly accumulated more specific information as to what German scientists were attempting. None of this leaked through to our level, except the disturbing worry that if some super weapon did emerge from the war, Germany would be most likely to come up with it because of the seven or eight year head start they had with preparations for a war.

After lights were out I made the following remark to whoever was awake and listening: ''This afternoon I talked to Lt. Atkins (the Gunnery Officer). He says there are rumors that Hitler's boys are workin' on a gigantic rocket that they can fire across the Channel.''

Rogers said, "It sounds like one of Goebbel's pipe dreams to me."

"The trouble is, Buck, these people have the brains an' the know-how to do it, if they get enough time," I answered.

Jim added, "They've probably been at it since 1936."

Lancia said, "Those Germans are damned smart. We can't sell them short. Ever raid I look around an' half-way expect to see something new thrown at us."

"Me, too," I said. "I've seen two extra large explosions recently up high. They had a brownish color and looked big enough to blow a group out of the sky if it burst in the middle of a formation. Has anyone else seen this thing?"

No one had and I hoped it was my imagination.

Pitts asked, "Well, suppose they can make a huge rocket. How are they goin' to hit anything with it fired from a distance?"

"It could be controlled by an aircraft near the target like a model airplane," Counce added.

"They think that Allied Intelligence will find out soon where it is being tested," I said.

Then there was silence except for an occasional snore, and the faint sound of engines on the distant flight line. Did it mean a mission in the morning? I never could sleep well when I thought a raid was shaping up.

CHAPTER XVI
Mission to Wessel

November 7 — Wessel, Germany   *Aircraft 808*

I wanted to get in a mission because the weather had slowed down the air offense. George Reese read the roster and the aircraft was number 808 from another squadron.

I asked George, "What kind of ship are we flyin' today?"

"It's a new G — only been on two missions."

Jim peeped outside, "Don't see much low hangin' mist — we might get off this morning."

I asked Counce to wait outside the Briefing Room while I went on out to the aircraft. Any time it was a strange ship I wanted more time to look it over and talk to the crew chief, as all aircraft had peculiarities that it was good to know about. It was a very dark morning and my flashlight quit working. I knew those planes well enough to feel my way along in the dark. I thought I was the first one at the plane. As I groped slowly forward in the waist area suddenly something very hard struck me on the head just above my eyes. I fell flat on the floor and counted a dozen stars from the pain. A flashlight came on and Wilson helped me to my feet.

"John! I'm sorry! Didn't know anyone was in the plane but me."

"What did you hit me with?" I inquired in a shaky voice.

"I jerked out my gun barrel just as you walked by in the dark."

"My head throbs! An' both eyes feel like they're swellin' shut. This is the first time you've been early since we got to England. From now on go back to bein' late."

I was still woozy and hurting when Gleichauf arrived. "What's the matter with you? Been in a fight?"

"Our brilliant waist gunner hit me in the head with a gun barrel in the dark."

"Can you make it today?"

"I'll make it — going to have two shiners — nothin' worse, I hope."

The rest of the crew arrived and it was time for the briefing. "The target is Wessel, in Germany, on the far edge of the Ruhr Valley, but we'll cut across the Valley and try to miss the worst flak. The temperature will be near fifty below, so watch yourselves for frostbite. We'll use the Pathfinder System[1] today, so we can drop through fog and not have to worry about clear weather at the target. We're glad to have Trapnell with us in the radio room. Once more — watch out for the low temperature.''

At twenty-eight thousand feet, I became concerned about the bitter cold.

''Turret to Navigator.''

''Go ahead, Turret.''

''How cold is it?''

''Minus forty-eight Centigrade.''

''Turret to Bombardier — with this low temperature, we may get some ice in oxygen masks — you might want more frequent crew checks.''

''Good idea, Turret. We'll have one ever' twenty minutes.''

The escort was on time and gave us perfect coverage. What fighters came up, if any, were quickly turned away and the formation was untouched. The bomb run was twelve minutes long, double the usual length.

''Bombardier! Are we goin' to drop or not?''

''No, we missed it, Paul. Looks like we're going around again.''

''Hope he drops this time — we stay around here too long an' fighters will get to us.''

''Bombs away'' was good news.

''Radio to Bombardier — Radio to Bombardier — bomb hung up in the bomb bay. Keep the doors open.''

''Turret to Bombardier — I'm goin' back to take a look at it.''

The hung up bomb was high on the outside rack and difficult to get to the shackle with a screwdriver. The problem was to keep the bomb from knocking me off of the catwalk when it fell free. On my fourth attempt it released.

''Turret to Bombardier, the bomb bay is clear. You can raise the doors.''

''Radio to Copilot — I think I'm gettin' frostbite on one hand — it's numb — no feeling.''

---

[1]The lead aircraft in each group, and the deputy lead also, were equipped with the special Pathfinder radar to aid the Navigator. Waves bouncing back from the ground were converted into a scan of the surface below that could be interpreted by a trained operator. He could in effect see the ground through clouds or darkness. Later the Americans dubbed the process ''Mickey.''

"Is your 'lectric glove workin' on that hand, Radio?"

"It's workin' but the heat is not on the fingers where I need it to handle cold metal."

My mike went silent and after a hasty change to a reserve mike, I called the Radio Operator. "Radio, can you hear me?"

"I can hear you."

"This ship has 'lectric gun heaters — turn on the gun heat and put your hand where the heat is."

I liked the idea of the Pathfinder System if we learned to hit a target with it. We would know after photo planes came up with a good picture of the damage in a day or two. That equipment showed promise of opening up the air offensive in poor weather. I could feel both eyes swelling almost shut and my head ached from the blow. The return to England was painful and tiresome. But I would trade two classic black eyes and a throbbing headache for an easy mission like that one any time. I was not going anywhere on pass for a while anyway, so I did not let the jibes and wisecracks bother me. The incident did not increase my affection for Carroll Wilson.

November 8

Jim Counce had girl problems that worried him. He had broken with a girl he had been seeing for a long time before his last furlough and became engaged to a girl he did not know very well. He was a bit bewildered by the speed at which it came about, but was serious, and had every intention of carrying out his pledge. He worried that there should have been more time to get to know each other better, but he was glad that his mother approved his choice.

Counce was our mainstay in the aft section of the aircraft. We needed at least one solid man with top notch mechanical aptitude back there. Balmore was excellent at his radio position, but he was helpless with some sudden mechanical problem for which there had been no specific training.

Wherever we were situated for a few weeks, Counce would find a temporary girl friend. He was the kind of man that women are attracted to. By late August he had two girls close enough to the base that no pass was needed. One interesting and unexpected entanglement worked out. An English mother liked Jim as much as her daughter did. He talked about that development with George but never mentioned it to me. Why? Perhaps he thought I would disapprove of the bizarre situation. I suppose that I never quite shed the image of being a little square.

November 9

Rain! Rain! Rain! It was bitterly cold and there was no fuel for the tiny stove. We had our hoarded crosscut saw, but it had to be kept out of sight. We could cut the King's trees only at night and when weather allowed. Did you ever try to saw wet wood? When the rain let up enough, two or three men would pedal into the nearby village and bring back copious amounts of cider and ale. Enough ale and the cold was less difficult to handle.

November 11

Stimulated by the success of my electric overshoes, I made a much better pair of electrically heated gloves. The heat was placed where it was needed instead of in the middle of the palm. Having to keep the fingers in constant contact with metallic controls, at temperatures that varied from thirty-five to sixty below zero centigrade, should have required that the electric heat be concentrated on the fingers where the contact was. But the equipment designers apparently had no conception of high altitude gunnery needs and put the heat in the palm of the hand. Of course, it was much better than nothing, but at the lower temperatures handling metal for extended periods overtaxed the crude design. My new gloves were ideal and for the remainder of my combat missions never needed repairs.

No matter what the conversation was, or the location, the bull sessions always led back to the one thing uppermost in the mind: where would we go tomorrow? How rough would it be? and the ultimate question: would we make it? I never deliberately let that question come up, but it was there in the subconscious mind day after day. The boredom for stretches of days at a time, the endless waiting for action we knew was coming, and too much time to think all combined to draw the nerves ever tighter.

November 13

Allied weather forecasters had a complex task in trying to decide what could be expected a day or two in advance with enough accuracy to guide Bomber Command in their planning. European weather is changeable and clear periods such as we are accustomed to are infrequent. For stretches of days at a time, clouds hover over the area of the European Continent. Sometimes a mission would take off with questionable visibility, and an hour later the operation would be scrubbed. One day during that period we were scheduled for a raid over Germany and so much murk settled in that there was no chance of the mission. The fog increased and created hazardous flying conditions. Three wings of airplanes were blindly groping their way down, hoping for a break in the clouds. We were lucky and found a hole in the swirling mists with a welcome airdrome in view. When we pulled up to an empty space, Counce said. "Look! Yonder is 'Tootsie Snoots,' " our one-time airplane. Her name now was "Dottie J" but to us she was still Tootsie. At that time she had twenty-five missions to her credit without a turn back for mechanical problems. In the 381st, few aircraft made that many missions. I examined the ship from close range for a long time with Jim and let my thoughts drift back to Herb Carqueville, and the high hopes of that day when we landed Tootsie on English soil. So much had happened that it seemed a long time. It was almost certain by now that Herb was gone. If he had bailed out and survived we would have heard about it. Every time I had to face that harsh reality I felt a dull stab of pain.

November 14

The call came at two A.M. Jim was ahead of me and when I got to Operations he said, "There's somethin' different in the air this morning. The Brass looked tense when they went into the Briefing Room."

"Any idea what may be comin' up?"

"No. But you can bet it's gonna be a rough one! Go on to the ship an' I'll wait until they pull the curtain."

When Jim arrived on the next transport truck, I was waiting anxiously. "What did it sound like?"

"The worst groan you ever heard — then dead silence — not another sound."

"Where do you think we're goin'? Schweinfurt again?"

"Could be Schweinfurt — or some other place just as bad."

When Gleichauf arrived I could see that he was keyed up. "Today it will be BERLIN!"

"Is this some kind of a joke?"

He shook his head.

Counce said, "We're not really goin' to Berlin?"

"We sure as hell are. There may be two thousand fighters close enough to hit us. This will be the first daylight raid ever on Berlin. S-2 says to 'expect the Luftwaffe.' It will be rougher than anything we've seen so far."

I had difficulty believing that Bomber Command would attempt what seemed to me a foolhardy venture. There were so many fighters in the Berlin area that the forces we could put up would be overwhelmed as I saw it. Perhaps in a few months, with two or three times as many B-17's and a swarm of long-range escort fighters, hitting Berlin in daylight would become feasible. But we did not have that kind of strength then and I think most 381st men knew it. George Reese assigned himself as our copilot. Either he knew something the rest of us did not know, or he had more courage than brains.

Two new gunners were flying our tail and ball positions. I did not resent them personally, but why did Operations have to stick us with two inexperienced men on a raid like this? Both of them were already so numb with fright that I doubted either would be worth much to us. I got Shutting, Counce and Balmore together for a minute and said, ''Those rookie gunners are scared so bad that the color has drained out of their faces. We got to do something to relax them.'' Turning to Shutting: ''Couldn't you put on a comedy act with your testical armor? Get them to help you assemble it. We got to get them over the shakes. The best way is some horse play.''

Carl was at his best. ''They're gonna be after me today! They think they goin' to shoot off my balls. No way! I got 'em fooled. They don't know about this armor doodad. I get it tied like this then stand on my armor plate.''

''But what if the flak bursts on your left side instead of below you?'' I asked.

''I got that figured out. If they burst on the left I get on the right side of the Bombardier. If it's on the right I get on his left side — use him for armor plate — we got a surplus of Bombardiers.''

George had some chalk and inscribed each bomb ''Herman,'' ''Adolf'' or ''Goebbels'' and obscene remarks about what we would like to do to each one of them personally. I watched the tension fade and the color return to the two young gunners. When they could laugh at the wisecracks and foolishness I felt much better about them.

Thirty minutes went by while the crews waited for the signal to start the engines. Suddenly I heard cheering echo across the field. The mission to Berlin was canceled. Did Bomber Command really intend to strike Berlin that day? I still have doubts. Was it a morale thing to break the monotony of idleness caused by bad weather and a slowdown awaiting a build up of long-range fighters? I thought so.

November 17

Two times recently we had been on missions flying #730 that had to be called off for weather reasons. On both flights number three engine developed heavy smoke, becoming increasingly denser as the aircraft climbed to higher altitude. At sixteen thousand feet the ball operator could see a suggestion of raw flame from the exhaust. To me this was a clear case of a malfunction in the air fuel mixture system, probably in the bellows valve of the carburetor, which adjusted the amount of fuel as the altitude increased and the outside air pressure being sucked into the carburetor became lower. I rarely had differences with the efficient ground crews at Ridgewell, but locked horns on that malfunction. The crew chief insisted that nothing was wrong because the engine ran fine at ground level. I don't think he understood the function of the bellows valve and unfortunately his line chief backed him up. I was dead certain they were both wrong!

That morning Major Shakley, the Squadron Commanding Officer, was leading the Group and riding with us in the copilot's seat. I knew the aircraft would not make it to the bombing altitude and managed to catch the major outside operations.

"Major, 730 won't make the mission! It has a bad bellows valve but the crew chief says I'm wrong an' won't change it. I thought you would want to know it."

"I'm leading and can't run the risk of an abortion. We'll switch planes. Stand by for a change."

The mission was cancelled over the North Sea but not before 730 got into serious trouble. At seventeen thousand feet number three engine blew off the cylinder heads and scattered broken parts over the sky. Her crew was lucky to escape more damage or a fire. The ground crew blew it that time, but it was one of the few instances of a mistake so serious that should have been avoided. I don't recall what crew was flying #730 but I was glad it wasn't us.

CHAPTER XVII
Mission to Norway and
Mission to Bremen

Norway — Johnny Purus Only   *Aircraft 878*
November 16

Johnnie Purus was drafted to fly with a new crew on their first mission. What did he do to deserve such an unenviable assignment? He must have become crossways with Franek because bombardiers were not in short supply. I am sure Franek would not have done that to most of the experienced bombardiers. It was one of those days when nothing went right. The first error was the faulty weather forecast. The second error was the information on the target, which was a plant in Norway located over a mine. The briefed altitude was thirteen thousand feet, but halfway across the North Sea they hit a weather front that was unexpected, and had to circle and circle up to nineteen thousand to get over it. When they reached the target area neither the lead navigator or bombardier could find anything resembling the plant supposed to be there. The intelligence relied on by Bomber Command might have been planted by the Germans. Both sides tried to lure the other into costly misadventures to waste manpower and materials. In frustration the Group made a wide three sixty swing back over where the target was supposed to have been. Again nothing!

But the boneheads for the day were not finished! The pilot was too inexperienced to realize the need to stay in formation so he was trailing along behind. Ten minutes from the Norwegian Coast the pilot made what turned out to be the fourth error of the day. He left the cockpit and headed for the radio room to confer with the radio operator. Pilots do not leave the cockpit in enemy territory without a compelling reason! On the catwalk near the door to the radio room he was shocked by the rattle of fifty caliber guns in action and a twenty M.M. cannon shell tore through the bomb bay, somehow missing the bombs, and took off part of his flight jacket sleeve. Eight enemy fighters had jumped the formation and hit the stragglers first as they always did. Another slug crashed into the top turret. The copilot belatedly decided to get into the formation and did a good job of flying to pull quickly into the protection of the defensive fire coverage. That was how new crews got shot down! They listened to the stories about fighters and did not buy them. "All of that junk about tight formation was for the birds!" Purus was lucky to survive.

November 26   Bremen

The raid was called on a raw, windy morning. Outside the sky was a mass of shifting clouds and blowing fog. After a quick look I went back into the hut and said, "We got weather problems today for sure. It'll surprise me if we get off the ground."

Balmore was still grounded for frostbite injuries, but he sat up and remarked, "Hope you fellows don't get another one of those blind climb ups through fog."

"If we go at all it looks like that is exactly what we will draw," I answered.

Balmore continued, "I'd rather have fighter attacks than sweat out those climb ups in fog."

Gleichauf gave us the story for the day: "The target is going to be Bremen. You know what the flak will be like! The weather over the Continent will be ice-forming so some of the fighters may not be able to get to us. The altitude will be twenty-six thousand feet and the temperature will be about fifty below." Shutting added, "There is a strong wind blowing at a hundred and forty miles per hour at our altitude. It is one of those winds that can shift directions and cause problems."

Gleichauf had one more comment: "The Copilot and Engineer must keep an eye on the engines for carburetor icing."

It was a bleak outlook. The biggest mistake of the day, and there were many, was the weather forecast. I knew there would be mixups in such turbulent skies. The takeoff proceeded on schedule thirty minutes before dawn. I was invariably fascinated by the sights and sounds of a group takeoff in the dark. There was an element of the theatrical with airplanes groping toward the lineup at the end of the runway. Pilots detested the severe risks of collisions or mishaps because B-17 formations were not really suitable for night flights.

Paul followed the flight course as briefed: A specified rate of climb and speed for so many minutes, then a forty-five degree turn, repeating the process until out of the murk. Theoretically the planes should come out in the clear close together so that the squadron could form quickly. If the fog was a thousand to fifteen hundred feet, the tactic would work fairly well. But if the overcast was up to eight or ten thousand feet it would create chaos.

"Pilot to Navigator."

"Go ahead, Paul."

"Can you see anything ahead?"

"Nothing! Blind as a bat."

"John, get in the turret an' watch out ahead. Lots of planes in this soup."

A little later: "Pilot to Navigator — what is our rendezvous altitude over splasher four?" (A radio beam projecting upward to aid navigation.)

"Five thousand feet."

At that height there was a clear space between banks of heavy clouds and the 381st was supposed to assemble over this radio beacon. Some aircraft were already there.

"Bombardier to Pilot."

"Go ahead."

"There's our signal light color high at seven o'clock."

"Good. I see it."

When we pulled close to the aircraft flashing the signal light that was intended to identify the 381st Group, it turned out to be another group, and a mixup on the signal light colors. It was just one of a number of mistakes the pilots would have to endure for the next two hours. Another aircraft with the familiar 381st Triangle "L" was also lured by the false signal. The pilot saw we were from the 381st and moved in on our right wing and stayed there.

"Hey, Paul, we got company," said the Copilot. "It's from our Group, but I don't recognize the ship."

"I wish to hell he'd get off of our wing! We got more fog comin' up."

But the aircraft hung in on our wing tight, much to our consternation. It was bad enough being in the soup with so many other ships flying blind. Later we found out the reason: that wing aircraft was without a navigator, and the confusion and awful weather was driving the pilot to desperate measures. It seems odd that Operations would have permitted a ship to take off under such conditions without a navigator.

"Pilot to crew — we're goin' on up to nine thousand feet — hope we can catch the 381st there — everyone watch out for other airplanes — Navigator! Navigator!"

"Go ahead."

"Let me know when we are approaching the rendezvous point."

Sometime later: "This is the Navigator. We're getting close to where they told us to go — can't see anything in this soup."

"This is one big mess, Navigator. I'll try to contact the Wing."

After another five minutes: "Pilot to Navigator — OK, they say go to twelve thousand feet over splasher four."

At twelve thousand feet it was the same — fog — fog — fog!

"Pilot to Navigator — this is no good either! Can't see anything. Let's try thirteen thousand."

But another thousand feet did not help, and we lost radio contact with the Group leader.

"Radio to Pilot — Radio to Pilot."

"This is the Pilot."

"Blasingborn says the 381st will pass over splasher four at fifteen thousand feet at nine hundred hours."

At the scheduled time we were over the radio beacon at the correct height and it was the same story — just blinding fog!

"Pilot to crew — we're goin' on up until we break out of this soup. Ships this high have lost contact — no telling how many lost planes are up here. Watch out for other aircraft."

The overcast broke at nineteen thousand feet. There were many aircraft milling around in confusion looking for a formation to join. The long climb up to this altitude had undoubtedly used up a lot of fuel.

"Turret to Copilot, do we have enough gas to join a formation without knowing for sure how long the mission will be?"

"Copilot to Pilot."

"Go ahead."

"We've burned up a lot more fuel than was expected. We got enough for a short mission, but not for a long one."

"I don't see any formation to join anyway. If we should find one later we would run a risk on gas! Navigator — Navigator."

"Go ahead, Paul."

"Give me a heading for Ridgewell."

Shutting knew that the wind might have shifted in the several hours since the weather briefing, but without visibility he had no means to check for drift. "Start letting down in wide circles, Paul, and I'll keep calling out the headings."

A long time later the aircraft broke under the clouds. We were over land near the North Sea.

"Navigator to Pilot, we were lucky. We could've come down far out over the sea the way these high wind currents can shift direction."

On this same goofed up mission attempt George Reese was assigned to Lt. Deering's crew as copilot on their first mission. Operations thought that with Reese in the cockpit Deering could stay out of trouble. The rookie navigator must not have paid much attention to the briefing because he evidently did not catch the hundred and forty mile per hour wind. It was odd that he could miss such navigational data, probably due to the fear and trauma of a first combat mission. When it was decided that it was impossible to proceed with the mission, the Navigator had to rely on dead reckoning[1] to get back to the base. The strange story came from George Reese: ''We were at twenty-one thousand feet when I told the pilot that the mission was scrubbed. I didn't pay too much attention for the next hour as the ship eased down through fog; I was worried mainly about a collision in the soup. I remembered that a high wind was blowing but I could not recall the exact direction from the briefing. Once or twice I called the Navigator to ask if he was allowing for the drift from that high wind, but could not get anything out of him. I was a little uneasy that he might be confused, but at that time there did not seem to be any good reason to ask the radio operator to get us a Q.D.M. I expected that we would need one when we broke clear of the fog. There were no holes in the ceiling and we came down blind. At six thousand feet the Ball called, 'Ball to crew — land below us.' ''

'' 'Pilot to Copilot, do you recognize the area? See anything familiar?' ''

'' 'Don't recognize it — Navigator.' ''

'' 'This is the Navigator.' ''

'' 'Watch for some landmark you can recognize from your charts.' ''

''Deering dropped down to a lower altitude. Sanford, a waist gunner, had quite a few missions, but neither of us could pick out anything familiar. Suddenly a tower appeared to the right. I recognized immediately that it was a German flak tower, but before I could say anything, a furious burst of shells exploded around us.''

'' 'Get the hell out of here — we're over the Continent.' ''

''But where over the Continent? It could have been East or West France, Holland, Belgium, North Germany or possibly Denmark. Stanford and the tail gunner did have the pleasure of strafing the German tower — one of the few times I know of that Fortress gunners could shoot back at the enemy manning those flak guns.''

''We flew North for ten minutes until we sighted what I thought was

[1]Dead reckoning means navigating strictly by instruments, speed, time, etc., without any chance to correct the course for changes in wind direction or velocity.

the North Sea. Suddenly twelve bursts of very accurate flak caught us almost dead center. I quickly grabbed the wheel and ducked out of that spot fast. I threw the ship up and down and took as much evasive action as I thought the crew could stand.''

'' 'Copilot to Navigator, we've got to find out where we are so you can give us a heading for England.' ''

'' 'Copilot to crew — Copilot to crew. Watch for fighters. They're goin' to hit us if we don't get out of here quick.' ''

"Back in the waist, tail and radio room, the ammunition had been thrown out of the cans and the men banged up a bit by the drastic evasive action. The gunners were frantically trying to get the ammunition straightened out. Deering turned west and flew parallel to the coast in the hope that Stanford or me would see something familiar. Thirty minutes of this and we turned southeast. High and inaccurate flak came up. A few minutes later a lone F.W. 190 appeared and made two passes. Fortunately both were against the tail where we have our best defense. Deering did a good job of evasive action.''

'' 'Copilot to Tail, good going back there! Let 'em have it when they come in.' ''

"Deering turned into land again. 'Copilot to crew, two fighters at two o'clock high — pour the lead to 'em if they try to attack us.' ''

"The pilot dodged into a cloud bank before the fighters could strike.''

'' 'Good work, Pilot. Stay in this cloud until we shake those fighters, but we got to find out where we are — we can't hang around here all day.' ''

'' 'Copilot to Radio.' ''

'' 'Go ahead.' ''

'' 'Do you know how to get a fix?' ''

'' 'I think we're too far away for a fix.' ''

'' 'I was afraid of that. Try anyway.' ''

"When we came out of the clouds, Deering turned inland again and headed for a sizable city in full view. Without warning all hell broke loose! Flak and small arms fire came up in a hail of lead.''

'' 'Copilot to Pilot. I know where we are. That is Calais! Let me have the controls.' ''

"I took more evasive action but not fast enough. I heard a loud noise underneath the aircraft. 'Copilot to Ball, where did we get hit? Any bad damage?' ''

'' 'The bomb bay doors were knocked down.' ''

'' 'Copilot to Top Turret, go back an' see if you can hand crank the doors back up.' "

"The doors would not come up, but it was not important. We had plenty of fuel."

" 'Pilot to Navigator, give us a heading for Ridgewell and be sure to allow for that heavy wind current.' "

"Deering took over and climbed to six thousand feet. Two more F.W. 190's came up from the rear. Both had belly tanks and one had a rocket chute."

" 'Copilot to Tail, watch that fighter with the rocket. When you see the rocket fire, follow the vapor trail 'an tell the pilot which way to move the airplane.' "

" 'Pilot, this is the Tail. It's gettin' in position about fifteen hundred yards behind us, slightly high. He fired it! It's comin' straight at us! Pull up! Pull up!' "

"Deering jerked the aircraft up an' the rocket passed under us real close."

" 'Tail to crew, fighter comin' in five o'clock level.' "

"I could hear the tail and waist guns hammering an' saw the fighter flash by below my window. It pulled up high and tried a nose attack."

" 'Pilot! Evasive action!' "

"The attack failed and the two fighters disappeared into the mists."

" 'Copilot from Top Turret, I think we hit that fighter — maybe knocked it down.' "

" 'I doubt it. Those 190's are heavily armored and can take a lot of punishment.' "

"The radio operator had been feverishly attempting to pick up a fix. He got a response all right, but the station failed to answer his challenge for the day. He knew then it was a German station trying to lure us in for a kill. That was a trick used by both sides. (The radio operators used Morse code which was easy to fake.) Actually we were a little too far away for a reliable fix. Halfway across the water that same F.W. 190 our gunners thought they had shot down appeared again. That persistent bastard followed us all of the way to the English Coast. Radio finally got in contact with a home station and established a Q.D.M. At the coast a Spitfire showed up and the F.W. 190 took off for Germany in a hurry. I was much relieved to see the outlines of Ridgewell show up. There was one final error: Radio was confused about the damage to the aircraft and had radioed ahead that our landing gear was shot out. When we came in to land I saw to my surprise ambulances, crash wagons and fire trucks standing by. The Old Man was plenty teed off! He blamed me for the mixups and damage to the plane."

November 18

During this period the 381st was constantly being infused with new crews, who had yet to learn the hard lesson that tight formation was as essential to their well-being as blocking is to a football team. We received new crews, but continued to lose experienced ones, and that meant an exhaustive effort to keep the quality high. Training went on but too many replacement crews lessened our ability to fly good formations consistently. Either the new pilots arrived with some high altitude formation experience or they had to start learning it on combat missions. Sure, we flew some formation practice, but there was no way that the 381st could provide the training that the crews were supposed to have had in the States. For quite a while the Group was losing as many men as it was gaining from new arivals. We did not have the time, or the aircraft, or the fuel to retrain those new arrivals.

November 27

The rain clouds cleared and there was a part of a moon. Eight or ten of us pedaled into a nearby village and enjoyed an evening at the pubs. At closing time we started back to the base. The men in the lead used their flashlights and the rest of us followed along in the dark. Between the local road and our quarters there was a swift running stream spanned by a narrow bridge. We were strung out in single file behind a Captain in the lead. Suddenly the Captain dropped his flashlight and everything went dark. I heard a wild yell and a splash as something hit the water. I switched on my light in time to see an officer's cap floating jauntily downstream bobbing gently in the water like a toy boat.

Someone yelled, ''Where's the Captain?''

Four flashlights scanned the empty water rushing by. An authoritative voice took command. ''All right! Jerk off your blouses! All of you! Now! Get in that creek! Couple of ya go downstream and work back. We gotta find him — and quick!''

The frigid water sobered me real quick. In one or two minutes someone located the Captain and we pulled him out of that freezing water. Fortunately he did not take on much water internally, and in ten minutes he was recovered enough to be out of danger. I was shaking with a bad chill by the time I got to the hut and into some dry clothes. The temperature was thirty-five degrees.

CHAPTER XVIII
Mission to Paris and Leverkusson

The month of November was frustrating because the weather kept the B-17's grounded for a week at a time. When a mission was called we fully expected it to be cancelled before takeoff, or in the air before we reached enemy territory. If clouds were almost certain to cover the target, there was no point in continuing the mission unless the drop was scheduled to be by Pathfinder equipment. Since the middle of the month we had taken off eight times back to back without getting in a mission. That was hard on morale. Being confined too much of the time to the small metal quarters, we became irritating to each other. Sometimes Lancia's noise became abrasive and Wilson's disorderly bunk was always revolting to a person like me, who wanted things neat and shipshape. There were days when Rogers withdrew into a morose silence and ignored the rest of us. When he was in one of those moods it was better to leave him alone. Tedesco's continual harping on Brooklyn and New York got on my nerves. Hadn't he ever been anywhere else before he was drafted into the service? The least offensive occupant of our hut was Hubie Green. He was such a nice, gentle young man I could find little to resent about him.

December 1 — Leverkusson, Germany   Aircraft 730

Jim climbed wearily out of bed and groaned, ''Another false alarm I suppose. Will we ever get in another mission?''

''We haven't flown a completed raid since early November,'' I said. ''At this rate we'll be here another year.''

Harkness added, ''But we've been in sight of enemy territory four times before we turned back.''

Gleichauf intercepted me at Operations. ''We're carryin' a General with us this mornin' so get things in good shape before we get there.''

I did not like the idea of high ranking brass on a mission. It meant extra trouble and having to be more careful over the intercom. As soon as I examined the cockpit of aircraft 730 I made a run for the perimeter road and was lucky to hail down a passing jeep. ''Get word to Operations real quick that aircraft 730 has no extra cockpit oxygen outlet — can not handle an extra passenger in the cockpit."

When Gleichauf arrived he said, "They switched the General to another ship. The target is Leverkusson, at the edge of the Ruhr Valley."

There were groans from the crew.

"Cut the bitching. Major Hall, the Group Operations Officer, will lead the 381st." He turned to Harkness. "Watch close for flak damage under the engines."

With Hall leading I knew it would be a smooth, well executed mission if the weather permitted. The takeoff was efficient and on time. The weather had improved so much it looked like we might be able to proceed with the operation.

"Pilot from Navigator."

"Go ahead."

"We'll hit the Coast at eleven hundred hours. Fighters can show any time."

The P-47 escort arrived as we crossed the coast and shortly afterward the intercom came on: "Ball to Copilot — fighters at four o'clock low comin' up."

"Tail to Ball, what are those fighters tryin' to do? I've never seen them circle around down below us before?"

"Don't know. Maybe it's a new tactic against the 47's."

"Copilot, I can see at least thirty from the turret."

I looked up in time to see eight 47's streaking down at high speed followed by the remainder of the escort. For a few minutes there was a marvelous view of about forty P-47's tangling with about fifty M.E. 109's. It was the biggest dogfight I ever saw — a gigantic twisting, turning, diving battle that was soon out of my range of view.

At the I.P. I saw the first B-17 go down from a fighter attack. Suddenly ice began to form inside the turret glass and cut my vision to zero. Where was the moisture coming from? The cockpit windows and windshield were clear.

"Copilot to Turret — Copilot to Turret — four fighters crossing in front of us at ten o'clock high — let 'em have it."

I scraped the ice furiously. When I could see, they were too far away to get in my sights. Gleichauf was caustic. "Why in the hell didn't you shoot? They were right in front of you!"

"Ice! The turret glass is iced up — barely see out of it. Scraping it off as fast as I can. Don't know where the moisture came from."

The aircraft was another of those old "E" models with small Ball and Top Turret oxygen tanks. "Ball to Waist. Ball to Right Waist — "It's time to refill the ball oxygen tank."

"OK, Ball, turn it around forward and hold it there. Don't move that ball until I tell you it's clear."

"Got it, Jim."

Remembering what happened the day we flew Tinker Toy, Jim had George standing by with a walk-around bottle in case ice should form and hold the valves open. When he tried to remove the filler valve it would not release. Realizing that he would have to run back to the waist and get a screwdriver to prize it off, Jim went on intercom: "Waist to Ball, do not move the ball — repeat — do not move the ball, until you hear me say clear."

All Harkness heard distinctly was the word clear. "Thanks, Jim," he said, and whirled the ball back into action and snapped off the filler line. The oxygen pressure in the left side aft system of the Waist and Tail vanished as the gas spewed out. Fortunately the pressure in the ball held firm.

"Radio to crew. Radio to crew. The left rear oxygen system is gone. Switch to the right system."

My ear phones were so poor that I could not pick up what was going on in the aft section of the ship. Really it was no serious matter, as the mission was relatively short. We had plenty of oxygen but Sanford, flying left waist, failed to hear the warning and keeled over and passed out. Counce quickly switched his hose to the right side regulator and he revived.

"Bombardier to Waist."

"Go ahead."

"Is everything OK back there?"

"I think so. I can't tell about Legg. I think he's OK 'cause he looks like he's sitting up at his position."

"Bombardier to Tail."

"Bombardier to Tail — Bombardier to Tail — come in."

There was no response.

"Waist?"

"Go ahead."

"Go back and check out the Tail Gunner."

When Jim got to where he could see Legg clearly he realized the tail gunner was in very serious condition, and had to have oxygen fast or he was going to suffer brain damage or worse! Jim struggled valiantly to untangle the gunner's hose and switch him to the undamaged right side system, but Raymond had collapsed so that he was lying on his hose. There was only room in the tail for one man. Counce knew that man had to have oxygen quickly. Without a moment's hesitation he unhooked from his portable bottle and plugged Legg into it. He knew he would probably pass out before he could get back to his waist position, and he did. But Sanford quickly revived him and no harm was done.

"Tail from Waist — Tail from Waist."

"This is the Tail, go ahead."

"Are you all right?"

"I guess so — a little dizzy — but I'll make it."

"Keep your regulator on the right side system. The left system is empty."

"OK — Waist — that's what the trouble was? Thanks for straightening me out."

While Legg was unconscious he suffered a severe electrical burn on his leg where the electric suit pressed too tightly against him. When off of oxygen for an extended period, the bodily resistance to high or low temperature plummets.

"Ball to Copilot, my electric heat has gone out — hope I can keep from freezing a foot or hand."

"Use straight oxygen. That'll help some."

In the ball the gunner had less room for bulky clothes so he depended more on his electrically heated equipment than the rest of us. I felt the bombs fall away. It told me we would be free of that miserable flak in a few more minutes. That was the main thing I wanted right then.

"Turret to Ball, exercise your hands and feet as much as you can. A little exercise can stave off frostbite."

"Turret to crew. Turret to crew — Fighters at one o'clock high."

The attacks were directed to the high squadron and I did not have a good opportunity to fire.

"Tail to crew, another Fort going down at eight o'clock low — four chutes."

A Fort nearby caught heavy damage to number three engine. An oil or fuel line was ruptured and a long stream of flame shot back as far as the tail. Several men dropped out of the waist hatch. One unfortunate crewman pulled his ripcord too soon and the silk blossomed up into the flame. It instantly began to blaze. I watched in stunned horror as the condemned man started his terrifying plunge toward Earth five miles below!

"Copilot to crew — that's the third Fort I've seen go down so far."

The fighters kept circling the formation making sporadic passes. They were by no means a hot interceptor group. I suspected they were green German pilots. It was time for the attrition of war to begin decimating the excellent pilots with whom Germany had started the war. Ten minutes from the coast the intercom came on: "Tail to crew — another

B-17 dropping down at five o'clock.''

"Copilot to Ball — do you see it?''

"Yes. I see it. No chutes so far. It looks to be under control.'' After some more questions Kels announced, ''That must have been Nixon's plane. I guess he knew he could not make it across the Channel.''

The way I saw it Nixon decided to give the crew a chance to bail out rather than risk a water ditching. Those men were old friends and it was depressing to see them lost. Well, it would be better for them to jump if they couldn't make it to England. With bad visibility shaping up the chances of getting picked up from the water before dark were poor. Few survived a night drifting on the cold Channel.

The total loss was twenty Forts, which was too high in view of the moderate opposition.

December 5 — Paris   *Aircraft 730*

Jim Counce and I were scheduled to ride with the crew of Lt. Deering, the pilot George Reese was with when they accidentally came down over the Continent. I suspect that the assignment was to give Deering a little experience in his crew, but there was not always any particular reason for assignments. The raid would be Deering's second attempt and I was leary of him as a pilot. Of course Jim, as well as myself, was annoyed at being put with a green crew. The Paris area always threatened to throw Goering's crack ''Yellow Nose'' squadrons at us, and they were as mean as fighters could be. If they caught us near the target, with a pilot throttle-jockeying the formation, it would send out a clear signal of ''green crew — hit it first.''

Riding in the rear of the personnel truck in complete darkness to the perimeter where the aircraft were parked was a different experience each mission morning. Some days the men were morosely silent, lost in speculation of what the next few hours would be like. Or they were gabby, covering their anxieties with the bravado of inane chatter. That morning I did not see them get into the truck so they were only voices in the darkness.

"Why the hell didn't they send someone to tell us they were loading bombs last night? We closed the Goddam pub. I feel like hell.''

"Some pure oxygen will snap you out of it — always works for me when I got a hangover.''

"The way you soaked up the ale last night I bet you piss in your pants down in the ball today.''

"Hey, you remember that red headed broad we saw at the pub last week?''

"Yeah — she looked good."

"I had her out two nights ago."

"How was it?"

"Allllll right! Her ole man only gets home every three weeks and she can't wait that long."

"We got us a new boy flyin' Navigator today. Our Navigator's got the clap — on that last pass to London I guess."

"They can cure the clap easy now with that sulpha stuff — dries it right up."

"Let's hope it stays dried up."

We got out at aircraft 719 and as the truck pulled out I could hear the conversational drivel still going on. "Hey, let's go to Ridgewell tonight — there's a blond bitch you'd go for . . ."

The crew chief headed my way with a glum look on his face, "Sorry, but 719 is redlined for today."

"Damn! We draw a green crew an' now the airplane's cancelled out."

Jim asked, "What's wrong with it?"

"Number three is vibrating too much — real rough."

"Did you call Engineering?" I asked.

"Yeah, they're sendin' a truck to pick ya up."

Jim growsed, "Another one of those delays — not enough time to get the guns ready — and on top of that a new crew."

The wait for the truck wasted precious time needed to get the aircraft, whatever one it would be, ready for a mission. When we finally piled out at the replacement airplane it was near engine starting time. Deering arrived at the same time we did.

"Pilot," I said, "we don't have time left to get the guns ready. How about calling Operations and telling them that we will be late taking off because of a last minute change of aircraft?"

Operations told Deering to try to catch the formation over the Channel and set up a rendezvous time. Of course formations were rarely that close on timing. A minor mechanical problem added another ten minutes to the takeoff delay.

When the aircraft finally became airborne we were twenty minutes late. It was time consuming for the process of squadrons to gather their planes, then for the groups to form and the wing to assemble into proper positions. Deering had instructions to head straight for the final rendezvous over the Channel. When we got to the Channel the 381st was in sight but so far ahead that to try to catch up was impractical. We trailed the rest of the way over water midway between two groups. I think

Deering still hoped to overtake the 381st.

"Top Turret to Pilot."

"Go ahead."

"Fighters can show up any time now. Not good being out of a formation."

He did not reply.

Ten minutes later he still had made no move to get into a formation. That was how aircraft got shot down. Flight Engineers do not tell pilots what to do, but something had to be done right away.

"Top Turret to Pilot."

"Go ahead."

"There's a vacant spot in the high group to our left — it's always better to be in the high group if fighters attack."

"Good idea — don't think we can catch the 381st."

"No chance of that."

A few minutes later Deering pulled into the high group and I felt a hundred percent better about the situation.

"Pilot to Copilot."

"Go ahead."

"I hope they don't raise hell about us bein' in the wrong group."

So that was what had been worrying him. I suppose he did get chewed out for that episode with Reese and he did not want to get back on the carpet on his next flight.

"Top Turret to Pilot. Don't worry about that. Planes fly with other groups all the time when they can't find their own outfits. You got a good excuse. Operations didn't really expect you to catch our Wing when they saw you take off twenty minutes late."

"Thanks."

After that Deering relaxed and did what I thought was an excellent job for a pilot with so little formation experience. We got off in such a hurry that all I knew about the target was that it was an aircraft plant somewhere near Paris.

"Copilot to crew — I've got good news for you. Today we're gonna have a P-51 escort. How about that?"

Super news! At last we were getting what had been billed as a long-range fighter that would be a match for the best Germany could throw at us. We would soon find out if the P-51's were that good.

"Tail to crew — fighters at six o'clock high."

As soon as they were close enough I saw what they were. "Top Turret to crew — they are P-51's."

They were beautiful airplanes. I wondered if the Germans knew we had P-51's in England and what they thought about them. The secret had been well kept from the bomber crews. I watched with glee as the 51's drove off a handful of Jerry fighters and stayed with us to the I.P., where a group of P-47's with the larger disposable fuel tanks took over escort duties. Shortly afterwards seven F.W. 190's came poking up toward us. The 47's dived after them and the action moved beyond my vision. As far as I saw there were no fighter attacks against the formations. Visibility was zero over the target. The weather forecast missed completely.

"Pilot to Bombardier — we going to drop the bombs?"

"Not on this target — they may try an alternate."

The soup covered Europe, and by that time Bomber Command in England knew it. The B-17's turned back to England with no blow struck against Adolf. It was a frustrating day, with so much effort expended for no results. At one-thirty we touched down at Ridgewell Airdrome. Seven more raids would put me over the top. With those P-51 beauties, my prospects looked far brighter.

The P-51 Mustang Fighter began as a mediocre low-level fighter used mainly for strafing. The original Allison engine was replaced with the Rolls Royce Merlin engine. Other modifications were made and it emerged as the finest propellor-driven fighter plane of World War II. With disposable fuel tanks, the plane could go with the bombers to the deepest targets.

After the landing I singled out Lt. Deering. "I want to compliment you for the way you held tight formation today. That is the best I've seen for a new pilot since I arrived in England. If you keep that up, your crew will be OK."

December 6

When newspapers from the U.S. occasionally found their way overseas, there were distorted stories and statements about the war that were irritating. I remember one silly news article: a U.S. Senator said the German Air Force was almost eliminated. That was 1943 when the Luftwaffe was at its height. A Congressman orated that the war would be over by June, the date of the Normandy Landing. An American newspaper was an object of both nostalgia and derision at some of the fanciful tales.

December 8

If a Sunday was free I sometimes attended Chapel Services on the base. The Chaplain was named Brown and he got along well with the

English people who lived nearby. I can remember the familier sight of the farm families from close by walking down the runways on Sunday mornings to church. One Sunday about time services were to begin, a large, awkward soldier in oil-stained coveralls and muddy shoes stumbled down the aisle and took a front seat. Obviously, he came directly from work. That was certainly all right, but it seemed to me he should have taken a back row seat in his soiled clothes as the civilians were dressed in their best. A few minutes later that big bear of a man with grimy hands stood and faced the audience. "Suddenly he was transformed: the notes of the "Lord's Prayer" in a powerful and beautiful baritone voice filled the Chapel. It was a magnificent solo, as good as any of the top rated baritones of that day could have done. When the last notes died away, his shoulders sagged and he was once again a weary G.I. mechanic. He nodded to the Chaplain and was gone. Who was he? With such a voice he had to be a highly trained professional singer. I never discovered his name or saw him again around the base. In this time of war any man in uniform might have been a well-known name that one did not recognize among the thousands wearing military garb that made us all look a little alike.

Eight months earlier, when we were a newly formed flight crew at Boise, Idaho, I arrived at the aircraft site for a night flight ahead of the rest of the crew.

The instructor pilot was already there, so we went through the pre-flight inspection procedure, and I picked up the aircraft flight form to write in the names of those on the flight.

"Sir, may I have your name, rank and serial number?"

"Oh, let me have it and I'll fill it in. That way I know I'll get the serial number right," he replied.

There was a wearisome two hour flight with six of us crowded into the cockpit space. A week later I was in the P.X. Barber Shop getting a haircut when the same instructor pilot came in. I noticed that he went out of his way to nod to everyone nearby.

"That officer must be a politician in civilian life," I whispered to the barber.

"Don't you know who he is?"

"Sure. The name is Stewart — instructor pilot."

"Don't you recognize Jimmy Stewart, the movie actor?"

CHAPTER XIX
Mission to Emden

December 11 —
Emden, Germany   *Aircraft 719 — Hellcat*

Our aircraft was ready to fly again, we hoped, and the question was, would it handle as well as it did before the damage? It was snowing when Gleichauf pulled the wet nose of 719 into the air and the thick gray soup. Pilots detested that nerve-wracking procedure that could at any time so easily end in a head-on crash with another plane. The flight of airplanes could not be held precisely to the exacting specifications of the briefing plan, and especially with so many pilots short of flying experience.

"Pilot to crew — keep alert — it's going to be thick today — Bombardier."

"Go ahead, Paul."

"Watch ahead — if you see anything call out quick."

He turned to me. "Get in the turret and help us look — keep a sharp eye above us."

"I know how many green pilots are taking off this morning all over England. That's what bothers me most in this stuff," I said to George Reese, who was our copilot for the mission.

"Bothers both of us," he replied.

"Pilot! Pilot! Eleven o'clock level — that dark blob! What is it?"

After intense scrutiny it turned out to be a splotch of darker cloud. But with nerves drawn tight we were ready to see the dark form of an aircraft on a collision course.

At nine thousand feet we broke through into brilliant sunshine and a sparkling sky. The world atop the fleecy billowing clouds was one apart from the winter drab and mud below. I had not seen the sun in so long it was reassuring to know it was still shining, and that the sky was as blue as I remembered it.

"Navigator to crew — Navigator to crew — the temperature will be only thirty-eight below today. We'll have an escort of P-51's at the German Coast and we'll sic them on those Jerry fighters and sit back and watch the fun."

The target was the port facilities at Emden, Germany, from an altitude of twenty-three thousand feet, lower than usual. We were scheduled to fly with a high composite Group made up of elements from several groups in order to add extra strength. The slow climb to nine thousand feet through fog disrupted the timing enough that our squadron missed the Group we were supposed to be part of. That left the decision of what to do to the Squadron Commander and he elected to go on alone.

A little before ten o'clock we started across the North Sea toward Germany bucking a strong head wind that required heavy power on the four engines. Even so, the crossing consumed two hours, because the velocity of the head wind subtracted from the air speed of the ship.

Emden was not regarded as a difficult target, but the formation that day turned out to be ragged, with aircraft throttle jockeying back and forth.

"Damn these new pilots — I can't keep up a steady air speed — one minute I'm drawing too much power and the next minute we're barely above stalling," fumed Gleichauf.

"Cline's raisin' hell every time you dogleg," said the Copilot.

"Navigator to Pilot, there's the Freisian Islands right at one o'clock."

A voice cut in on the intercom. "Hey, Bombardier, drop some bombs on that seaplane ramp and watch the Krauts scatter."

"Copilot to crew, cut the unnecessary chatter."

"Bombardier to crew, single fighter coming from the South at nine o'clock high."

The solitary M.E. 109 circled us cautiously for a few minutes.

"Bombardier to crew — flak at twelve o'clock level."

Fortunately it did not amount to much, then the Navigator spotted something. "Fighters at ten o'clock — about thirty-five of them."

The enemy interceptors came in to five thousand yards and after a few minutes pulled away to the left and were soon out of sight. For some reason not known to us they elected not to attack. It could have been that they were at the far end of their fuel range.

"Pilot to Navigator, where did you say the escort would pick us up?"

"At the coast, Paul. If they are comin' we oughta see 'em soon. In five minutes we'll swing to the right inshore then make two left turns to come in over the target downwind."

Fifteen minutes went by and Purus called, "We're starting the bomb run."

"OK, Bombardier."

Flak began popping at us as we approached the target. There was a loud crashing sound from the rear section of the aircraft.

"Copilot to Waist, anyone hurt? Any damage?"

"This is Jim — big chunk struck where I was standin'. The armor plate deflected it. Otherwise would have got me. No serious damage."

Bombardier to Radio, stand by to watch bomb bay doors down."

George, as usual, was standing with the front radio door open to watch the bombs fall out. "Radio to Bombardier — Radio to Bombardier, over."

"Go ahead, Radio."

"Three bombs hung up in the racks. Thousand pounder stuck on the bottom rack an' two five hundred pounders on top of it."

"Turret to Bombardier, I'm goin' back to release the bombs."

"OK, John — Radio, stand by to see if Turret needs any help."

The bomb load was mixed. Thousand pounders were carried on the lower racks while five hundred pounders were hung on the middle racks. Above those were clusters of either incendiaries or fragmentation bombs held in place by small steel cables. The situation in the bomb bay was a weird mess. One thousand pounder had failed to release on a rack well below the catwalk. Resting on top of it two five hundred pounders were also hung up on the loose cables used to hold the fragmentation bombs in the racks. To trip the rack shackle on the lower bomb a screw driver had to be used, but access to the shackle was blocked by one of the five hundred pounders directly on top of the big one. I caught a glimpse of Balmore in the radio room motioning me to return to the cockpit.

"Turret to Bombardier, it'll take two of us to clear the bomb bay."

"OK. We'll wait 'til we are down to fifteen thousand feet."

It would have been foolish to attempt the release at high altitude because of the limited working time of the portable walk-around bottles, and the risk of losing oxygen and tumbling out into space. A few minutes later I called Purus again. "The thousand pounder is stuck on the lowest inside rack below the catwalk. The two five hundreds are resting on top of it and tangled up in the loose cables from the frag cluster."

"When we release the thousand pounder, will the two fives fall free?"

"It's impossible to tell for sure. We may have to cut them loose," I answered.

"How can we cut those steel cables?"

"I always carry some hack saw blades, Bombardier. One of us is going to have to hang down below the walk and slip a screwdriver between the big one and the fives on top of it."

"I'm smaller than you so I'll do it while you hold my legs."

"OK. I will straddle the catwalk and lock my legs around it. You hang down in front of me so I can get a good hold on your legs. We got to be careful that when that big one falls out the fives don't knock us off of the catwalk."

At fifteen thousand feet we cut loose of oxygen and began the risky procedure that had to be done. An airplane could not land at an airfield with hung up bombs. The risk was too great to the other aircraft and base facilities. I sat on the narrow catwalk and locked my legs around it. Purus climbed over me and slid head down so I could grasp his legs. There was barely enough room between the bombs to work. Johnny carefully pushed the long screwdriver, working by feel in the cramped space between the bombs. When he got the tool in position to attempt the release he looked back at me, and I increased my grip on him and the narrow beam we were sitting on. We did not know which way the two upper bombs would move and had to be ready. When he pushed the shackle release the big one let go smoothly and the other two bombs shifted their hang positions slightly but not enough to endanger us. That was a tremendous relief! But not for long! The two five hundreds began to swing back and forth on the cables, striking the vertical support beams on each swing. Theoretically they were not supposed to explode as long as the impellor was in place, but I would have preferred not to put the theory to a test.

Now it was my turn. With Purus holding me I leaned far out and began sawing away at the steel cable holding the closest of the two remaining bombs with a hacksaw blade. Meanwhile we were speeding across the North Sea assisted by a terrific tail wind that Purus and I had forgotten about. At the moment the first five hundred pounder broke off and fell free I caught a frantic signal from Balmore at the door of the radio room. He pointed down: to my horror that bomb was headed straight for an English sea plane base on the Coast of England. All I could do was watch in shocked consternation. As it neared the base the bomb appeared to the eye to veer slightly seaward and struck the water fifty yards from the ramp. It was frightfully close to a disaster! Gleichauf turned back over the sea and circled until I cut the last bomb hazard loose.

When I returned to the cockpit Gleichauf was visibly upset. "What were you trying to do? Wipe out an English base?"

"We forgot about that strong tail wind."

"We had been trying to stop you back there," he replied testily.

"You can't hear much in an open bomb bay with that deafening wind noise."

"We'll get chewed out when we get back to Ridgewell — maybe some disciplinary action — you can bet on that!" And he was right. We knew the English would get our aircraft number and lodge an angry complaint.

When the Bombardier raised the doors a limit switch failed to shut off and the circuit began to sputter and smoke, but fortunately I was nearby and saw it quickly. That circuit fuse should have blown out instantly, breaking the current connection. I had no choice but to reach in with my fingers and pull out that hot fuse to avoid a fire. It was painful and I had bandaged fingers for a week, but was far better than what a cockpit fire could have done to us. It would be interesting to know what the odds were against two malfunctions on the same circuit at the same time.

Forts out ahead of us ran into trouble and fourteen B-17's were lost. Our gunners claimed the ridiculous figure of one hundred and thirty-seven German fighters shot down. My guess was that thirty-five would have been a high kill. With so many duplicated gunner claims our figures for enemy aircraft shot down were becoming a joke. No one who knew first hand how tough those fighters were paid serious attention to our extravagant claims.

An incredulous major at Group Operations the next day was caustic!

"You say a thousand pound bomb stuck on the lower racks and two five hundreds on top of it tangled in loose cables from the fragmentation clusters carried on the top racks?" the Major asked.

"Yes, sir."

"And you just happened by some odd chance to have some hacksaw blades on hand? Is that what you expect me to believe?"

"Yes, sir — we always have some hacksaw blades."

He looked at us in disbelief, "You always carry hacksaw blades! No other crew in England does! You expect me to repeat this wild tale to the English?"

"But we are telling you the straight truth, Major," Purus insisted.

That night I repeated the conversation to Counce at the hut. "I wouldn't have believed it either," he said, "if I was in his position. Two bombs hangin' up on cables at one time must be a million to one chance."

"Jim, do you remember how we wondered why the people at Boeing Aircraft recommended a half dozen hacksaw blades as part of what flight engineers should carry on missions, along with the other tool list they made up at our request?"

December 12

One very cold night in London I was with Jim in a cab about two A.M. returning from Kensington to our hotel. The night was exceptionally dark under the blackout common at that period of the war. The two small slits in the headlights that were permitted gave the driver little illumination to negotiate the maze of twisting streets. I had no idea where we were and do not see how Jim could have known either. He turned to me. "Pay the driver my part of the fare and I will repay you tomorrow. I'll meet you at the club about noon. OK?"

I looked at him in amazement. "What are you talking about?"

"Driver, let me out here, please."

He got out and disappeared into the blackness of the bitterly cold night. "See you tomorrow."

Had he completely gone off of the deep end? There was no way he could have known where we were. There was not a thing open at that time of night in the area he chose to get out. The next day he met me at noon in a bright, cheerful mood as if nothing unusual had happened. He made no move to explain his unorthodox behavior and, since it was none of my business, I did not ask him. Neither of us ever mentioned the incident. Jim was like that. When I thought I had him figured out he would shock me with some bizarre act totally out of context with his character or usual habits. Jim shared my taste for good music so we saw some excellent musicals at the Prince of Wales Theater. One evening we were fortunate to get tickets to a fine performance of the opera La Traviata.

CHAPTER XX
Mission to Bremen

December 13 — Bremen   *Aircraft 730*

Reese flicked on the lights and his voice broke the silence: "All right! Let's go! Out of that sack! Lancia, don't screw up today — this is your twenty-fifth — good luck."

Green asked Lancia, "How do you feel?"

"Lousy! Couldn't sleep last night — wide awake — but I'm gonna make it today."

Ugo had been sweating out this mission for several weeks because of some illness that had him temporarily grounded. As we left the hut everyone shook hands with Lancia and wished him the best of luck. The trip would make twenty missions for me and should have been good news except for a strange phenomenon: luck ran out for so many men in the 381st Group in the final quarter of the game. We have talked about a jinx airplane and for a while it looked to us like the 381st might have been a jinx group. Why was it so difficult for a 533rd man to complete twenty-five missions? Why had nearly every man who approached the finish line met with disaster? Only a handful had succeeded in running the twenty-five mission hurdle. Was it merely coincidence? What about the Fortress taking off with nearly all the crew on their twenty-fifth and exploding? It was like an evil force hovering over the 381st ready to cut men down just as they neared success. That day Ugo was on a crew composed mainly of men reaching for the elusive last raid. We were anxiously awaiting the verdict, hoping they broke through the hard luck syndrome we had seen too often. Rogers and Balmore were still adamant that it was the odds catching up that explained the heavy loss of men nearly through. Regardless of what the real reasons were, a psychic wall was slowly developing in the minds of those who were getting close to the magic number. Combat men tended to be superstitious and watched with dismay as the pattern repeated so many times that it no longer appeared to them to be a series of coincidences.

Takeoff time was nine o'clock into a dense cloud bank fifteen hundred feet high. Above the weather was bright and clear.

"Pilot to Navigator — that fog was extra thick — you think it will dissipate by the time we get back?"

"I hope so, but it don't look like one that'll burn off as soon as the sun heats it up."

There was no use worrying about it. If it hung on until we returned it would create pure chaos with so many planes trying to land in a short time period. At eight thousand feet the Wing turned out over the North Sea and began a steady climb to the scheduled altitude.

"Pilot to Navigator — why are we making a left turn?"

"We're starting a three sixty to balance the timing of the Wings because we're fifteen minutes early."

After the formation circled the Copilot came on intercom: "The wing ahead is gettin' hit by fighters — I can see the cannon flashes."

"Turret to crew — they lost a Fort at nine o'clock low — I see two chutes."

"Ball to crew — two more chutes opened up before it exploded."

"Bombardier to crew, three Forts aborting the wing ahead — I don't see any feathered engines or smoke."

I watched them drop down just over the cloud layer, as if they intended to use the clouds if necessary. The abortion looked suspect to me — a severe breach of discipline. Meanwhile the formation passed Bremen to the right and made two left turns to pick up downwind currents over the target for maximum airspeed. We knew what the flak would be like and I am sure the rest of the crew was dreading it as much as I was.

"Waist to Turret."

"Go ahead, Jim."

"My gloves an' shoes just went out an' we got a long way to go before we come down."

"Try to find out which unit is burned out and use your short circuit plug." (The heated suit electrical system was a series circuit, like old time Christmas tree lights. If one unit burned out it broke the circuit and knocked out the rest of the units. I made some special plugs that could be used to shunt the current around a defective unit to restore power to the other units.)

"The plug is in my electric suit. Remember that they couldn't locate my suit at Equipment Check Out this morning and gave me this spare?"

"I'll pass my short circuit plugs back to Radio an' you can get them from him — Radio?"

"Go ahead, this is Radio."

"Meet me on the catwalk."

Ten minutes later Shutting called: "Navigator to Pilot."

"Go ahead — this is the Copilot — Paul's on command."

"Tell him the I.P. is coming up right away."

I expected the usual flak spectacular but this time special tactics were used in an attempt to reduce flak damage. Three wings were sent over Bremen at closely timed intervals and widely varying altitudes to confuse the anti-aircraft gunners.

"Bombardier to crew, flak ahead — it's coming up all over."

The expected flak intensity was there, but the plan did work. Even though the volume of fire was as heavy as usual, the accuracy was nothing like the last time we were over Bremen.

"Navigator to Copilot, look at that formation of B-24's at twenty thousand feet — they're taking a lot of flak off of us."

"Bombardier to crew, fighters ten o'clock low."

"Ball to crew, Focke Wolfe 190's six o'clock low."

"Turret to crew, vapor trails very high catching up with us — P-47's I think."

"Waist to crew, Fort goin' down at three o'clock low — Jerry fighter on fire and out of control."

Dogfights erupted at high and low levels. Fast thinking saved an unknown P-47 pilot. A Jerry fighter got on the tail of the 47 and hung there; the pilot had an inspiration. He dived straight down toward the edge of the Fortress formation with the Jerry still on his tail and unaware of what awaited. When the 47 flashed by us at short-range, fifty guns slammed into the enemy fighter turning it into flaming debris.

"Tail to crew, B-17 pulling out of formation — engine feathered. Hey! Wait a minute! Three 47's are coming down and slowing to his speed — they're flying along side to give him protection."

The 47's stayed with that crippled ship until the formation pulled so far ahead that I could no longer see them.

"Waist to Turret, Ugo just about has it made."

Twenty more P-47's arrived to relieve the first Thunderbolt escort. It was hard to remember that only a few weeks ago the short-ranged escort was ineffective. Now with long-range fighters and larger disposable fuel tanks it was a different war. I would have liked to have bought a drink — a big double — for every escort pilot who helped keep the Bogies off of us.

"Bombardier to Copilot, I can see fighters hitting the wing ahead of us."

"This is the Navigator, there goes another Fort."

I saw only four Forts go down that day. It must have been some kind of record. The total loss for the mission was eleven aircraft, which was modest in view of the tough target for the day.

"Waist to crew, I know Lancia has it made now. We're nearly to the coast. He's going to break the jinx."

"There will be a big celebration tonight," Wilson added.

When the aircraft landed the procedure was normal. I turned around to pick up some equipment and the brakes failed. Gleichauf turned off into the mud to let it stop the aircraft. It was a muddy mess but there was no damage to the ship. Later the crew chief told me that a hydraulic fitting snapped off from the landing impact.

The celebration started before I got back to the barracks, after the guns were put into good order for a possible raid the next day. Some men from the 533rd Squadron had finally completed twenty-five missions! It could be done! The black clouds dispersed and a collective sigh of relief rolled over the Squadron. That night the nearby pubs were packed with celebrants and glasses were raised to the six men who swept away the barrier. There was now little doubt in my mind that I would soon join the selected band. I expected Ugo to put on a wild demonstration, but to my surprise he was quiet and somber. Perhaps the full impact had not yet had time to come through to him.

Air Sea Rescue (No Mission)   *Aircraft 765*
December 14

The night before, The Royal Air Force made a raid against Germany and encountered heavy opposition. On the return a number of Lancasters were forced down at sea shortly before dawn. Any R.A.F. men who made it into rafts might have survived that day, but they had small chance to last out that night. The area covering all of the water where they could have ditched was divided into search areas by grid lines. One aircraft was assigned to each search area. The plan was an exacting one for the Navigator, Lt. Smith. He certainly was a busy man, carefully calling out headings to the pilot so that all of the area was checked. The constant staring at the waves became nauseating. For hours we were just above the wave tops peering intently at the water for some signs of a rubber raft.

"Pilot from Nose — Pilot from Nose, what's that black spot at nine o'clock?"

"I don't see it."

"I see it from the turret."

We came around over the spot and it was a water soaked piece of timber. Later the Tail called, "There's somethin' at five o'clock — I think — not sure — it looks like — well, I don't know—."

It proved to be nothing except a dark blob of water and an imagination.

"Navigator to Pilot, if there are any rafts out here I hope we can spot them."

"I guess we are all thinking the same thing — next time it might be us out in that cold water," replied Gleichauf.

We knew that whoever was there and still alive had only an hour or two of daylight left and would never survive the night if not found before visibility faded out. For eight hours we scanned the waves. Nothing! Just empty water! At some time during the day we were not too far from the Coast of Denmark. The danger was slight because we were too low for radar to spot us and it was highly unlikely that there would be armed patrol planes over the area. By dusk every man on the ship was half sick. The sensation was similar to seasickness. The unfortunate R.A.F. crews who were hopefully waiting for rescue were not located. Perhaps none of them made it out of the Lancasters in time. The big British bombers were less sturdy than the Forts and more likely to break up in the process of ditching. We were more than glad to help in the rescue act because the R.A.F. pilots frequently provided escort for us, and without some escort the bomber groups would have suffered an intolerable casualty percentage.

December 17

Ugo Lancia left for the port of embarkation to the U.S. and in spite of his noise and gusto, I was reluctant to see him leave. Without his lively spirit the hut would not be the same, indeed it would be too quiet. Instead of the wild celebrating I expected him to do, Lancia was restrained and quiet his last days at the hut, as if torn between relief that combat duty was over and a sense of belonging with the rest of us. Until then I had relished the idea of more peace and quiet, but now I would have traded it for the noise and confusion Ugo created. I had become fond of that big, brash Italian but I never got around to letting him know it.

There was an unspoken feeling among men who have lived together and fought side by side that has no parallel in civilian life. We all went to the train to see Ugo off. I realized that barring some unforeseen coincidence I would never see him again. Oh, we mumbled words like "we'll write and keep in touch" but it would not happen, and we knew it. Separated by time and distance, the letters and cards we intended to write would get sidetracked until the relationships would fade out. Tucked away in a far corner of the mind a flicker of remembrances would surface at odd moments, but by then the addresses would be lost or obsolete.

That night things were depressed after the departure of Ugo's exuberant personality. Tedesco remarked, "Well, it's the beginning of the end for Cahow's crew.''

Someone asked, ''How many missions does Cahow need?''

''I don't know for sure — three I think,'' Tedesco answered.

Jim Counce and I had the same number of missions completed, but Balmore trailed by five, due to recurrent frostbite injuries that grounded him three or four times.

''John, you and Jim will finish way ahead of me, and I'll end up as a spare radio for whatever crew needs one.''

''Now wait, George Reese is your friend and he'll see that you get on decent crews.''

''But you and Jim will go back to the States and we will get separated an' you know what that means.''

''You're probably right,'' Counce added, ''but I know the three of us will keep in touch and get together now and then after the war is over.''

December 18

Three days earlier Carroll Wilson had been on a rough raid with another crew and he suffered internal injuries from the banging around in the waist caused by the pilot taking severe evasive action to blunt the effectiveness of fighter attacks. In spite of his goof-offs, which were legion, he was a likeable youngster with good potential. All he needed was some responsibility to bring out his merit. When the going was extra tough, Wilson reached back into the reserve that some people are born with and came up with whatever was needed for the day to see it through. Compared to that, what else really mattered? He was transferred to a recovery hospital at another base and it was depressing to see him go. I knew there was a good chance I would be gone from Ridgewell before he returned.

CHAPTER XXI
Mission to Bremen

December 20 - Bremen   *Aircraft 730*

Harold Harkness was back with us in the ball turret after recovering from the painful glass in his eye injury. It was good to have a competent man watching things below the aircraft. Raymond Legg was grounded, due to burns suffered when he became unconscious for too long in the tail. Wineski, a member of the Free Polish Air Force, was with us on the tail guns. He had escaped from Poland when the Germans invaded his country and joined the R.A.F. for a while before he was transferred to the American Air Force. He was an experienced gunner and we were glad to have him. La Buda was on the left waist guns taking Wilson's place.

The aircraft lifted from the runway at eight thirty, just as dawn was breaking. Shutting called the Copilot. "Did you ever see a more beautiful sunrise?"

Before he could answer Gleichauf cut in, "Keep the intercom clear — no personal conversation."

"Navigator to crew — Navigator to crew, the altitude today will be twenty-nine thousand, five hundred feet and the temperature will be sixty below. Watch yourselves for frostbite."

It turned out to be the coldest temperature I have ever had to endure. At nine thirty we went on oxygen and the long climb began. At ten thirty the Wing headed over the North Sea toward Germany. The target was Bremen again, with that awful flak. When I saw the coast approaching, I called the Navigator. "What is our altitude and temperature?"

"We are at twenty-seven, five hundred and the temperature gauge is against the stop — low as it can register — sixty-two degrees below."

"Navigator, how cold is that on the Fahrenheit scale?"

"About eighty below — an' we got another two thousand to climb. It's goin' to be between eighty and ninety below Fahrenheit at our top altitude — real balmy — you can take off your shirt and get a good suntan in the turret."

"Turret to crew, at this temperature if any of your electric units go out, it will take heavy exercise to keep from freezing, so watch it."

"Bombardier to crew, we'll take more frequent oxygen checks today."

Fifteen minutes into Germany Purus came on intercom: "Oxygen check — report in."

"Turret an' cockpit OK."

"Radio, rajah."

"Ball OK."

"Navigator OK."

"Waist OK."

"Bombardier to Tail — come in."

"Bombardier to Tail — Bombardier to Tail — report in."

There was no response.

"Bombardier to Waist."

"This is Jim, go ahead."

"Go back and check out the Tail."

"Rajah, will do."

Counce snapped his mask into a walk-around bottle, picked up a reserve constant-flow oxygen container and headed for the tail. Jim found Wineski passed out and immediately started working on him. Then his own regulator froze and cut off his oxygen supply. The demand-type regulator was supposed to be impervious to freezing at any temperature, so Jim thought his mask had frozen and hastily went through the procedure to clear a frozen mask. By that time he was too far gone and collapsed on top of the tail gunner. La Buda, the other waist gunner, could not see into the Tail with Jim blocking the view.

"Bombardier to Waist, what is Counce doing? Everything OK?"

"Something is wrong back there! Counce is not moving — repeat — Counce is not moving!"

"Waist! Get back to that Tail quick an' revive those men."

"Radio!"

"Go ahead."

"Take over the waist guns and let us know what is happening back there."

Three to five minutes went by and a frantic Balmore called, "Bombardier! Bombardier! La Buda just passed out an' fell on Counce. For God's sake, send John back there quick! I don't know what to do. Don't let these men die!"

"I'm on my way, Radio. Calm down and keep your mask clear of ice. We can't have another man down."

"Pilot to Copilot, get in the turret until John gets back."

My mind was in a turmoil. I kept asking myself, "What is happening in that tail that has knocked out three experienced men? Anything different today from other days? Yes, the temperature. But that shouldn't cause major trouble. The demand regulators are not affected by low temperature.[1] But what if the regulators are freezing?'' Those thoughts raced through my mind as I got out of the turret and plugged into a walk-around bottle. Instantly my oxygen failed. Hastily I switched back to the turret hose and tapped the walk-around bottle several times hard with a heavy screw driver. I switched back to the bottle and it worked. So that was the problem! The demand regulators were freezing.

"Turret to crew — Turret to crew — listen carefully. The demand regulators are freezing! Repeat: the demand regulators are freezing! If it happens to you, tap the regulator several times with anything handy. A screw driver works fine."

Grabbing four or five bail-out bottles and two walk-arounds, I went aft as rapidly as possible. I kept telling myself, "You must not make any mistakes — if you do some people are going to die — watch what you are doing — no mistakes—."

I heard the nose and turret guns chatter over and over. "All right, keep your mind on what you're doing. Forget the fighters." George was slowly going insane with three men needing help so badly. He had the mental ability to know that if he rushed back to the tail, there would be four men unconscious in short order. When he saw me he was like a man reprieved. I could see a change come over him as he regained his mental composure.

When I reached the tail, La Buda had to be revived first to get him out of the way so I could get to the other two men. Both of their faces were black as coal. The tail gunner looked like he was dead and Jim looked almost as bad. I poured oxygen down La Buda continuously until his color returned and he revived enough for me to clear his regulator and readjust his mask. With La Buda on his feet and helping, we pulled Jim out to where I could get to him. He was awful to look at. The unreal blackness of his usually pale face was terrifying. I had never seen a person off of oxygen that long at thirty thousand feet. "Oh, God," I whispered as a stream of oxygen coursed down his throat, as much as I felt he could stand, "let

[1]The demand type oxygen regulator opened and closed by means of inhaling and exhaling. Up to that time it had been considered impervious to freezing, but the temperature that day was extremely low, perhaps a little beyond the capacity of the regulator to handle. It was the lowest I encountered in seventy five missions over Europe.

him come back — please! Don't let him die!'' When I saw the first signs of color returning, I felt a surge of joy. He was going to make it! As soon as he came to enough to move, we got his mask in position and his regulator working. I sent La Buda to help Jim back to the waist and turned hurriedly to Wineski. There was no doubt in my mind that the tail gunner was dead. His face was coal black, like something out of a bad dream. He was not breathing, because the slightest breath could be seen in that intense cold, and he had already been off of oxygen longer than the medics told us a man could continue to live at thirty thousand feet.

La Buda returned and helped me pull him out of the cramped tail space. Hopeless or not, I had to make every conceivable effort to revive him. I rammed a tube down his throat and injected extra heavy doses of oxygen for a full minute with no success. I knew that if he had the slightest chance it would require some desperate measures! I increased the oxygen pressure, deliberately running the risk of serious if not fatal injury. Those bottles held eighteen hundred pounds of pressure and too much could have ruptured his lungs. It seemed to me that the risk was necessary. That went on for another minute and I had given up all hope when I had a vague feeling of slight movement. At first I thought it was my imagination playing tricks. No! He did move! I was sure I felt something. Then there was a sharp twist of his left leg, and there was no longer any doubt. The man was going to revive. I would not have given him one chance out of a hundred a few minutes earlier. The color slowly returned to his face and I reduced the amount of oxygen and timed the intakes to coincide with my breathing rate. It was a great feeling to see a man return from what I believed to be death. When his color became normal I began working on his regulator with my free hand, while continuing to keep oxygen flowing with the other. Physically, he was coming along well, but I could see from the wild look on his face that he was mentally disoriented. I hoped that it was not a matter of brain damage. Suddenly he drew back his fist and struck me hard on the jaw. I failed to see the blow coming and it knocked me backward and my head hit a metal joint so hard that for a couple of minutes I was mentally out. Counce, who by now was fully recovered, ran back and straightened my mask and helped me up. Meanwhile, Wineski had passed out again when he lost the oxygen I had been feeding him. We got his mask in place and the regulator working normally and watched him closely until sure that his brain was once again functioning. In another five minutes he was back on the tail guns, OK as far as I could determine.

The aircraft was bouncing around so I knew we must be in the middle of the flak. I hoped we were past the target and would quickly get out of the anti-aircraft gunner's range. I was working my way forward carrying an armload of empty oxygen containers To enter the radio room from the waist, one used the top of the ball turret as a step because it was directly in the way. Harkness chose that exact moment to whirl the ball around. Both feet went out from under me and I took a nasty fall. The worst part was that two of the heavy cylinders bounced into the air and struck me on the head with stupefying force as I lay prone on the deck, feeling like a losing fighter just before the referee stops the fight. Two knockout blows in ten minutes — it was not my day!

When I climbed wearily into the turret we were past the target on the way home. I knew from the sounds of gunfire that there was a brisk battle while I was in the tail. The report said that sixty fighters jumped us and I missed the action. The only good thing about the mission was that I did not have to look at the detestable flak over the city of Bremen.

"Radio to Turret."

"Go ahead, George."

"It was close. You got back here just in time. Little longer, an' both Jim and Wineski would have been gone. Right?"

"Yes, it was close for Wineski. He was partly inside the Pearly Gates — or that other place."

"Tail to Turret, was it that close?"

"At first I did not have any hope you would come out of it — how are you feeling?"

"OK, except for a bad headache."

"Navigator to Turret, Tinker Toy got it while you were in the tail."

"Was it flak or fighters?"

"A 109 slammed into her waist and both ships went down locked together, turning end over end."

"It's hard to believe. I thought Tinker Toy would always make it back."

Some of the men heard Lord Haw Haw predict that they would shoot down Tinker Toy. Did the Jerry pilots have some special vendetta for that aircraft that might partly explain her jinx reputation?

"Turret to Navigator, were we supposed to have P-38's on the return?"

"Yes, but they didn't show."

A strong head wind was slowing down the return.

"Bombardier to crew, fighters at twelve o'clock low."

The enemy made two passes and vanished without doing any damage.

"Tail to crew, that B-17 strugglin' behind the formation is about to get it — four fighters are ganging up on her."

I turned around to watch that Fort put up a furious battle and hold off the attackers. I believe it was the only time I ever saw a B-17 survive a fight with that many interceptors. The American papers were full of stories about wounded Fortresses holding off ten or fifteen fighters. Most of those stories were purely imaginary. In the real life of combat over the Continent, it simply did not happen against experienced fighters.

Halfway across the North Sea the tail gunner reported, "Lone 109 closin' fast from the rear."

"What is he goin' to try?" asked the Bombardier.

"Don't know — but he's goin' around to our left."

That audacious fighter pilot pulled ahead of the formation, circled to eleven o'clock, and with guns blazing whipped straight at us.

"Navigator to crew, look at that bastard — did you ever see such guts?"

What did a military formation do to a gallant airman blithely taking on deadly odds? The book said shoot him down, but that went against the grain of American admiration for courage beyond the ordinary. And in a hopeless cause. We easily could — and perhaps from a military point of view should — have destroyed that fighter. But there was some chivalry left in the American makeup. Without a word of consultation with each other, all of our gunners came up with the same decision: they held their fire. The formation opened up to let him blaze through. How could we kill a man with such foolhardy courage? It is seldom that men see an example of pure nobility. That German expected to die on his assault. It was foolish of course but, like the British Cavalry's "Charge of the Light Brigade," it was a thrilling spectacle to watch.

Landing time was three P.M. and I was saddened to learn that a top turret gunner died during the mission from oxygen failure. Bomber Command listed twenty B-17's lost to fighter attacks. I saw little of the action so could not judge if the loss was excessive.

Jim Counce sustained a frozen hand when he removed a glove to try to clear ice he thought was in his mask. The damage was severe and it was certain that he would be grounded for several weeks to a month. He was depressed when he found out about the damage, because it meant that he would be grounded for an extensive period and would drop far behind in his missions.

December 21

After Jim left for Braintree Hospital, I felt lost and depressed. We had been together so long — well, not that long by the calendar, but so much had happened in those eleven months that it seemed more like years.

"George, I hated to see Jim leave. I may be finished and gone before he gets back to Ridgewell."

"I'm afraid you're right. The doctors told Jim his hand is in bad shape. You know, there is a chance it will have to be amputated."

"Where did you hear that?"

"Jim told me last night after they finished examining the hand."

"It's not gonna be the same, with him gone, in this hut."

"Before long, John, I'll be the only one left in this hut out of the two crews. You an' all the rest will get through before me. How many missions you need now?"

"Four. Shutting needs four, and Purus needs three. Don't know about Gleichauf. I think he needs either two or three."

"It will be lonesome around here when all of you guys are gone. Cahow's men will be finishing too, but I'll be here with a hut full of new gunners."

Later that day I went to the flight line to do something to 719 and passed by the empty hardstand where Tinker Toy had been parked since the 381st arrived at Ridgewell. At times I had imagined that she thumbed her nose at me as I pedaled by her when I was new to the base. She seemed to say, "Another one of those screwed up gunners they send over here to ruin good airplanes like me." Her end was as weird and spectacular as her reputation. A ship with such a bloody and storied record could not have had an ordinary ending like other airplanes. The Copilot saw her go. "That fighter spun out of control. It hit Tinker Toy in the waist just behind the ball — it went halfway through her like a giant arrow! They tumbled end over end — I saw flame and about a thousand yards down she exploded and I could see metal and bodies all over the sky."

The stars were out that night. I liked that very much because it meant a hard freeze and out of the mud for at least two or three days. Also, it sent a message to the combat crews: get ready for a mission in the morning. With that in mind I set out my mission clothes and equipment. Most combat men developed superstitions about clothes or some special talisman they always carried on a raid. I remember one gunner who wore the same coveralls each trip and refused to have them washed. Somehow the unwashed coveralls had become his security blanket.

After turning in, I lay in the sack and let my mind replay the events of the last six months. There was one strange thing I had problems understanding. In that cold, damp climate, and many hours at extreme altitudes and temperatures, I had been remarkably healthy. There had been no colds or sinus difficulties such as I had expected. Barring a hangover I awoke each morning feeling exceptionally good.

CHAPTER XXII
Mission to Osnabruck

Pitts was the first man up when the call came, "Aw right! Get outta that sack. This is Cahow's twenty-fifth."

Tedesco muttered, "He's been so nervous all week that I hope he don't screw up something today."

"That's not like Cahow," I said, "I remember how cool he was on the raid to Schweinfurt."

Green added, "When they get down to one or two they all start to sweat — they've seen too many blow it at the end."

"After this run, five or six of us are goin' to start sweating," Pitts remarked.

George waited to pick up the sounds from the Briefing Room so I could go on to the aircraft. We were flying a ship I knew nothing about. When I unloaded at the aircraft I asked the crew chief, "Does 419 have any peculiarities I ought to know about?"

"Yes, there are two things. You got to keep the cylinder head temperature of number two below two fifteen or you'll get detonation. And there's a vibration between seventy an' eighty on takeoff. It don't hurt nothing, so don't worry about it."

I always wanted words with the crew chief because every plane, like every flier, had its own eccentricities.

The target was Osnabruck, known to me previously for its cheese. Gleichauf was leading the squadron and we were flying the low position in the Group.

"Well, we got the purple heart corner again today," said Balmore.

The first ship got off at ten thirty and pulled steadily up through an overcast. The tail gunner flashed a red "L" signal with a bright lamp to guide other aircraft to form on the lead plane with less loss of time.

"Bombardier to Turret, pull the bomb fuse pins."

A few minutes later, "Turret to Bombardier, pins are pulled — rack switches are on."

"Radio to Turret."

"Go ahead."

"My oxygen regulator is not right."

"What's the problem?"

"It just don't look right. I don't think it is working."

I knew it would be better to get George settled about his oxygen system before we reached enemy territory.

"Turret to Copilot, I'm going to the radio room for a few minutes."

A mechanic had hooked up the regulator backwards, but it made no difference. It was working fine. As soon as I got back to the turret, I called George.

"Your oxygen supply is OK. It does look odd but don't worry about it."

At twenty thousand feet we headed out over the North Sea. The temperature was minus forty-two degrees, but otherwise it was a nice day for a mission. The clouds thinned and visibility was adequate below.

"Tail to Turret, my electric heat went out."

"Which circuits are gone? Hands and feet or the body circuits?"

"All of them are out."

"Check the plug on the end of the cord. You may have a poor connection."

"Can't see anything wrong with it — I've tried plugging it in and out several times."

"One other thing you can try — scrape the prongs on the plug with any kind of metal you have back there. A screw driver will do fine. Try to get any corrosion off the plug."

"Bombardier to Tail, it's going to be better than forty below at our full altitude today. You think you can make it?"

"I'll make it — some way."

"Copilot to Tail, exercise those hands and feet."

"Not much room in the Tail to exercise, but I'll find some way to do it."

"Turret here, now keep up that exercise no matter what. One mission I had to go up and down for four hours to keep my feet from freezing."

"Copilot to Turret, the damn airspeed indicator went out."

"What's the altitude?"

"Twenty-two thousand."

"It could be in the instrument or it could be that some trash in the air caught in the pitot tube. Can Gleichauf fly lead with no air speed?"

"It will be rough. We would be better off flying a wing position. If Paul can't cut it, we'll drop back and let the deputy lead take over."

"Navigator to Pilot, enemy coast in ten minutes."

"Bombardier to gunners, test fire your guns."

I listened to the chatter of the guns as each position rattled off a burst and thought how lucky I had been to be with such a solid crew of ordinary men who became extraordinary when they had to. It all boiled down to three things: a first class pilot who was good at tight formation, a good crew, and those much appreciated escort pilots.

"Radio to Turret, I'm getting dizzy. I told you this regulator wasn't working right."

"George, listen to me. I think you're imagining trouble and are over breathing. Now relax. Breathe normally and quit taking in deep gulps of air. Try it and see if you feel better."

"OK, I'll try it."

"Bombardier to crew, fighters at eleven o'clock low."

"Copilot to crew, don't let them slip in on us."

Sleek 109G fighters, the latest German interceptor to appear against us, circled the formation warily and made several passes but none directly against our Squadron.

"Tail to crew, the escort at six o'clock high."

"Copilot to Navigator, look at those dogfights! How I'd love to be flying one of those fighters."

I could think of many things I would prefer to do. The fight between the 47's and 109's was a swirling panorama of tracers, cannon flashes, and smoke plumes. Then the "Bogies" vanished and for a little while we had the 47's overhead. When they reached the end of their fuel range, they dipped wings and turned North. P-38's were due in a few minutes and I hoped more Bogies would not hit us in the interval. I was already starting to worry about my last three missions.

"Copilot to Navigator, this formation is so lousy, a group of hot fighters could tear us apart. How long to the I.P.?"

"About twenty minutes."

"Navigator to crew, fighters at nine o'clock low."

They climbed to our level and began to circle the Group picking out targets.

"Copilot to crew! Fighter coming in twelve o'clock high."

I had some good shots but could not tell if I inflicted any serious damage. I could hear the ball guns hammering away below. When the firing ceased, I called Harkness. "Are you all right down there?"

"I'm OK — they keep coming up at us — I spray 'em an' they break off the attack."

The 381st took a beating as we approached the target and three Forts went down. I saw one chute but the unfortunate man pulled his ripcord too soon, and the silk flared out quickly and hung on the rear of the Fortress. It was a sickening sight to watch that pitiable drama that could end only in a prolonged agony of terrifing struggle and a horrible death unless somehow that silk shook loose from the tail where it was caught. The last I saw of the striken Fort, that doomed man was still trailing along helplessly in the slipstream. Nearby, two P-38's blasted a 109 and I noticed a brown parachute blossom from it seconds before it went into a dive out of control. One of those P-38's had to execute a frantic turn to avoid flying into that chute.

"Navigator to Pilot."

"Go ahead."

"They are sure cracking that wing ahead of us."

Balmore picked up the three words "cracking the wing" and his blood pressure went out of sight. In the radio room he could see little of the action. About that time the aircraft caught some propellor wash from a plane ahead and lurched sickeningly. George thought the wing was coming off and grabbed his chute and headed for the exit door in the waist. La Buda, flying as waist gunner for us that day, stopped him, but George insisted on examining the two wings from the waist windows before he would return to his position.

"Radio to Turret, is something wrong with one of our wings?"

"Not that I know of — why do you ask?"

He did not reply, but I could sense his relief.

"Turret to Copilot, is the air speed still out?"

"Yes — shows nothing."

"How is the Pilot doing?"

"Rough. He's estimating the speed by watching the squadron ahead. Could the pitot be frozen?"

"It could be, or something in the air clogged it up. Or the instrument may have gone out."

"Bombardier here, did you see those two 109's up above try to throw their bellytanks at us? They'll try anything."

"No, couldn't see it from the waist, but two Forts at three o'clock high came damn close to colliding. That could've knocked out half of the squadron. A 109 just clobbered a 38 at four o'clock low."

"This is the Copilot. I saw it. The 38 got careless. You can't do that with those damn Krauts."

"Bombardier to Pilot — Bombardier to Pilot."

Kels motioned Gleichauf to switch from command to intercom.

"Go ahead, Bombardier."

"We're starting the bomb run."

Flak began bursting around us. It was not heavy, but it sure was accurate. As usual, I cringed when the shells burst close by.

Wham! It was just below us.

"Copilot to Ball — are you all right?"

"I'm OK — it was close but didn't hit me — we got damage between the waist and tail."

I felt better when the bomb load fell free.

"Radio to Bombardier, the bomb bay is clear."

"Tail to crew, the fighters are fading away — fuel getting low is my guess."

"Navigator to Pilot — Cahow has about got it made."

The formation droned placidly along with no opposition. I kept alert for another fighter group to come screaming up, because we were vulnerable with our loose erratic formation. This time, the 533rd Squadron was throttle jockeying like the rest because Gleichauf was guessing at his air speed.

"Navigator to Pilot — ten minutes to the coast. Now I know Cahow has it made."

I knew his men were happy for him and so was I. He was one of the best. The coast slid by and the North Sea was a welcome sight, like the causeway when I was coming back to Corpus Christi by way of Aransas Pass. We were almost home again.

I relaxed and began removing some of the equipment, especially that uncomfortable oxygen mask. After five or six hours, my face was raw from the pressure of the mask and the low temperature. I found out early in the game that a mask was worse when the whiskers needed shaving. If I thought a mission was likely, I often shaved at night to lessen the discomfort. The realization came over me that I was tired. It was not the usual exhaustion of the early missions; I had become acclimated to the routine. It was a built-up weariness of months of altitude and combat tension. For the first time I understood why twenty-five missions was set as the completion point of a combat tour. It was the time when crews would begin to lose mental and physical effectiveness. I suspected the accumulated fatigue was due more to mental strain than to physical weariness.

As we approached Ridgewell, Kels punched me and pointed down. "Cahow is buzzing the field." Indeed he was. At the 381st it was customary to permit a pilot returning from his twenty-fifth mission to buzz the field in celebration of a job well done.

That day we lost seventeen Forts to German fighters. To my thinking the loss was excessive. It was the familiar pattern of late: loose, erratic formations inviting Jerry to attack. The accumulated losses in men and aircraft during the summer and fall of 1943 were staggering and beyond expectations. The replacement crews were put through speeded up training procedures, by no means as thorough as the original 381st received. The predictable result was that inexperienced pilots and crews predominated, and the price we paid was higher casualties than should have been necessary. In the air as on the ground, raw troops rarely fare well against seasoned battle-hardened forces. But an attrition factor was working for us: we were thinning out the experienced pilots of the Luftwaffe. When a veteran German pilot with eight or ten years of training plus experience in numerous campaigns was lost, they could not replace him any faster than we could create his counterpart in the U.S. or England. The advantage in attrition gradually shifted to the side with the largest manpower and industrial facilities. Fortunately, that was the combined might of the Allied Forces.

December 23

Lt. Cahow had finished his twenty-five missions! The dangers were all in the past. He had nothing more to worry about now except getting back to the States. However, Operations assigned him, along with Pitts (Engineer), Parsons (Co-pilot) and Dubois (Navigator) to take a B-17 to a Modification Base 30 or 40 miles away. They were to return another B-17 that had been modified, back to Ridgewell. There was a solid overcast at 500 feet but no problem. The navigator gave Cahow a heading of 190° going over. Coming back, the navigator gave him another heading of 195°. The pilot should have recognized that to be an error, but it was a fun flight and they were all joking on the intercom, not paying too much attention to what they were doing. All of a sudden Cahow began getting interference on his head set. It got worse and worse. Something was definitely wrong with the radio — the noise became increasingly louder. Suddenly Cahow saw that he was flying between heavy steel cables that would have sawed the wing right off an aircraft that hit one of them. To his horror he realized he was in the middle of a balloon barrage near London!! He could not see the balloons because they were hidden in the overcast above. That loud noise was his IFF (Identification Friend or Foe) sending out a warning signal of the balloons and cables, and the flak guns down below, ready to blast any unidentified aircraft from the skies. Lt. Cahow turned that big Fortress around like it was a fighter plane and carefully dodged those cables until he was back in the clear.

There were few signs of Christmas on the base at Ridgewell Airdrome. Some cards and a few packages had arrived, and some scattered decorations were hung here and there. It was a half-hearted effort to do lip service to the Prince of Peace while we went about the grim task of killing and destruction. I had a good idea of how I would spend Christmas Eve, no doubt in dropping off a Christmas package for Uncle Adolf. Our gift would be twelve giant firecrackers a bit larger than the ones I used to explode Christmas mornings. Peace on earth and good will toward men would have to wait until the killing was finished.

It was extremely cold and it had been weeks since the last distribution of coal to our area. During the morning we tramped the nearby woods searching for small trees that might be sneaked out for firewood without attracting attention. There was a risk if caught, but weighed against no heat in the middle of winter, it was a slight deterrent. Most of the wood cutting with our crosscut saw was done at night to lessen the chance of getting into trouble. Two hours after dark we had a sizeable stack stashed away for the next two weeks. With the fire going again that night, it was cozy in the hut. Balmore asked, ''John, you are down to three missions?''

''That is correct — three and I got it made.''

''How many does Purus need?''

''Two I think — not sure.''

''I noticed he's been nervous the last week. That's not like Johnny.''

''They all go through that emotion. Gleichauf will finish one raid ahead of me so I will have to fly my last one as a spare — and I don't like to think about the possibility of having to do the last raid with a new crew,'' I added.

George continued, ''I wish I was up there with you. I need so many missions, I'm bound to draw some lousy crews.''

Watching others approaching twenty-five missions, I had seen the tension building up, but I did not expect it to happen to me. I was older than most of the men flying combat missions and I thought that I had more disciplinary control over my mental processes. I resolved that I would not let it happen to me.

CHAPTER XXIII
Mission to Calais[1]

December 24 - Calais   *Aircraft 730*

When I heard the Jeep coming some distance away, I got up and started dressing, because the signs were clear the night before that we would go out today if the weather cooperated.

"You would think we could do without raids on Christmas Eve," growled Balmore. "What we do today isn't going to change the war much."

"But Mars is more powerful than Jesus — I don't think the burghers are goin' to like the presents we have for them today," I answered.

We waited outside the Briefing Room after drawing equipment. A loud cheer echoed through the closed door.

"It must be a super milk run," George said.

"That's fine with me. I hope my last three runs are milk runs."

An hour later Kels arrived with a grin on his face.

"All right! Let's have it. Where are we goin' today?"

"Maybe I should wait an' let Gleichauf tell you," he toyed.

"Come on! Where we goin'?"

"Today we raid Calais!" he answered.

"Calais? I can't believe it."

"It is Calais — we will go over in small nine-plane formations to try to destroy some construction sites the Allied Command thinks the Germans are building to launch long-range rockets across the Channel. There can be a lot of fighters but Spitfires and P-47's will fly low cover to keep them from getting up to us. Major Fitzgerald will be flying as Copilot and I will go along as Observer."

"I've heard about observers but you are the first live one I've ever seen. What the hell are you supposed to do?"

[1]The official roster of missions shows Cocove, France. My diary shows we went to Calais Dec. 24, 1943.

"Try to see what the bombs hit an' how much damage they do."

"We already got a whole squadron of tails and balls who can see the bomb drop a lot better than you can see it from the cockpit."

At one P.M. the Squadron cleared the English Coast and turned toward the Continent. It was a beautiful day for wintertime Europe and the altitude was only twenty thousand feet.

"Bombardier to crew — stay alert — don't get cocky an' think we can't get hit over Calais — test fire guns."

"Navigator to crew — heavy flak ahead."

Calais had a large number of flak guns and I dreaded the barrage at our lower altitude, because all of their anti-aircraft guns could reach twenty thousand feet with accuracy. The squadron circled to the right slightly in an effort to go around the main field of fire. All at once the bursts caught us dead center. With perfect visibility and the low height, the Jerry gunners were at their best. Burst after burst exploded in the middle of the Squadron. It was incredible that with so much accuracy and so many shells thrown at us, no direct hits were made. The fuse timing was perfect: every burst was exactly at our level. It was the best example of the art of anti-aircraft fire I ever saw. At times the other planes in our small formation were obscured by the smoke of the bursting shells. Only pure luck prevented one or more of the Squadron aircraft from taking a direct hit. At times I cringed down behind the Sperry Computing Sight, as if that would do any good. There was no way to guess which way the lethal fragments were coming from.

I heard a loud crashing noise on the right wing. A heavy fragment struck it under a main fuel tank.

"Turret to Ball — do you see any serious damage like a fuel leak?"

"No — nothing that amounts to anything."

Flak struck the armor plate that Balmore was standing on and knocked him to one side. A few seconds later a fragment caromed off the rim of the radio hatch a few inches from his head.

"Radio to Copilot — they're dustin' me off from two sides — that last one missed my head by two inches."

Four pieces of large shrapnel smashed through the cockpit to my rear with a fearsome noise. I turned around to look for damage and another piece whistled by my ear; it slammed up from below, went through the turret and out the top, sounding like a cannon exploding when it pulverized the plastic glass above me. Fortunately, I had on sun glasses. One lense was broken and the other scarred by the flying glass fragments.

"Copilot to Turret — are you OK."

"I'm OK."

BAM! A huge chunk struck where number two main tank was located. I held my breath for several seconds waiting for the telltale signs of fire.

"Copilot to Ball — can you see sign of a fuel leak?"

"No — I guess we are lucky."

"Sometimes they self-seal an' sometimes not."

Wineski was on his twenty-fifth mission and it was almost his last day again. Big hunks of flak tore by him so close they damaged his clothes.

"Bombardier to Pilot — we're not going to drop — a small cloud has the target covered — we'll have to do a three sixty an' come back over it."

"I wish that we could get out of this damned flak," Gleichauf muttered.

The second bomb run was better, although I did not know what the target was. My concern was that fighters would arrive if we stayed around too long. But once the bombs were released, we were quickly over the Channel on the way home and raid number twenty-three was tucked away.

The remnants of Cahow's crew were with Schultz on our right. They picked up two hundred holes. We had only fifty-five, but many of ours were exceptionally large for flak shrapnel and in vulnerable spots.

Bill Kettner and Ray Bechtel finished their twenty-five that day. What a great Christmas present for them! No question but that tension was mounting more than I expected. How could I suppress it knowing that so many good men had failed at the finish line? The question kept coming back: was it purely coincidence? No doubt it was, but at the time imagination, frustration and superstition allowed phobias to build up.

Recently two men were reputed to have predicted their own deaths with accuracy. What mental processes were involved that defy rational understanding? There must be undiscovered capacities of the brain that perhaps some day we will understand. But how did they know what was coming for them? It is possible that many men made such predictions in error. When one of them turned out to be correct, it attracted intense interest. But such instances were bewildering and unsettling. They were shocking and the mind groped for a reasonable explanation. The recognitive phenomenon confused and fascinated at the same time.

My experience was in the opposite direction. I had tried to psyche myself to help provide a basis for courage that might otherwise have been lacking. I just somehow knew — or made myself think I knew — that I would make it through the war. I felt that if I had to jump, I knew parachutes well enough to make it down safely. I was confident that if I could avoid capture upon landing I could make it back to Allied territory, because I had some familiarity with European customs.

December 25

Christmas Day! It turned out wet and foggy, so no missions were planned. All day the station loud speaker resounded with Christmas music, but the best thing for me was the return of Jim Counce. His hand turned out to be better than first expected. Jim was depressed because the rest of the crew was getting ahead of him and would be breaking up after one more raid by Gleichauf.

Anne had sent a full-sized fruitcake loaded with nuts in a tin container with the lid soldered. There was no other way a cake could have made the trip. Whatever food goodies came from home were shared with the others in the hut. That cake was the big event of the day.

While we were opening packages I heard some unusually loud profanity from Bill Pitts' corner. When it died down he sputtered in a rage, "Look what my Aunt sent me — a five pound can of spam!"

The day before, several men not on the battle order for the day went into Cambridge on the supply truck and brought back large sacks of ale and hard cider bottles from one of the wholesale liquor houses. So mostly that day we sat around the little stove, drank ale and listened to Christmas music on the radio. And of course talked about the raids. We could never stay off of that subject very long. Late that night the President's Christmas message was rebroadcast: it was a typical Roosevelt speech, with his magnetic warmth and assuring us that right would prevail over tyranny.

Bill Kettner and Ray Bechtel spent the day packing and giving away accumulations too bulky or heavy. They had sold their bicycles and we refunded their share of the radio. Whoever took their bunks would have to cough up part of the common ownership of the radio. Watching them, I realized that two more missions would put me in the same position. I had seen Gleichauf that morning and he was noticeably nervous and tense.

Christmas Day 1943 was the most somber one I can remember. Mostly the men were withdrawn, lost in memories of happier times. Americans were asked to stay off of the trains and public transportation facilities during the season so that the English soldiers and war workers would have an easier time getting home for a few hours. It was a reasonable request because we had nowhere special to go.

December 26

Weeks ago huge boxes were placed in the Post Exchange and other spots about the base for men to drop in candy or presents suitable for the

English children who could expect little for Christmas. I watched men file by and drop all of their P.X. rations of candy and chewing gum, which the children loved, into the boxes. Many of the English youngsters had no recollection of prewar days. I was on a mission when the party for the nearby village kids was given. Trucks brought them to the base. Jim was there and told us about it. ''You should've seen those kids. When they saw the candy and chewing gum and other things, they squealed and danced with joy.'' Many of them had never seen such an abundance of goodies. At least we did one thing right during Christmas week.

December 29

Bechtel, Cahow, Bell and Wineski left that day for transportation to the United States. It was my impression that Wineski, a citizen of Poland, was being granted special status for American citizenship because of his service in the Allied and American Air Force. He deserved it but almost did not survive to make it two times I knew of. He would be an asset to our country — no question about that. We shook hands and said the usual things about keeping in touch.

The weather was decent enough the last two days but I was bypassed. The main thing now was to get those last combat missions over with. But the pace seemed to have slowed down recently. That day General Doolittle succeeded General Eaker as Commander of the 8th Air Force. Although it was unfair to the new Commander, the news was received with misgivings. All we knew about Doolittle was the raid on Tokyo that seemed to us like a publicity stunt, with the certain loss of aircraft and men not remotely justified by the insignificant damage one such puny raid could inflict.

CHAPTER XXIV
Mission to Ludwigshaven

The call was welcome because I was anxious to put the last two missions behind me. I looked outside and said, "You won't believe this — it's clear outside. We're going to get in a mission today."

Jim raised up in his bed and said wistfully, "I wish I was goin' with you — hell, I don't know when they'll turn me loose to fly again."

"Just two more, Jim, two more an' my war is over."

Counce could have stayed in bed, but he got up and went out to the airplane with us. It was a habit hard to break.

When Gleichauf arrived, he gave us the pertinent information. "It's Ludwigshaven! We're goin' for the I.G. Farben Chemical Works in Happy Valley. You know what the flak will be. We could draw two hundred fighters but there will be three groups of escorts — Spitfires goin' in — P-38's over the target — and P-47's comin' back — you all know this is my twenty-fifth so don't screw up on anything today."

I could tell Paul was nervous because he was easily irritated. It was harder to tell about Purus. He was so much the same day after day. I will wager he had spent some sleepless nights in the last week.

Shutting turned to Purus, "If those Jerries intend to hit your ass they better get with it. I hear they have been putting in special gunnery practice this week. They know it's your last mission."

"You've only got two to go — who are you goin' to give your special testical armor to?"

"Some Navigator who don't want his voice to change suddenly."

The first streaks of dawn lighted the horizon as the ships took to the air and the sunrise was beautiful. Thirty minutes later the formation began to climb up to high altitude. My mind tried to cover all possibilities. "We must be careful! Watch what you are doing. Above all else don't let any Jerry fighters slip in on us out of the sun — you know how many men have been lost on their twenty-fourth or twenty-fifth — but I'm different — I'm going to make it — I can feel it — yeah? Those men who got it probably had the same feeling. Calm down! I know Gleichauf is nervous and not at his best but he'll be good enough for today. But what if he gets too tense and screws up? Forget it. We're one of those crews that had the sign from the first raid that we would survive. Oh, come now! You know better than that. You say you've got something special going for you! You can't believe that — not really. Oh yes, I do!''

My inner dialogue was interrupted as we made several diversionary turns then headed in the direction of the target. I expected a rough day. Two times before in that area the opposition had been fierce. A cloud cover underneath worried me, because I could see no Pathfinder planes, and that meant enough visibility was necessary to drop visually. We would be the first group over the target, so whatever reception the Germans planned we would likely catch the worst of it.

As the flight passed east of Calais and the enemy coastline, I expected fighters to intercept us in the next few minutes. Surprisingly we droned on for a while without opposition. A fifteen degree turn to the right brought us in line with the I.P. and at that point, Gen. Galland's defense commanders could narrow their estimate of the possible targets we could strike. If our strategy was good enough it gave us two advantages: one, it forced Jerry to put fighters over several targets, thus reducing the number that would intercept us. The second thing it did was to force Jerry to use up his dwindling fuel.

''Pilot to crew — Pilot to crew, a large formation of fighters is due to hit us in a few minutes — get ready for them.''

The information must have come from the Wing Commander. Did it mean that the ban on radio silence was being lifted? I hoped so. It seemed to me that we had carried the ban too far. What difference did radio silence make when Jerry had us on radar?

''Navigator to Pilot — Navigator to Pilot.''

''Go ahead.''

''We'll cross the German border in about five minutes.''

''Bombardier to crew — fighters at eleven o'clock low.''

''Ball to crew — about seventy fighters — they look eager.''

At first the interceptors circled the formation, searching warily for the weakest spots. Gleichauf pulled in tighter. At all costs he did not want to attract attention on his last mission.

''Bombardier to crew, three fighters coming in head on twelve o'clock — let's get them.''

They barrelled through us with cannons blazing, were hammered by seventy guns and turned into flaming wrecks. No flying machine could withstand that kind of punishment and continue to be an airplane.

''Navigator to crew — Spitfires high at eleven o'clock.''

When the Spitfires approached, the German fighters surprised me by taking off for safer territory. Perhaps they did not have enough fuel left to mix it with the R.A.F. pilots. No other Bogies showed up and the Spit escort stayed as long as they could.

"Bombardier to Pilot — we're approaching the bomb run."

"Radio."

"This is Radio."

"Watch the bomb doors down."

"Doors are down."

"Copilot to crew — flak at ten o'clock level."

Anti-aircraft gunfire was mild and scattered but devilishly accurate. We were bounced around from the concussion of some close ones.

"Copilot to Pilot."

"Go ahead."

"That new joker on our left wing is hangin' in tight. He's going to be a good one."

"Right. I told him to stay the hell on that wing — an' he's doing it."

"Bombs away."

"Radio to Bombardier — bomb bay clear — you can raise the doors."

We were improving! Another drop with no bomb release malfunction. The bomb shackle release problems were finally getting under control.

"Copilot to crew — Paul just heard that the radio operator on the plane to our right died from an oxygen failure."

Death from any cause was final and irreversible. It seemed to me it would be preferable to be able to report to the family that the man died from enemy fire in the defense of his country. I would have been reluctant to write his family and have to tell them he died by accident from an equipment failure. I remembered how close we came to losing Wineski from the same kind of failure.

"Bombardier to crew — the P-47 escort is with us."

Purus and Gleichauf almost had it made now. Kels called, "Paul take a look at France. Next time you see it maybe you'll be a tourist."

The Navigator came on intercom: "Hey, Johnny! Those Krauts only got a few more minutes to hit your ass."

Ten minutes later I could see the glistening water ahead. They had made it. There was no way that Jerry was going to hit us with an escort above and friendly water below. We came out southwest of Le Havre.

As soon as he saw the English Coast, Gleichauf began to whoop and sing snatches of songs. He was a happy man. It was something to lift the tension of combat flying and put it in the background. That was the only time I saw Paul Gleichauf act up in the cockpit of a B-17. After we crossed the coast the men from the rear came forward to congratulate Paul and Johnny. Both were popular, not only with our crew but others on the base. Paul broke out of the formation and began his triumphant buzzing of the airdrome and an unexpected thing took place.

"What's the matter with that left wing ship? Can't he see I'm going to buzz the field?" Gleichauf asked in exasperation.

"You told him to stay on your wing and that is exactly what he is doing," Kels answerd.

"But he oughta know I didn't mean on a buzz."

"You didn't mention the buzz and he thinks this is some special test for him."

"Well, he'll break out of it when I go into the dive."

He was wrong! That persistant wing man hung in tight and cozy down to fence height altitude. I do not know what he thought was going on, but it was probably the only time in 381st history that two B-17's zoomed over the field at ten feet elevation flying in tight formation. I imagine there were explosions of unprintable words in the control tower.

Jim, Legg, Chamberlain, and many others were waiting when the aircraft stopped. Gleichauf was popular with the ground crews because he always treated them with special respect. Most of the crew chiefs showed up to offer congratulations. The Squadron C.O. and the Operations Officer were there. Major Shackley had a bottle of good scotch and passed it around in honor of the event.

While our celebration was starting, the friends and associates of two hundred and nine men were numbed by their loss. Twenty Forts were missing, one radio operator was gone, and eight escort pilots paid the price.

That night Gleichauf and Purus celebrated wildly. Those of us still on flying status had to break it off and get to bed at a reasonable hour because we were subject to call the next morning. My sweat-out of mission twenty-five started in earnest the next day. I went to Operations and cornered George Reese. I wanted to know what kind of crew I could expect on the last raid, now that I was unfortunately just a spare top turret operator.

"Now look, John, we're goin' to get a first class crew trying to finish up and a good pilot — isn't that what you want?"

"You're damn right that's what I want. When?"

"I can't tell you the date now. Give me time to work it out."

"Well, don't keep me on the fence too long."

"Oh, how would you like Ferrin for your pilot?" he asked. "You know him him well?"

"Real good. Who else?"

"What's left of Cahow's crew an' I'll dig up some more who are ready to finish."

"That will be great if you can arrange it."

"Now just relax and leave it to me."

He was right and I would do that. No need to worry about a thing. Reese was working up the best deal available. I would not allow myself to get in a sweat. It was just one more mission. I tried to make myself believe I could forget about it until the morning they called me for the last one.

December 31

That night as I lay in the sack my mind went through fanciful twists: "Goodby 1943! And thanks for your help. I hope 1944 will be as good to me as you were. I am not listed in 'Who's Who,' but I am listed in "Who's Still Around' which is more important. I want to thank you for that, 1943. It could so easily have been a different story! Do you have any influence with 1944? You do? Great! Please do me one more favor and ask her to give me the same breaks. You know I will likely be back in combat somewhere in 1944, so ask her to keep my luck simmering on the back burner until I need it. Again, 1943, thanks for your help!"

The first thing the next morning I was back on that twenty-fifth mission syndrome. There was too much time to think about it. "Will it be tomorrow? Will it be a good solid crew, or will Franek make up the assignments and throw me on a new crew that needs a gunner? I don't want to wait forever. Let's get it over with. I have been very lucky so far. Will my luck hold one more time? How can I sleep tonight without knowing if I am on the battle order? Now wait! Here I go again, overplaying this thing. Remember it is only one more raid. Why not calm down and take it like all the other raids? Sure, that is what I'll do. Not going to let it bother me. I will forget the whole thing until they call me. George promised he would get a good crew together, but I haven't heard a word from him. He may have forgotten all about it and I am just a spare gunner on the extra board waiting for whatever the dice roll. . ."

We went into the village that night and I caught the bartender diluting our scotch with cheap potato whiskey, which was common later in the evening when we would not notice it, and got into a heated argument. But George cooled it down and we moved to a table with some more men from the Air Base.

"You are sweating out your last mission? No wonder you are so edgy

— I've only got five — how I wish I was in your shoes," one of them said.

"But Operations won't give me that last call. What am I supposed to do? Why don't they let me get it over with?"

"When was your last raid?" the other gunner asked.

"December 28."

"That was only three days ago. You missed two runs and now you're bitching about it? Give them time to put you on a good one."

Jim said, "That is what I keep telling him — cool it down. Let it come when it comes and quit worrying about it."

January 2, 1944

I was wide awake when the Jeep stopped outside to wake up the crews. I flipped on a light to catch the time and saw it was an early call. Did that mean a long mission? For hours I had been unable to sleep. The far off sound of engines being run up kept telling me a mission was shaping up. Normally I would not have heard it. Hopefully waiting for the call to come, I heard the Operations people pass our hut and familiar noises as nearby huts came alive. That made the third time they had passed me up. Why? Maybe they did not have a mission mean enough! What were they waiting for? Another Schweinfurt or Berlin? My mind was operating in an irrational manner. Operations was doing me a big favor by holding me off until a good mission developed if such a thing existed. I should have been grateful, and in moments of lucid thinking I was, because extra considerations were uncommon in military operations. But the opposite pull was an almost insatiable desire to get it over with.

About mid-morning Jim came back from Operations with bad news. "A Fort blew up on takeoff this morning and killed the whole crew. Three men were on their twenty-fifth. The others were on their twenty-third."

"Did we know any of them?"

"They were from another squadron but we've seen them many times around the mess hall or Operations. They must have got here about the same time we did."

"What a hell of a thing to happen! Makes you sick to think about it."

"John, suppose you had to write to their families. Would you tell them it was just a lousy accident?"

"They are just as dead, no matter how it happened," George added.

"Yes, but think about the families wondering about how the accident came about, if it was carelessness on the part of someone."

"Why are you holding your neck so stiff?"

"I don't know what it is — maybe it's a kink that will be OK tomorrow. Today it's dealing me a fit."

"You better go to the Infirmary and see the Flight Surgeon. You don't want to come down with the flu or some bug an' get yourself grounded for two or three weeks."

"Man, I can't get grounded now — the worst thing that could happen. You are right. I'll go see what the Infirmary says."

The Flight Surgeon examined me and asked a lot of questions: "How many missions do you have?"

"Twenty-four, Sir."

"Are you getting nervous about the twenty-fifth?"

"Oh, not much — some men sweat it out, but it doesn't bother me."

"All right, Comer. I think I know what your problem is. I'm going to give you some pills. Take one when the pain bothers you and before going to bed at night."

He went into the adjoining room, but I could see him reflected in a mirror over a lavatory. He was laughing! An orderly handed him a bottle and he resumed a serious expression and returned to the room where I was waiting.

"Here you are. Now take these and I'm sure you will be OK in a week or two."

That laugh told me all I needed to know. My problem was nerves. The pills were no doubt some harmless concoction. They went into the first trash can I passed. The only pill that would help me was one more mission. The pain in my neck and shoulders got worse. It was painful to turn my head either way. Well, I had to live with it a little longer. Otherwise they might ground me for a while if the Infirmary found out how bad it really was. That night I had the greatest difficulty finding any position where the pain would permit sleep. I heard every noise in the area for hours, but it was not a matter of expecting a call. The signs, as best I could read them, said no mission in the morning.

January 3

The pains were definitely worse when daylight finally arrived. I remembered all of those futile resolves: "All of those great words! It was not going to get to you like other people. Where was the discipline? The Flight Surgeon spotted it right away. I hope it doesn't hang out for everyone else to see."

Reese was busy when I arrived at Operations. When he slowed down I asked, "Are you going to be able to work out that special deal for us?"

"Got it all shaped up. All I'm waiting on now is a target that won't be too rough. Just be patient a few more days.''

''With Ferrin?''

''Right. With Ferrin.''

That afternoon I pedaled into the village with Moe Tedesco to get some exercise and a couple of beers. The weather was quite cold, but we were used to that.

''John,'' Moe said on the way back, ''if they keep putting me off, I may get so nervous I'll crack up.''

''We'll get the call the first time Reese thinks it's a good run. He's looking after us and I'm damn glad. I would hate to draw another Schweinfurt.''

''Or Berlin!''

''In five or six months they can hit Schweinfurt with five hundred Forts surrounded with P-51's all the way to the target. Things are changing fast, but it won't do us any good.''

''You know where I would like to be right now?''

''Where?''

''Ebbetts Field watching the Dodgers beat the hell out of those damn Giants. You've never seen a ball game until you see those two square off. They hate each other. The Dodger fans hate the Giant players and scream at every Giant batter who comes up.''

''You really love the Flatbush, Moe?''

''Greatest place on Earth! I know that city. Her sounds are music to me 'cause I've heard them all my life.''

''I think this ale helps the pain in my neck some. Not quite as bad as it was earlier today.''

''What's wrong with your neck?''

''Nerves — from sweatin' out that last one.''

''With me it's tryin' to sleep. I lie awake — doze off — wake up — catnap all night.''

''About the same with me — haven't had a good night's sleep in a week.''

January 4

The pains were becoming so severe that I could barely turn my head, but I was determined to ride it out, because I could not afford to get grounded and have to keep putting off the final raid. I kept saying to myself, ''How long can I hold out? I need pain pills now and do not know how many more days. . .''

Since exercise helped a little yesterday, I talked Jim into the long ride to Ridgewell. The pains eased up a bit after two or three beers. Riding back to the base the clouds parted and it turned into one of those rare winter nights of clear weather.

"Jim, tomorrow is the day. I can feel it. Look at that sky and you know it will be clear in the morning. I'll get that last call."

"Don't bank on it. Franek has you working on that electric gadget he wants for the Operations Office and he may keep you waiting until you finish it."

"What are you saying? He wouldn't do that to me."

"He might if he thinks about it."

"When do you think you'll be released to start flying again?"

"I think it will be this week."

"That soon? You'll catch up real fast," I replied.

"Don't know about that, John. Me an' George are extras now and never know when they'll call us or who we will fly with."

CHAPTER XXV
Mission to Tours

I had a strong feeling it would be my day. From midnight on I heard every sound in the area. There was loud talk in the adjoining hut when two of the residents staggered in from a night at the pubs. On the distant flight line there was a faint roar of engines being revved up. It was an ominous sound that suggested "in the morning we go." Every hour Tedesco or I would sit up in bed and light a cigarette. The pains in my neck were so bad that aspirin no longer helped.

An hour after midnight I heard the faint wail of air raid sirens far to the east. Which way were they coming? I hoped the invaders would go to the north, but the next ring of sirens opened up closer to us. I lay there and pondered the situation as the sirens became louder. It began to sound like the target might be Ridgewell. "Well, Comer, what's it goin' to be? Are you goin' to stay here in the warm shack and bet they can't hit you? If you climb out where will you go? The slit trenches are full of water an' by now have a sheet of ice over them. Hell, you might as well stay in the sack. . ." Then the anti-aircraft guns and sirens in the nearby town opened up. The metal walls rattled and vibrated loudly and I knew a bomb had exploded somewhere not far away, but too distant to hear the sound of the explosion. The eerie sounds of German bombers overhead faded out and the sirens signaled all clear.

Then came dead quiet. But sleep for me would not come. If I was going out in the morning sleep was desperately needed. Just two or three hours of partial slumber would help. I tried all of the tricks to induce sleep I could remember, to no avail, and I lay there staring morosely into the dark. The seconds ticked slowly by. I flipped on a light long enough to look at my watch. The thing must have stopped running. It had to be later than that! No, the second hand was still operating. Would that night never end?

I caught the sound of the Jeep a mile away as it sped toward us. I followed the course of the noise as it halted on the loose gravel nearby. There were sounds of steps on the gravel paths between the huts. Muffled noises floated through the metal walls. I could hear the sound of voices and a cold water tap turned on. Someone tripped over a parked bicycle and knocked it against our hut with a crash. I heard cursing but could not recognize the voice. The steps headed our way. "Great! They're coming for us." The steps passed by on the gravel. "No! No! They're passing me by again! What is the matter with Reese and Franek? Have they forgotten I exist? The first thing in the morning I'm going to see Major Shackley — wait — the steps are coming back — hold it — maybe. . ." The door opened.

"All right! We gotcha a good one. Come on and get up you lazy bastards — Comer, Tedesco and Green — you're flying with Ferrin in five one four. This is it — good luck."

I bounced out of bed, although every move meant stabs of pain. Hubie Green and Tedesco were up with grins on their faces. "One way or the other this will be the big one," Green said. "That was the longest night of my life."

Moe answered, "I didn't sleep much either an' I saw John get up and smoke a cigarette two or three times."

"Let's check over that ship extra good and no foul ups — no mistakes today."

"Hey, Jim. What're you getting up for?"

"How could I sleep with that damn air raid, then you guys making noises all night? I might as well get up an' see you off."

So he went to the aircraft with us and helped get the guns ready for the Bombardier, who was also on his last mission. Jim said, "What I really came out here for is to watch Shutting put on his testical armor for the last time. I wish I had a picture of it for the *Chattanooga Times.*"

Ferrin and the rest of the officers unloaded and I waited expectantly. "OK, the target is Tours — about eighty miles southwest of Paris. We will have a fighter escort in and out." He was interrupted with cheers. "The altitude will be twenty-two thousand feet and the temperature will be twenty-three below. Stay alert. Nothing is going wrong today. We're all going to make it."

Opposition was expected to be mild so it sounded like a good mission for us. The Wing formation turned out over the Channel and the operation was finally on the way. Almost no chance existed now that it would be cancelled or called back.

"Navigator to crew — enemy coast in five minutes — start watchin' for fighters."

"Bombardier to crew. Let's have an oxygen check."

I listened to all positions report in.

"Turret to Bombardier."

"Go ahead."

"Do you want me to pull the bomb fuse pins?"

"Yes, go ahead an' pull them."

Five minutes later I was back in the turret:

"Turret to Bombardier, pins are pulled — bomb rack switches are on."

"Thanks, Turret."

The run going in was without incident. Believe me, no other crew on that mission was so alert and ready for trouble if it materialized. A few minutes inside enemy territory the P-47's appeared as briefed. They were a beautiful sight to me. Some persons might think the big Thunderbolts too heavy and massive to be pleasing to the eye. I saw them from a different perspective. They saved my life many times and I would never lose my gratitude to them and the men who flew them.

"Navigator to Pilot."

"Go ahead, Navigator."

"The I.P. in ten minutes. We'll do a sharp turn to the left and the bomb run will come up fast."

"Bombardier to Radio, when we go on the bomb run, watch the doors down."

Ten minutes went by and the Ball reported flak. It was light to moderate.

"Bombardier to Pilot, we're on the bomb run."

When I saw and felt the bomb load fall out, I felt good. All we had to do now was get back to England and it would be all over for me.

The Bombardier screamed over the phones: "Fighters! Twelve o'clock level!"

His call came too late. None of us saw them in time! They must have dived down out of the sun and were a hundred yards away before the first man spotted them. That is what happened on a mission when it was seemingly too easy and the Fortress crews relaxed their normal alertness.

"Copilot to crew! Fire! Dammit, fire!"

Three 109's screamed through the formation and caught the lead B-17 with a rocket directly in the cockpit. The Fort burst into flame and in seconds was on the way to oblivion. No one escaped from the doomed craft.

"Waist to crew — fighters are circling to get in front of us again."

"Copilot to crew — the sonnuvabitches are coming in! Fire! Fire! Fire! Pour the lead to them!"

They turned around and attacked again with cannon fire blazing from their wings. The aircraft shuddered from the impact of heavy firing. I could see my tracers striking the lead fighter.

"Tail to Copilot. Fort exploded behind us."

"Ball to Copilot, another Fort at four o'clock in bad shape."

The fighters vanished to the south as suddenly as they had appeared.

"Copilot to Turret, do you have sunglasses?"

"Yes, Copilot."

"Put them on an' watch the sun area."

For an hour nothing happened and I relaxed. The mission was about over and I exulted in the smug knowledge that I finally had it made. But Jerry had one last goodie in reserve to throw at me! Oh, hell! More 109's straight ahead! Where did they come from?

"Turret to crew! Turret to crew! Two 109's one o'clock high coming in!"

The fighters swooped down and leveled out too low for my guns to reach them. Two times on that mission Bogies had slipped in almost undetected. Two more Forts caught heavy damage. Suppose one of them had hit us a lethal blow less than twenty-five minutes away from the coast. It almost happened.

"Bombardier to crew, fighters eleven o'clock low."

"Navigator to crew, they are Spitfires — our escort home."

Well, I thought, surely I have it made now, with those R.A.F beauties criss-crossing below, ready to take on anything that looks German. A little later the sunlight reflecting on the Channel began to sparkle in the distance. It was almost over, but I wouldn't risk jinxing the crew by saying so — yet. I watched the coast slowly slide by below with mixed feelings. When it faded into the haze I knew for sure it was all over.

"Turret to Navigator, we got it made. We got it made."

"Pilot to crew, keep the intercom clear an' stay on your positions until we cross the English Channel. We are not taking any chances."

We had broken the 381st jinx again (if there was a jinx) and that would make a good many men feel better. Jim, George, and the others waited with congratulations. There was no way I could describe my relief and exulation. I turned to Shutting. "You made it without losing your balls."

"Yeah, but a couple of times it was close."

"What are you going to do with your special armor?"

"I'll find some deserving Navigator."

"I got a better idea. Take it home and hang it on the wall."

On the way to interrogation Jim asked, "How does it feel to have twenty-five made?"

"It would be great if I didn't have these miserable pains ever' time I move. It was murder when I had to look straight up today — like a knife stabbing me in the neck."

"You better go have it looked at."

"I will, first thing in the morning."

After interrogation, I had to go out to the plane and clean and stow the turret guns. With fair weather holding another day they might go out again the next morning. On the perimeter truck to the personnel site, I suddenly realized that I felt different. What was it? Then it dawned on me that the pains were gone. Just like that. It took an hour and a half after the mission for my ragged nerves to return to normal. The Flight Surgeon knew it would happen. Now I felt just great! Never before had I any conception of what effect tight nerves can create in an otherwise healthy body.

The celebration that night lasted until two A.M. and when the pubs closed, it resumed at the hut. I was through! ! ! The fighting part of the war was over for me! Now and then I would glance at Jim or George and it was clear that they felt left out of things now. But I had no doubt that both of them would come through fine. Reese would put them on the best available crews, so I did not let their gloom dampen my elation.

January 9

It was now a matter of awaiting orders for the port of return to the States. It was a proud moment to report to Col. Nazzaro and receive the Distinguished Flying Cross, awarded to men who survived twenty-five missions at that date. Studying the decoration, I pondered why my luck had held up and tried to recall the faces of those I knew well who failed. What was luck? Was it an inexplicable thing available to a few at times, but withheld from most men? Or was it a series of pure coincidences? Looking back at it today the latter seems far more likely, but I am not sure. In wartime some men and some crews, wore a charm one could almost see. I could spot them around the Operations area or the mess hall. I could spot others that I felt certain would never make it. How could that be? I developed the ability to sense those things. It was strange and puzzling to me that I could feel those predictions in advance and I never discussed it with anyone else. Of course, the majority of our combat crews fell into neither class. Only a few, on the opposite sides of what I call luck, generated those psychic impressions.

The feeling of elation at completing a combat tour was starting to wear thin. I was so bound to those men and to that place that I felt sad and a little depressed at leaving. Something inside me said, "You belong here until this thing is over," and I suppose a part of me will always remain at Ridgewell. One could not go through those experiences and walk away cold.

Meanwhile Carroll Wilson had recovered and arrived at the hut on combat duty again. It was good to see him once more before I left, because from the time he joined our crew I had a warm feeling for that complex and immature young man. As always, he was broke, so I loaned him another ten pounds in addition to what he already owed me. (When he returned to the States he sent me every cent of it.)

The weather turned nice and most of the men were out on a mission. The ground was dry enough for the English farm children to play outside our huts. A gunner named Pope was trying to teach seven or eight of them how to throw and kick a football. I can still remember his happy-go-lucky grin and cocky mannerisms. Kids took to him readily. When Pope entered a room the atmosphere changed. He was one of those people who had the knack of placing themselves in ridiculous situations. He had the look about him that suggested he would try anything at least once. I know he had been a star athlete somewhere but he never talked about it. His Georgia drawl lingers yet in my memory. The next day he failed to return from a mission. There was no report about what happened to the aircraft. I hope he got out in time.

That night George, Jim, Carroll and I were in a somber mood. We talked about our early crew days and the scary situation when we arrived at Ridgewell. Those men were more like a family than could have been expected from ten persons drawn from so many divergent backgrounds, and parts of the country. I was reluctant to see it break apart and scatter us about over the country.

I thought about a funny thing that happened on one of our missions. We were bouncing around in some flak and all of a sudden I was startled to hear the radio gun behind me cut loose with heavy firing. I whirled around expecting to help George hold off fighters diving down on us. Evidently a piece of flak had hit the inflating valve on one of our two life rafts. The big, bright yellow raft automatically inflated with gas and pushed out of the upper storage compartment, in front of the radio hatch where George was standing at his gun facing the rear. It tumbled into the slipstream, and the blast of air propelled it directly over the radio position. I turned just in time to see George pouring furious bursts at it as the huge contraption zoomed beyond the tail.

"Radio from Turret."

"Go ahead."

"Did you get that big yellow fighter?"

"Go to hell, Turret."

I developed such a brotherly love for that big man with his infectious Irish grin. He had so many strengths balanced with small weaknesses. One of the things I remember best about him is the one tap dance routine he knew and his soft voice singing, "Mary, Mary, plain as any name can be. . ."

After lights were out I said, "Jim, do you remember that night at Las Vegas when we got out of that bar just before the fight broke out and the M.P. Patrol wagon arrived?"

"Yeah, I recall the incident."

"What happened?" asked Wilson.

"One night we were having a drink in a small casino and bar and Jim went to the rest room. He returned in a hurry and told me to pay for the drinks quick and get out of there. From across the street we heard the sounds of a sizable brawl break out, and watched the paddy wagon cart off twenty or thirty civilians and service men."

George inquired, "How did you know the fight was going to break out?"

"Because I started it," Jim replied. "Some soldiers and sailors were arguing in the rest room. When I left I turned off the lights and pushed them together."

January 10

It was quiet my last night at the airdrome. I volunteered to check the canteen for signs of a mission shaping up for the next morning. It was the last thing I could do for them.

"Well, the key faces are missing so you can expect a call in the morning," I reported.

"You mean those who will go — they may not call us," said George.

"Or we may draw a green crew. Who knows what to expect from now on?" Counce added.

"I don't think either of you will have to wait too long. I don't see any surplus gunners or radios around."

Jim had been returned to combat status that day and was in better spirits, with a chance to run off the four or five missions he needed quickly. The door opened and Vernon Chamberlain walked in.

"I heard you were leaving tomorrow and wanted to say goodbye, John."

"Vernon, you have been a faithful friend to our crew and we appreciate it. You took chances many times to slip us the extra ammunition we needed," I said.

"I don't know what it was, John. At first it was Gleichauf, then all of you. Your crew became my team. I've been sweating out you guys so long it's going to be odd not to have someone on the missions that I feel a little bit responsible for. You guys were always the same, no matter where the mission was. Other crews came out to the plane nervous or silent or bitching about the guns when nothing was wrong with them. But you fellows always arrived in a good humor, kidding each other or some kind of horseplay. You were just different from the others — my kind of people, I guess. . ."

It was going to be difficult to leave all of those friends, not knowing if I would ever see them again. Certainly we planned to get together after the war, but would it really happen? Or would the occasional letters eventually die out?

Jim looked at me, "We have talked often about mental attitude — about fear. Tell me something honestly, John — have you overcome fear in combat?"

"No. I doubt if anyone ever does completely. But starting with the way it was when we arrived here, I have gone seventy to eighty percent of the way toward controlling it. That damn flak still bothers me at times."

"I haven't done near that well," said George. "I doubt if I have gone fifty percent of the way."

"It depends on what you mean by fear," I answered. "How do you tell when it starts and when it ends?"

"I don't follow you," Balmore said. "I'm either scared or I'm not."

"Look at it this way: you are flying along knowing that fighters are going to hit you. When? Where are they? Hope we see them in time. You build up anxiety, the first stage of fear. I wish the escort would get here before they do! We got to be careful and not let them slip in on us out of the sun! Tension builds up. There they are! About sixty of them. Where's the escort? The sensation of fear wells up. Here they come! Look at those cannon flashes! You pour bursts at them and excitement crowds out fear. The adrenaline is flowing. At two hundred yards your bursts get longer and closer together. Excitement increases. The fighters are now at one hundred yards, using their full assortment of weapons at you from close range. Your bursts are three times as long as they taught you at gunners school. You do not care if the barrels burn out. You are keyed up to your maximum performance — exhilaration! It's an emotional high that is a heady sensation unlike any other emotion you have ever experienced. A gunner could become addicted to it with enough experience. In time he might crave the kill-or-be-killed thrill as some people crave strong drugs. Maybe that's why some men become professional soldiers of fortune. Civilian life is too tame for them after years of combat and the high excitment that goes with it.''

There was silence for a while and Wilson said, ''You're getting close, John.''

Counce added, ''I never thought about it the way you break it down, but it's true that all of those emotions are involved in a fighter attack. I guess we all have a secret desire to flirt with danger, but each of us thinks that others will pay the price — not him.''

''What do you say to all this George?'' I asked.

''In the radio room I hardly ever get to see any of the attackers until it's over and they flash by. Most times they roll under the wing and I don't see them at all. I hear the intercom scream, 'COMING IN.' I hear the bursts getting longer and longer and I'm petrified back there, seeing nothing that is going on! If I had more chances to fire at the fighters, it might be different.

That last night at Ridgewell I was caught in the ambivalence of twisted emotions. Of course, I was glad to have escaped the hazards of air combat. But the attractions of exhilarating combat experience lingered in the subconscious mind. Stateside military duty, whatever my assignment might be, by contrast with Ridgewell would, I knew, be too dull and stagnant. And there was regret at having to leave these men, with whom I had relationships that could not be repeated in civilian life. After lights were out I lay there in a state of gloom. What should have been a happy contemplation had turned sour.

CHAPTER XXVI
Goodbye to Ridgewell

January 11   James Counce and George Balmore Only —
On different aircraft

At five-thirty A.M. the lights came on and roused me from a deep sleep. I listened to the roster: "Counce flying 888 with Cline — Balmore flying 912 with Crozier . . ."

I raised up in bed. "Those are good crews. Right?"

"We could have done a lot worse," Counce answered.

"Well, since I'm already awake, I might as well go out and see you jokers off."

The personnel truck let George out first. "Good luck! I'll see you back in the States when this thing is over." A handshake and he was gone.

I helped Jim get the guns ready until it was time to start engines. "Good luck, Jim. Let me know where you are stationed when you get back to the States."

He gave me that big grin and closed the hatch. I watched the ship pull away and almost wished I was going with them.

I had to hurry to get my bags ready for the truck that was to take us to the nearby station. Just before the train arrived, I looked up as I heard a formation overhead.

"Take a good look, Carl. That's the last time we'll see the 381st in action."

"Good luck, boys," he said. "Go get 'em."

It was a long, slow train ride across England to Chorley, on the west coast, the embarkation point for service personnel who were returning to the United States. Nearly all of these men were wounded, or for some other reason were no longer needed in the combat area.

When men completed a tour of combat duty and returned to the States, quite a few of them did become highly nervous for a while. The condition was brought about by too many traumatic experiences buried deep in the subconscious mind and seeking an outlet. The excitement, and the motivation created by the need to defend all that was good in our civilization, was abruptly withdrawn, and replaced by a hum-drum military existence. The change was too sudden and drastic for the mind to accept it right away. So those men continued to dwell mentally in the immediate past for a while. The falling aircraft, the explosions, and the hideous flak were strongly imprinted and needed to be worked out of the subconscious mind. In time, the nervousness would wear off for most of those who were affected. The need to talk about the war would fade, to be replaced by the daily trivialities of civilian life, from which they had escaped for a brief time into high adventure. For the majority of those men there was no lasting damage. Slowly they returned to what we call normal. For a few, perhaps more sensitive than others, the memories were too indelibly planted. For them, more time and treatment was needed. In severe cases of neurosis, and continuing anxiety, injections of sodium pentathol were used, along with the help of a psychologist, to pry troublesome memories out of the subconscious mind. The patient was induced to talk at great length, in response to questions about those lingering nightmarish experiences. The drug helped to release the deeply buried tensions. Most times it worked.

January 14

I was standing in the snack bar at Chorley when I saw Lt. Ferrin walk in. He was a few days behind me getting away from Ridgewell.

"When did you leave the 381st?" I asked.

"Yesterday. Got here this afternoon."

"I read that the January eleventh mission had high losses. How did the 381st come out?"

"There was a mixup and the planes were called back. Some of 'em didn't get the message and went on and got clobbered."

"How many did the Group lose?"

"Quite a few. I didn't get the exact number, but it was bad!"

"You know Jim Counce and George Balmore."

"Sure, I know 'em."

"They were with Crozier and Cline on that mission. Did both of those ships get back OK?"

"The loss startled Col. Nazzaro because it was unexpected."

"How about Cline and Crozier?" I sensed he was avoiding my question.

Ferrin took a deep breath and looked me in the eye. "Crozier and Cline both went down, Comer."

I listened in a state of shock and disbelief. For a minute I could not say anything.

"Were there any chutes — either plane?"

"Croziers plane was seen to explode.[1] There was hardly any chance for a survivor." There was an icy feeling in the middle of my chest. When I recovered enough, I asked almost in a whisper, "And the other plane?"

"Cline's ship was last seen badly damaged and engines burning — it is not known if any of the crew got out. No chutes were observed."

At least there was a chance that Jim had time to jump, but I knew too well how fast the explosions came after engines caught fire. If anyone got out, surely Jim would be one of them, for he was close to the waist escape hatch.

"Have you seen Shutting?"

"Yes, I ran into Carl an hour ago."

I turned away from Ferrin and stumbled blindly from the crowded bar. He followed and told me the meager details that were known. But I had quit listening. My mind was in shock. Right then I could not talk to anyone. The night was bitterly cold and it was raining. I walked blindly in the rain without cap or raincoat for a long time becaue a man does not cry in front of other men; I walked until I was soaked and shaking with the cold. What Ferrin said kept coming back. "The 533rd Squadron was almost wiped out. The mission was aborted but they did not get the message and were hit by a devastating fighter attack." One squadron all alone so far inland was unbelievable!

There was no possible sleep for me! All night I stared into the blackness and groped for the means to accept the inevitable. At such times the mind tries to find ways to avoid the truth when it is too bitter to accept. There is some mistake! They will turn up! The word will seep back that they got out and are prisoners of war.

January 15

It was a bad day for me. The weather was cold and rainy. I kept thinking about Jim and George. I supposed that it was futile to keep trying to delude myself that George got out in time. I had to accept the facts, and they were that the aircraft was seen to explode and no chutes were reported. But surely Jim had a chance. He was in the closest position to an escape hatch. No one saw the aircraft explode and it was under control at

---

[1]At a 381st Reunion at San Antonio I met Gordon Crozier, pilot of the aircraft that George was in. Gordon told me that all of the crew was able to bail out except Balmore. He personally examined Balmore and confirmed that he was dead. All other crew members survived as prisoners of war.

the last report. Yet, I had a strange feeling — some extra sense — that Jim was gone! It was the same psychic premonition that I often felt about combat crews and was almost always correct. No matter how I tried to rationalize his escape, I knew there was no hope.

January 16

In a state of depression I looked up Shutting. I had avoided him the day before because I could not talk to anyone about it until I accepted the facts.

"I tried to find you yesterday, John," he said. "That was terrible about Balmore and Counce. They were the best."

"It hit me hard. One of them would have been bad enough, but both the same day on different planes!"

"Maybe Jim bailed out."

"No! He's gone. Don't ask me how I know, but I do. I'll try to see Mary Balmore if we land in the vicinity of New York and the Counce family later when I can."

"John, we were just lucky that we made it. Think about how many we knew who didn't."

January 20

In the dim predawn light, I stood high on the stern deck of the S.S. Frederick Lykes and watched the shoreline of England dissolve in the distance. As I stared into the dark swirling mists, memories began to cloud my vision. Once again I saw the Forts flying in perfect formation with long trails streaming far behind them in the sky. Once more I heard the distinctive drone of Fortress engines. And I saw faces — unforgettable faces I would never see again: Herb Carqueville, Pete Ludwigson, Major Hendricks, Feigenbaum, Pope and many others. All lost over Europe. More than anything, I saw Jim and George. I could almost hear their voices, those comically contrasting accents of the Bronx and Mississippi. We had shared a unique and special brotherhood, forged by circumstances and tested by adversity. It was a gift of friendship beyond anything I had experienced before. And I knew it could not be replaced.

As I remembered them, I felt an overwhelming sadness, and turned away from the others nearby to hide the tears that I could not blink away. At that moment I experienced an intuition of startling clarity. Suddenly I realized that we would meet again. I did not know how or when, but I knew! "Death is not the end, but only the beginning of a new dimension." How many times had I heard that Christian refrain? But I had never fully accepted its meaning until that moment. There was no longer any doubt. I felt a certainty and a peace. The sense of gloom lifted and I was a different person.

Yes, we would meet again. And until we did, I vowed to keep my memories of them from fading. I named my firstborn son James Balmore Comer. And because of them and their families, I wrote this book.

After the War

Paul Gleichauf, Pilot: Remained in the Air Force and retired as a Lt. Colonel in El Paso, Texas, where he died from a brain tumor several years ago.

Herbert Carqueville, Copilot: M. I. A. No trace of the aircraft or crew was ever found.

Carl Shutting, Navigator: Became a practicing psychologist at Chattanooga, Tennessee, where he died ten years ago from a heart attack.

John J. Purus, Bombardier: After a 1951 reunion in New York with the Comer and Balmore families all contact was lost.

George Balmore, Radio Operator: K. I. A. January 11, 1944.

John Comer, Flight Engineer-gunner: Was a sales manager then a zone manager for a large manufacturer retiring at Dallas, Texas, where he still lives.

James Counce, Waist Gunner: K. I. A. January 11, 1944.

Carroll Wilson, Waist Gunner: Completed his missions as a radio operator on another crew. He retired from the service as a Master Sergeant and presently lives at Nashville, Tn.

Nickalas Abramo, Ball Turret: Was wounded, recovered, and resumed combat action. He was wounded again, had to bail out and became a P. O. W. Unconfirmed information is that he died several years ago.

Harold Harkness, Ball Turret after Abramo was wounded: No contact.

Buck Rogers, Tail Gunner: He was grounded when he did not recover from severe injuries early in his missions. After the War no contact.

Raymond Legg, Tail Gunner after Rogers: No contact.

John Kels, Copilot after Carqueville became a first pilot: No contact.

George Reese, original Copilot: Operations officer during the action and once in a while our Copilot — a lawyer in New Orleans.